MAKING

Making creates knowledge, builds environments and transforms lives. Anthropology, archaeology, art and architecture are all ways of making. In this exciting book, Tim Ingold ties the four disciplines together in a way that has never been attempted before. Instead of treating art and architecture as compendia of objects for anthropological or archaeological analysis, Ingold advocates a way of thinking through making in which sentient practitioners and active materials continually answer to, or 'correspond', with one another in the generation of form.

Making offers a series of profound reflections on what it means to create things, on materials and form, the meaning of design, landscape perception, animate life, personal knowledge and the work of the hand. It draws on examples and experiments ranging from prehistoric stone tool-making to the building of medieval cathedrals, from round mounds to monuments, from flying kites to winding string, from drawing to writing.

Tim Ingold is Professor of Social Anthropology at the University of Aberdeen, UK. His books for Routledge include *Lines*, *The Perception of the Environment* and *Being Alive*.

'In his latest book, Tim Ingold persuasively argues for anthropology's transformational capacity and promotes serious reflection on the need for anthropologists to correspond *with* the world. His focus on handwork in art, building, and the making of tools beautifully illustrates "thinking through making" and learning by doing. This accessible book makes an excellent and timely contribution to a core area of anthropological research, and invites the reader to engage with the fascinating work emerging from it.'

Trevor Marchand, *School of Oriental and African Studies, UK*

'Ingold is a joy to read. With *Making*, he continues to enliven the social sciences with his distinctively compelling and critical reflections on anthropological, archaeological, architectural and artistic practices. This volume will be useful to all who are striving to integrate art and research, making and thinking, practice and theory.'

Ian Alden Russell, *David Winton Bell Gallery, Brown University, USA*

'For architects it is an absolute must to discover and absorb the work of this friendly outsider whose ideas touch the heart of what we do.'

Lars Spuybroek, *Georgia Institute of Technology, USA*

'Unafraid to ask bold questions and propose daring answers, Tim Ingold has developed a distinctive voice. In the process, he has staked out an increasingly influential position that touches on a wide range of disciplines.'

Webb Keane, *University of Michigan, USA*

MAKING

Anthropology, archaeology, art and architecture

Tim Ingold

Routledge
Taylor & Francis Group

LONDON AND NEW YORK

First published 2013
by Routledge
2 Park Square, Milton Park, Abingdon, Oxon OX14 4RN

Simultaneously published in the USA and Canada
by Routledge
711 Third Avenue, New York, NY 10017

Routledge is an imprint of the Taylor & Francis Group, an informa business

© 2013 Tim Ingold

British Library Cataloguing in Publication Data
A catalogue record for this book is available from the British Library

Library of Congress Cataloging in Publication Data
A catalog record for this book has been requested

ISBN: 978-0-415-56722-0 (hbk)
ISBN: 978-0-415-56723-7 (pbk)
ISBN: 978-0-203-55905-5 (ebk)

Typeset in Bembo
by HWA Text and Data Management, London

Printed and bound by CPI Group (UK) Ltd, Croydon, CR0 4YY

For Anna

CONTENTS

LIST OF FIGURES

PREFACE AND ACKNOWLEDGEMENTS

In my mind, and to everyone I have ever talked to about it, this book has always been known as *The 4 As*. The 'A's in question are Anthropology, Archaeology, Art and Architecture. I had been teaching a course by this name to mixed groups of advanced undergraduate and postgraduate students for several years, and the idea was to turn it into a book so that I wouldn't have to teach it any more. 'Simple', I assured myself, sometime in 2007. 'I have all my lecture notes and I've read the stuff – it's just a matter of writing up.' In the late summer of 2008 I started writing in earnest, in the couple of months that were left of a period of research leave. I drafted what are now Chapters 3 and 4 of the present work ... and then my time ran out. For the next three years I was saddled with the job of being a Head of School. 'You're a manager now, Tim', said one of my superiors one day – a Vice-Principal, no less – with an evil grin; 'you're one of us.' I shuddered, and thought of *The 4 As*. Would I ever return to them again, I wondered, or had I crossed irrevocably to the 'other side'? I had intended to finish the book first, and then move on to my collection of essays, *Being Alive*. But as it turned out – with many of the essays already written or in an advanced state of completion – the prospects of getting at least the latter book finished looked more realistic. Once again, *The 4 As* was shelved, while in the windows of time I could find, especially during the long hot summer in 2010, I concentrated on *Being Alive*. That left me with a problem, however, because I found that in my haste to complete the essay collection I had 'stolen' many of the ideas that were to have gone into *The 4 As*. It was no good relying on old notes. I would have to move on.

Looking back, I can only be thankful that circumstances forced me to do so. Although the book has been so long in coming, I could not have written it sooner, not least because it builds on ideas that have taken their time to take root, and which have grown through conversations I have had, and work that I have been able to read, only in the last year or two. For example, the idea of correspondence, which plays a central role in this book, only occurred to me in the final stages of revision for *Being Alive*. The result is that the present work is no longer the 'book of the course' that I might have written, based on my lectures, but has become something altogether different. I suppose it has turned into a kind of statement of my personal philosophy and, at the same time, a protest against the overwrought, puffed up and self-serving phrase-mongering of so much that nowadays passes for scholarship. Words are precious things; they deserve our respect. The inspiration for the book still comes from the course on *The 4 As*, which was by far and away the most rewarding I have ever taught, and my most immediate thanks must go to all the students who have participated in the years since 2003–2004, when I first introduced it. It has been fun, as all teaching should be, and I have learned a huge amount. What eventually made it possible for me to write the book, however, was the leave granted to me after finishing my three-year stint as Head of School. This leave, which commenced in October 2011, is funded for two years by the Leverhulme Trust, and I am immensely grateful to the Trust for its support, without which this book could not have been written. And now that it is finished, I promise to write the book I said I would write in my application! That's the next one.

I started my leave, however, with a very considerable backlog, and it was not until the end of April 2012, during a two-week visit to the University of Vienna, that I was properly able to resume work on this book, which had now assumed the official title of *Making*. Though I had a certain affection for *The 4 As*, I was advised that rather like the creatures of science fiction which can do everything conceivable in the universe except climb stairs, state-of-the-art electronic book distribution systems cannot cope with titles which have numbers in. Moreover *The 4 As* would have been an enigma to anyone not already familiar with the background to the book, whereas *Making* is transparently what the book is about. Its argument is that all four disciplines – anthropology, archaeology, art and architecture – are, or at least could be, ways of thinking through making, as opposed to the making through thinking that, in institutions of higher education, has tended to place theorists and practitioners on opposite sides of the academic fence. I also argue, however, that making things is tantamount to a process of growth. The same applies to writing books. Rain is good for growth, and as the wettest Scottish summer in living memory wore on, the manuscript gradually swelled. But it needed some sunshine for ripening, and once again – as happened with *Being Alive* in the summer of 2010 – the little cottage on the shore of Lake Pielinen, in eastern Finland, came to the rescue. Three weeks of July sunshine, in idyllic surroundings, helped me through the last two chapters. By this stage the book was already telling me what to write rather than the other way around. It is curious how books have minds of their own. All their authors can do is to find the ways they want to go, and follow them. Indeed, I believe this is true of making generally, and one of my principal themes in this book is to demonstrate that this is so. In a nutshell, my thesis is that making is a correspondence between maker and material, and that this is the case as much in anthropology and archaeology as it is in art and architecture.

As ever, for inspiration and assistance in writing this book, I have more people to thank than I could possibly enumerate. To all of the following, however, I owe a particular debt of gratitude: Mike Anusas, Stephanie Bunn, Jen Clarke, Anne Douglas, Caroline Gatt, Cesar Giraldo Herrera, Wendy Gunn, Rachel Harkness, Elizabeth Hodson, Raymond Lucas, Christel Mattheeuws, Elizabeth Ogilvie, Amanda Ravetz, Cristian Simonetti and Jo Vergunst. I am also indebted to Lesley Riddle, commissioning editor at Routledge, for her unfailing support and patience in the face of an author who has so consistently promised and failed to deliver on time, and to Katherine Ong for bearing with me through to the production process. For some of the chapters, I have raided material that I have presented or published elsewhere, though not without substantial revision. Thus a fragment of Chapter 1 comes from my chapter 'The 4 As (anthropology, archaeology, art and architecture): reflections on a teaching and learning experience', in *Ways of Knowing: New Approaches in the Anthropology of Knowledge and Learning*, ed. M Harris, Oxford: Berghahn, pp. 287–305, 2007. Some sections of Chapter 2 appear, in a rather preliminary form, in my article 'Toward an ecology of materials', *Annual Review of Anthropology* 41: 427–442, 2012, and parts of Chapter 5 appear in two introductory pieces ('Introduction: the perception of the user-producer', in *Design and Anthropology*, eds. W. Gunn and J. Donovan, Farnham: Ashgate, pp. 19–33, 2012; and 'Introduction', in *Imagining Landscapes: Past, Present and Future*, eds. M. Janowski and T. Ingold, Farnham: Ashgate, pp. 1–18, 2012). Chapter 6 owes a certain amount to my chapter 'The round mound is not a monument', in *Round Mounds and Monumentality in the British Neolithic and Beyond*, eds. J. Leary, T. Darvill and D. Field, Oxford: Oxbow Books, pp. 253–260, 2010. Chapter 7 incorporates a couple of paragraphs from the *Annual Review* article cited above, and a few paragraphs of Chapter 9 come from my 'Introduction' to *Redrawing Anthropology: Materials, Movements, Lines*, ed. T. Ingold, Farnham: Ashgate, 2012, pp. 1–20. The rest is new.

I dedicate this book to my most constant supporter and most unsparing critic in all things, who – by the time this book is published – will have put up for over forty years with an incorrigibly academic husband whose thoughts are always somewhere other than where they ought to be.

Tim Ingold
Aberdeen, August 2012

1

KNOWING FROM THE INSIDE

Learning to learn

Know for yourself! That was oftentimes the only advice my companions would offer when, as a novice fieldworker among Saami people in north-eastern Finland some forty years ago, I was stuck as to how to proceed with some practical task. At first I thought they were just being unhelpful, or unwilling to divulge what they knew perfectly well. But after a while I realised that, quite to the contrary, they wanted me to understand that the only way one can really know things – that is, from the very inside of one's being – is through a process of self-discovery. To know things you have to grow into them, and let them grow in you, so that they become a part of who you are. Had my companions offered formal instruction by explaining what to do, I would have had only the pretence of knowing, as I would find out the moment I tried to do as I was told. The mere provision of information holds no guarantee of knowledge, let alone of understanding. Things, as proverbial wisdom has it, are easier said than done.

It is, in short, by watching, listening and feeling – by paying attention to what the world has to tell us – that we learn. My companions did not inform me of *what* is there, to save me the trouble of having to inquire for myself. Rather, they told me *how I might find out.* They taught me what to look for, how to track things, and that knowing is a process of active following, of *going along.* These were people who had always lived by fishing, hunting and herding reindeer, so for them the idea that you know as you go – not that you know by means of movement but that knowing *is* movement – was second nature. To me it was not, and yet it must have somehow wormed its way into me, without my even realising it at the time, for when I look back I can see how it has guided my thinking and my preference for some philosophies over others. Would I be thinking in the same way had I not undergone this formative experience of fieldwork very early on in my career? That is impossible to say. I would have to rerun the past four decades without that experience to see whether the results would be the same or different. But for my part, I can find no other explanation.

Our task, in a situation such as that in which I found myself, is one of learning to learn. Gregory Bateson – anthropologist, cybernetician and general intellectual maverick – called it 'deutero-learning' (Bateson 1973: 141). This kind of learning aims not so much to provide us with facts *about* the world as to enable us to be taught *by* it. The world itself becomes a place of study, a university that includes not just professional teachers and registered students, dragooned into their academic departments, but people everywhere, along with all the other creatures with which (or whom) we share our lives and the lands in which we – and they – live. In this university, whatever our discipline, we learn *from* those *with* whom (or which) we study. The geologist studies with rocks as well as professors; he learns from them, and they tell him things. So too the botanist with plants and the ornithologist with birds. And anthropologists? They also study with those among whom they stay, if only for a while. Learning to learn, for them as for the practitioners of any other discipline, means shaking off, instead of applying, the preconceptions that might otherwise give premature shape to their observations. It is to convert every certainty into a question, whose answer is to be found by attending to what lies before us, in the world, not by looking it up at the back of the book. In thus feeling forward rather than casting our eyes rearwards, in anticipation rather than retrospection, lies the path of discovery.

This book is anchored in the discipline of anthropology. Surely the most anti-academic of academic disciplines, anthropology could not be sustained were it not for the institutions of learning and scholarship in which most of its practitioners spend the greater part of their working lives. Yet at the same time, it is largely devoted to challenging the principal epistemological claim upon which the legitimacy of these institutions is founded, and that continues to underwrite their operations. This is the claim of the academy to deliver an authoritative account of how the world works, or to reveal the reality behind the illusion of appearances. In the academic pantheon, reason is predestined to trump intuition, expertise to trump common sense, and conclusions based on the facts to trump what people know from ordinary experience or from the wisdom of their forbears. The mission of anthropology has long been to turn this pantheon on its head. It is to start from the presumption that if anyone knows anything about the ways of the world, then it will be those who have devoted their lives – as have their ancestors – to following them. Therefore, say anthropologists, it is by seeking to understand these ways of life, and by acquiring for ourselves some of the knowledge and skills required to practise them, that we have most to learn. Armed with this learning, and with the critical perspectives it opens up, we can turn our sights back on the academy and, as it were, cut it down to size by revealing the limitations inherent in its own knowledge practices.

Anthropology and ethnography

In anthropology, then, we go to study *with* people. And we hope to learn *from* them. What we might call 'research' or even 'fieldwork' is in truth a protracted masterclass in which the novice gradually learns to see things, and to hear and feel them too, in the ways his or her mentors do. It is, in short, to undergo what the ecological psychologist James Gibson calls an *education of attention* (Gibson 1979: 254; cf. Ingold 2001). But besides subjecting themselves to this kind of education, many fieldworkers are committed to documenting the lives and times of their host communities. This work of documentation is known as *ethnography*. More often than not, anthropologist and ethnographer are combined in one and the same person, and the tasks of anthropology and ethnography proceed in tandem. They are not the same, however, and their persistent confusion has caused no end of trouble. We need to sort this trouble out.

It helps to be able to think through an example, so I have made one up for the purpose. As an amateur cellist I used to dream, quite unrealistically of course, that I would one day go to study with the great Russian master of the instrument, Mstislav Rostropovich. I would sit at his feet, observe and listen, practise and be corrected. After a year or two of this, I would return with a much enriched understanding of the possibilities and potentials of the instrument, of the depths and subtleties of the music, and of myself as a person. This, in turn, would open up paths of musical discovery that I could continue to travel for years to come. Now suppose that instead, having perhaps read for a degree in musicology, I decided to carry out a study of prominent Russian cellists. The idea would be to find out what factors had set them on this particular path, how their subsequent careers had unfolded, what the major influences had been on their lives and ways of playing, and how they saw themselves and their work in the contexts of contemporary society. I would plan to spend some time with Rostropovich, using my cello as a kind of entry ticket to gain access to him and his circle, and in the hope of gathering information relevant to my study, whether through casual conversation or more formal interviews. I would do the same for a number of other cellists on my list, albeit not so famous. And I would come home with a lot of material to work on for my projected thesis: *Bears on Strings: Cellists and Cello-Playing in Contemporary Russia*.

I do not mean to deny that a study of the latter kind could make a valuable contribution to musicological literature. It could increase our knowledge of an otherwise little-studied topic. It might even have earned me a doctorate! My point is not that the first project is better than the second, but simply that they are fundamentally different. Let me highlight three differences that are crucial for what I want to say, by analogy, about ethnography and anthropology. First, in project one I study *with* Rostropovich and learn *from* his way of playing, whereas project two is a study *of* Rostropovich in which I learn *about* it. Second, in project one I take what I have learned and move *forward*, all the while of course reflecting on my earlier experience. In project two, by contrast, I look *back* over the information I have collected, in order to account for trends and patterns. And thirdly, the impetus that drives project one is primarily *transformational*, whereas the imperatives of project two are essentially *documentary*. To put it rather crudely, these are also the differences between anthropology and ethnography. Anthropology is studying with and learning from; it is carried forward in a process of life, and effects transformations within that process. Ethnography is a study of and learning about, its enduring products are recollective accounts which serve a documentary purpose.

Now in proposing this distinction, I do not mean to belittle ethnography. Many colleagues, I know, will protest that to regard ethnography as mere documentation is to take far too narrow a view of it. They will insist that ethnography is a much broader and richer endeavour than I have made out, and even that it should be taken to include everything that I have just brought under the rubric of anthropology. Not only anthropology but also ethnography, they will say, is transformational: the ethnographer is changed by the experience, and this change is carried forward into his or her future work. Hence in their view, ethnography and anthropology are practically indistinguishable. But to this I answer that there is nothing 'mere' about descriptive documentation. Ethnographic work is complex and demanding. It may even be transformational in its effects upon the ethnographer. These are side effects, however, and are incidental to its documentary purpose. Indeed, if anything belittles ethnography, or makes it seem less than what it really is, it is the usurpation of its name for other ends. After all, 'description of the people' is what ethnography (from *ethnos* = 'people'; *graphia* = 'description') literally *means*. If ethnography has in practice become something different from description, then by what name should the task of description be known? It can be hardly more emphatically devalued than by being left nameless and unrecognised. Nor is that all, for as I shall show in a moment, to conflate the objectives of documentation and transformation is to leave anthropology impotent in the fulfilment of its critical mandate.

For the present, I wish only to insist that the distinction – in terms of objectives – between the documentary and the transformational is absolutely *not* congruent with that between empirical and theoretical work. It is almost a truism to say that there can be no description or documentation that is innocent of theory. But by the same token, no genuine transformation in ways of thinking and feeling is possible that is not grounded in close and attentive observation. This book is a case in point. It is not an ethnographic study, and indeed makes very little reference to ethnography at all. That does not, however, make it a work of theory. Rather, my entire argument is set against the conceit that things can be 'theorised' in isolation from what is going on in the world around us, and that the results of this theorising furnish hypotheses to be applied in the attempt to make sense of it. It is this conceit that sets up what the sociologist C. Wright Mills, in a celebrated essay on intellectual craftsmanship, denounced as a false separation between ways and means of knowing. There can, Mills argued, be no distinction between the theory of a discipline and its method; rather, both are 'part of the practice of a craft' (1959: 216). Anthropology, for me, is such a practice. If its method is that of the practitioner, working with materials, its discipline lies in the observational engagement and perceptual acuity that allow the practitioner to follow what is going on, and in turn to respond to it. This is the method, and the discipline, known in the trade as *participant observation*. It is one of which anthropologists are justly proud. Participant observation, however, is a practice of anthropology, not of ethnography (Hockey and Forsey 2012), and, as I shall show below, anthropologists do themselves a disservice by confusing the two.

Participant observation

It is not anthropology's purpose to describe the specificity of things as they are: that, I have argued, is a task for ethnography. But nor is it to generalise from these descriptions: 'to account', as anthropologist Dan Sperber (1985: 10–11) would have it, 'for the variability of human cultures' by resort to 'ethnographic data'. It is rather to open up a space for generous, open-ended, comparative yet critical inquiry into the conditions and potentials of human life. It is to join with people in their speculations about what life *might* or *could* be like, in ways nevertheless grounded in a profound understanding of what life *is* like in particular times and places. Yet the speculative ambition of anthropology has been persistently compromised by its surrender to an academic model of knowledge production according to which lessons learned through observation and practical participation are recast as empirical material for subsequent interpretation. In this one, fateful move, not only is anthropology collapsed into ethnography, but the entire relation between knowing and being is turned inside out. Lessons in life become 'qualitative data', to be analysed in terms of an exogenous body of theory.

Whenever positivistically minded social scientists speak of 'qualitative and quantitative methods' – or even more obscenely, of 'quant/qual' – and point to their essential complementarity as though a mix of both would be advantageous, this inversion is at work. To make matters worse, they then recommend participant observation as an appropriate tool for collecting the qualitative component of the dataset. This is to add insult to injury! For participant observation is *absolutely not* a technique of data collection. Quite to the contrary, it is enshrined in an ontological commitment that renders the very idea of data collection unthinkable. This commitment, by no means confined to anthropology, lies in the recognition that we owe our very being to the world we seek to know. In a nutshell, participant observation is a way of knowing *from the inside*. As science studies scholar Karen Barad (2007: 185) has eloquently put it: 'We do not obtain knowledge by standing outside the world; we know because "we" are *of* the world. We are part of the world in its differential becoming.'[1] Only because we are already *of* the world, only because we are fellow travellers along with the beings and things that command our attention, can we observe them. There is no contradiction, then, between participation and observation; rather, the one depends on the other.

But to convert what we owe to the world into 'data' that we have extracted from it is to expunge knowing from being. It is to stipulate that knowledge is to be reconstructed on the *outside*, as an edifice built up 'after the fact', rather than as inhering in skills of perception and capacities of judgement that develop in the course of direct, practical and sensuous engagements with our surroundings. It is this move that – by situating the observer on the outside of the world of which he or she seeks knowledge – sets up what is often alleged to be the 'paradox' of participant observation, namely that it requires of the researcher to be both 'inside' and 'outside' the field of inquiry at one and the same time. This paradox, however, does no more than restate the existential dilemma that lies at the heart of the very definition of humanity which underpins normal science. *Human beings*, according to science, are a species of nature, yet to *be human* is to transcend that nature. It is this transcendence that both provides science with the platform for its observations and underwrites its claim to authority. The dilemma is that the conditions that enable scientists to *know*, at least according to official protocols, are such as to make it impossible for them to *be* in the very world of which they seek knowledge. It seems that we can only aspire to truth about this world by way of an emancipation that takes us from it and leaves us strangers to ourselves.

In any appeal to data, whether quantitative or qualitative, this division between realms of knowing and of being is presupposed. For it is already taken for granted that the world is given to science not as part of any offering or commitment but as a reserve or residue that is there for the taking. Disguised as social scientists we enter this world either by stealth, feigning invisibility, or under false pretences by claiming we have come to learn from teachers whose words are heeded not for the guidance they have to offer but as evidence of how they think, of their beliefs or attitudes. Then, as soon as we have filled our bags, we cut and run. This, in my estimation, is fundamentally unethical. It is to turn our backs upon the world in which we live and to which we owe our formation. With all the data at our fingertips, we think we know what can be known; yet knowing all, we fail to see or take our counsel from the world itself. With this book my aim is to restore knowing to where it belongs, at the heart of being. This is to turn once again *towards* the world for what it has to teach us, and to refute the division between data collection and theory building that underwrites normal science.

As anthropologists we currently find ourselves in a double bind. How can we do justice to the ethnographic richness and complexity of other cultures, while simultaneously opening up to radical, speculative inquiry into the potentials of human life? The alternatives seem to lie between abdicating from our responsibility to engage in critical dialogue around the great questions of how to fashion our collective humanity in a world that is teetering on the edge of catastrophe, or turning the people among whom we have worked into unwitting mouthpieces for philosophies of salvation that are not of their own making. Neither alternative has served anthropology well. The first leaves the discipline on the margins, condemned to the retrospective documentation of indigenous worlds that seem always to be on the brink of disappearing; the second only fuels the popular belief that the traditional wisdom of native people can somehow rescue the planet.

An anthropology that has been liberated from ethnography, however, would no longer be tied down by a retrospective commitment to descriptive fidelity. On the contrary, it would be free to bring ways of knowing and feeling shaped through transformational engagements with people from around the world, both within and beyond the settings of fieldwork, to the essentially prospective task of helping to find a way into a future common to all of us. When we go to study with great scholars in the course of our education, we do so not with a view to describing or representing their ideas in later life, but to sharpening our perceptual, moral and intellectual faculties for the critical tasks that lie ahead. Why, I wonder, should it be any different for anthropologists when they go to work with other people? The truth is that in finding ways to *carry on* we need all the help we can get. But no one – no indigenous group, no specialist science, no doctrine or philosophy – already holds the key to the future, if only we could find it. We have to make the future for ourselves.

The art of inquiry

We cannot make the future, however, without also thinking it. What then is the relation between thinking and making? To this, the theorist and the craftsman would give different answers. It is not that the former only thinks and the latter only makes, but that the one *makes through thinking* and the other *thinks through making*. The theorist does his thinking in his head, and only then applies the forms of thought to the substance of the material world. The way of the craftsman, by contrast, is to allow knowledge to grow from the crucible of our practical and observational engagements with the beings and things around us (Dormer 1994; Adamson 2007). This is to practise what I would like to call an *art of inquiry*.

In the art of inquiry, the conduct of thought goes along with, and continually answers to, the fluxes and flows of the materials with which we work. These materials think in us, as we think through them. Here, every work is an experiment: not in the natural scientific sense of testing a preconceived hypothesis, or of engineering a confrontation between ideas 'in the head' and facts 'on the ground', but in the sense of prising an opening and following where it leads. You try things out and see what happens. Thus the art of inquiry moves forward in real time, along with the lives of those who are touched by it, and with the world to which both it and they belong. Far from answering to their plans and predictions, it joins with them in their hopes and dreams. This is to adopt what anthropologist Hirokazu Miyazaki (2004) calls the *method of hope*. To practise this method is not to describe the world, or to represent it, but to open up our perception to what is going on there so that we, in turn, can respond to it. That is to say, it is to set up a relation with the world that I shall henceforth call *correspondence*. Anthropology, I believe, can be an art of inquiry in this sense. We need it in order not to accumulate more and more information *about* the world, but to better correspond with it.

By and large, however, practitioners of the art of inquiry are to be found not among anthropologists but from among the ranks of practising artists. And this prompts a reassessment of the relation between art and anthropology. There is of course a long and distinguished tradition of study in the anthropology of art. Scarcely a region of the world remains whose native productions have not been subjected to exhaustive analysis and interpretation. Much of the resulting literature overlaps with writing in the fields of material and visual culture. It also suffers from the same biases. In the study of material culture, the overwhelming focus has been on finished objects and on what happens as they become caught up in the life histories and social interactions of the people who use, consume or treasure them. In the study of visual culture, the focus has been on the relations between objects, images and their interpretations. What is lost, in both fields of study, is the creativity of the productive processes that bring the artefacts themselves into being: on the one hand in the generative currents of the materials of which they are made; on the other in the sensory awareness of practitioners. Thus processes of making appear swallowed up in objects made; processes of seeing in images seen.

Likewise in the study of art, anthropologists have tended to treat the work of art as an *object* of ethnographic analysis. 'The anthropology of art would not be an anthropology of *art*', as Alfred Gell has written, 'unless it were confined to a subset of social relations in which some "object" were related to a social agent in a distinctive, "art-like" way' (Gell 1998: 13). By this, he means that it should be possible to trace a chain of causal connections, in reverse, from the final object to the initial intention that allegedly motivated its production, or to the meanings that might be attributed to it. In a word, it is to place the object in a social and cultural context. In thus taking the artwork to be indexical of the social milieu and cultural values of its makers, the anthropology of art has merely taken on the mantle of art history. It is true that anthropologists have gone out of their way to distance their endeavours from the propensity of many art historians to make evaluative judgements on the basis of criteria that appear value-laden and ethnocentric. Nevertheless, in so far as they continue to treat art as a compendium of works to be analysed, there can be no possibility of direct correspondence with the creative processes that give rise to them.

I contend that this reverse-reading, analytic approach represents an intellectual dead end so far as the relation between anthropology and art is concerned. The source of the blockage lies in what could be called the 'anthropology *of*' formula. The problem is that whenever anthropology encounters anything outside itself, it wants to turn whatever it is – say kinship, law or ritual – into an object it can analyse. Thus when it encounters art, it wants to treat art as a collection of works that are in some way caught up in a texture of social and cultural relations that we can study. Yet while we might learn much *about* art from the analysis of its objects, we learn nothing *from* it. My aim, to the contrary, is to replace the anthropology *of* with an anthropology *with*. It is to regard art, in the first place, as a *discipline*, which shares with anthropology a concern to reawaken our senses and to allow knowledge to grow from the inside of being in the unfolding of life. To carry out anthropology *with* art is to correspond with it in its own movement of growth or becoming, in a reading that goes forwards rather than in reverse, and to follow the paths along which it leads. And it is to link art and anthropology through the correspondence of their *practices*, rather than in terms of their objects, respectively historical and ethnographic.

To date, with a few notable exceptions (e.g. Schneider and Wright 2006, 2010), collaborations between anthropologists and arts practitioners have been few, and those that have taken place have not all been entirely successful. Once again, the source of the difficulty lies in the identification of anthropology with ethnography. For the very reasons that render arts practice highly compatible with the practice of anthropology are precisely those that render it incompatible with ethnography. On the one hand the speculative, experimental and open-ended character of arts practice is bound to compromise ethnography's commitment to descriptive accuracy. On the other hand, the retrospective temporal orientation of ethnography runs directly counter to the prospective dynamic of art's observational engagement. Precisely as arts practice differs in its objectives from the history of art, however, so anthropology differs from ethnography. It is here, I believe, that the real potential for productive collaboration between art and anthropology lies. Could certain practices of art, for example, suggest new ways of *doing* anthropology? If there are similarities between the ways in which artists and anthropologists study with the world, then could we not regard the artwork as a *result* of something like an anthropological study, rather than as an *object* of such study? We are already used to the idea that the results of anthropological research need not be confined to written texts. They may also include photographs and films. But could they also include drawings, paintings or sculpture? Or works of craft? Or musical compositions? Or even buildings? Conversely, could not works of art be regarded as forms of anthropology, albeit 'written' in non-verbal media?

Doing things ourselves

These were the kinds of questions we set out to address in a seminar that began life over fifteen years ago, when the seed for this book was first planted. At that time, in the mid-1990s, I was still working in the Department of Social Anthropology at the University of Manchester. More by accident than design, the Department included a number of research students with backgrounds in either art or architecture, or both.[2] I thought it would be interesting for us to meet on a regular basis to talk about issues on the interface between art, architecture and anthropology. This we did, rather successfully – indeed the seminar ended up running in fits and starts for a full three years, until 1999, when I left Manchester to take up my current position in Aberdeen.

It was, at least for me, a very remarkable seminar, and I have never known anything quite like it. We began in the usual way, in a seminar room, listening to each other talk, but after a term of this we felt that we had reached some kind of impasse. For it became clear that the issues that concerned us could not be addressed in a vacuum. We had to be *doing things ourselves*.

Obviously, without the benefit of prior training (which some of us had), we anthropologists cannot snap our fingers and, as if by magic, turn ourselves instantly into artists or architects. But we could at least try to ground our discussions in something practical, so as to give the ideas we came up with some foundation in experience. And we did all manner of things! We wound string and wove baskets, made pots and fired them on a home-made kiln, we practised the Alexander technique and discovered how heavy a head or limb can be when it is completely relaxed. We helped a farmer rebuild a drystone wall, held a workshop on polyphonic singing, tried our hand at architectural drawing, visited artists' studios and exhibitions, and so on. Some of the things we did were a bit mad, and they did not always lead anywhere. We never had a coherent agenda. However, we were all agreed that the quality of the discussions we had while doing things was quite unlike anything experienced in an ordinary seminar, and that they were tremendously productive of new insights. But while this was undoubtedly the case, it was not so clear *why* this should be so. The question is: what difference does it make if discussion is grounded in a context of practical activity?

When I moved to the University of Aberdeen in 1999 to revive the anthropology programme there, one of my ambitions was to carry forward some of the ideas arising from the Manchester art, architecture and anthropology seminar. Initial discussions with colleagues at the School of Fine Art and the Visual Research Centre at the University of Dundee led us to put together a proposal for collaborative research under the rather cumbersome title, 'Learning is understanding in practice: exploring the interrelations between perception, creativity and skill'. To our considerable astonishment, the project was funded for a three-year period (2002–2005).[3] One component of the project was to look at the way in which the skills of fine art are taught and learned in the course of studio-based practice, and involved participant observation with fine art students in Dundee, following their learning experience (Gunn 2007). Alongside and complementing this study, however, we set out to explore the potential applicability of practices of teaching and learning, in both fine art and architecture, within the discipline of anthropology.

It was in this context that we developed a course for advanced undergraduate and postgraduate students in anthropology at the University of Aberdeen, entitled 'The 4 As: Anthropology, Archaeology, Art and Architecture'. The course was introduced and taught for the first time in the spring semester of 2004, and with one or two interruptions, has continued to be offered ever since. I shall say more below about what the course covered and how it was delivered, as well as about the philosophy of teaching and learning that underpinned it. Before doing so, however, I should explain what brought the four disciplines together, beyond the happy coincidence that they all began with the letter A! I have already devoted some attention to differentiating one of them – anthropology – from the practice of ethnography. I had to do this in order to establish the conditions for anthropology's correspondence with art. But it is also necessary, as we shall see, for its correspondence with architecture and archaeology as well.

The four As

While much work has been done in the anthropology of art, the anthropology of architecture remains little developed. The literature in the former is voluminous; in the latter it is almost non-existent. The reasons for this are unclear. It can surely be no reflection of the relative importance of art and architecture in people's lives. One possible explanation is that on account of their scale and portability, works of art are more collectable than those of architecture, and have therefore found their way into the museums and galleries of the western world, where they have naturally attracted the attention of scholars disinclined to travel to their regions of provenance. I have no evidence to support this hypothesis, however, and no doubt other factors are involved. In any case, of the few studies that do exist, most adopt the same general stance as studies of art, visual and material culture in equating 'architecture' with built structures that are then treated as objects of ethnographic analysis.[4] These are studies *of*, rather than *with* architecture. In combining it with art and anthropology, I propose instead to think of architecture as a *discipline* that shares with art and anthropology a concern to explore the creative processes that give rise to the environments we inhabit, and the ways we perceive them. Taken as the practice of such a discipline, architecture is not so much *about* as *by means of* buildings. It is, in short, an *architecture of inquiry*. Included in it are questions concerning the generation of form, the energetics of force and flow, the properties of materials, the weave and texture of surfaces, the atmospheres of volumes, and the dynamics of activity and of rest, of making lines and making place. To answer every one of these questions entails a way of knowing from the inside, and we shall be exploring some of these in the chapters to follow.

It was in the move from Manchester to Aberdeen that the three As of art, architecture and anthropology were joined by the fourth, archaeology. This was in part a reflection of my own interests, which have long spanned the boundary between archaeology and anthropology. But I was also convinced that no discussion of the relation between art, architecture and anthropology could be complete if archaeology were not included as well. With their unifying themes of time and landscape (Ingold 1990) and in their mutual concern with the material and symbolic forms of human life, anthropology and archaeology have long been regarded as sister disciplines, even though they have not always been on speaking terms. Moreover there is an obvious affinity between archaeology and the histories *of* both art and architecture, in their common interests in the artefacts and buildings of antiquity. In a sense, I suppose, architects and archaeologists could be regarded as procedurally equal but temporally opposed: after all the very same tool – the trowel – that the builder uses to fabricate the architectural forms of the future is used by the archaeologist, in the excavation of a site, to reveal the forms of the past. If one begins with designs of what is to be put up, the other ends in plans of what has been unearthed. With all these parallels and connections, indeed, it seemed only natural that archaeology should be along as the fourth A.

However, if archaeology is to join with anthropology not as a positive science but as an art of inquiry, and similarly if it is to join with art and architecture conceived as disciplines rather than as compendia of objects for historical analysis, then the terms of engagement have to be renegotiated, in two respects. Firstly, just as we have been compelled to distinguish anthropology from ethnography, so, likewise, archaeology must be distinguished from the kind of pre- or proto-historiography that has as its objective to arrive at descriptively plausible reconstructions of everyday life in the past. Though the pros and cons of using ethnographic analogies to fill the gaps in such reconstructions have been extensively debated, this issue – crucial to the relation between ethnography and prehistory – is of no particular consequence for the relation between anthropology and archaeology. Secondly, we need to recognise that archaeology's core practice of excavation, understood in the broadest sense as an engagement with materials embedded in the earth that carry the traces of past human activity, can no more be reduced to a technique of data collection than can the corresponding practice of participant observation in anthropology. Just like participant observation, excavation is a way of knowing from the inside: a correspondence between mindful attention and lively materials conducted by skilled hands 'at the trowel's edge'. It is from this correspondence, and not from the analysis of 'data' within frameworks of 'theory', that archaeological knowledge grows. In the practice of excavation, as Matt Edgeworth has recently put it, archaeologists are obliged to *follow the cut* – to 'see where it goes, and in what direction it takes us' – not passively but actively like hunters tracking their prey, ever alert and responsive to visual and tactile clues in an intrinsically variable environment (Edgeworth 2012: 78, see Ingold 2011a: 251 fn. 4). In effect, the cut is a line of correspondence.

The course

Many years ago, asked by a university bureaucrat how he would describe the objectives of his teaching, anthropologist Heonik Kwon responded that he would endeavour to turn his students into good hunters. It was a typically inspired response, and while it left the bureaucrat completely flummoxed, as a summation of the principles underlying the design and delivery of the course on the 4 As, it could not have been bettered. The aims of the course were to train students in the art of inquiry, to sharpen their powers of observation, and to encourage them to think *through* observation rather than *after* it. Like hunters they had to learn to learn, to follow the movements of beings and things, and in turn to respond to them with judgement and precision. They would discover that the path to wisdom lay in this correspondence, not in an escape into the self-referential domain of academic texts. And like hunters, too, they were encouraged to dream. To dream like a hunter is to become the creatures you hunt and to see things in the ways they do. It is to open up to new possibilities of being, not to seek closure. The world of dreams, as indigenous hunters tell us, is no different from that of waking life. But in the dream you perceive that world with different senses, while moving in different ways and perhaps in a different medium such as in the air rather than on land.[5] On waking you then see the familiar with new eyes (Ingold 2011a: 239).

In the official documentation we were obliged to provide for reasons of bureaucratic accountability, we stated that the 4 As course aimed 'to explore the connections between anthropology, archaeology, art and architecture, conceived as complementary approaches to understanding and shaping how people perceive and relate to their surroundings, in currents of space, time and movement'. In hindsight, however, one of the more remarkable and slightly unexpected outcomes of presenting the course has been that although planned as an explicitly interdisciplinary inquiry, in practice the boundaries of the disciplines simply vanished, if indeed they ever existed. Students did not have the experience of having to relate four distinct fields, but rather found themselves following a series of pathways in which the concerns of anthropology, archaeology, art and architecture seemed naturally and effortlessly to converge. This was perhaps because the course was as much *anti-disciplinary* as *interdisciplinary*. It was anti-disciplinary because it overturned the normative understanding of the academic discipline as a delimited domain of inquiry, the boundaries of which are coterminous with those of the class of phenomena (A) with which it deals. This is implied whenever a discipline is described as the study *of* A (e.g. art or architecture). But from our perspective of studying *with*, the entire terrain of knowledge is reconfigured. Instead of a territorial surface segmented into domains or *fields of study*, we have something more like a rope, wound from corresponding strands or *lines of interest*. In binding these lines together our aim has been to undo the territorialisation of knowledge implied in the way disciplines are normatively understood, and to celebrate the openness of knowing from the inside.

The course was delivered through a combination of lectures, practicals, project work and workshops, spread over a period of ten weeks. Following a general introduction, lecture topics included (in this order): design and making; materials; objects and things; gesture and performance; craft and skill; the senses in perception; lines; drawing; notation. Normally, courses offered at this advanced level comprise one lecture and one tutorial per week, each of an hour's duration. While the lectures for the 4 As followed a fairly traditional format, the tutorials were replaced by weekly practical sessions. In each session students would discuss the issues arising from that week's lecture, along with the accompanying readings, at the same time as carrying out specific practical exercises that helped to place these issues in an experiential context. Some of these exercises are described in the following chapters: they included collecting objects, messing with materials, flying kites, string-making and knotting, a walk on the beach, forging signatures, and constructing notations for observed movements.

Besides attending lectures and participating in practicals, students were also required to carry out a project. Project work proceeded throughout the course. Each student was asked to select a 'thing'[6] such as a building, a bridge, a bench, an ancient monument, a piece of public sculpture, or a landmark (for example a tower, fountain or prominent tree). The student was advised to spend about an hour with the chosen thing every week, focusing on a specific aspect, and to make notes on what had been observed or discovered. For example, they were asked to attend to the thing's history, whether it is finished or still growing or under construction, the materials it is made of and their histories, what plants are growing on it or animals living in it, how people and animals move in, over, through or around it, and what it sounds and feels like at different times of day, after dark or in varying weathers. They had to draw or sketch it and make plans of it, and reflect on how their drawing affected their observations. And they had to make a model from readily available raw materials, and consider what model-making could teach about the thing, bearing in mind the differences of scale and materials between the thing and the model. At the end of the course, these notes, along with drawings, model and supporting documentation, were to be assembled into a dossier to be submitted for assessment. The final component of the course comprised a series of three half-day workshops, including an outdoor session on weaving with willow, a visit to an artist's studio, and a walk in the countryside to address issues of landscape perception.

In its design and delivery, the 4 As course was part of an effort to introduce ways of teaching and learning in anthropology that are consonant with what we know from anthropology about the processes of learning and teaching. For many years I have taught undergraduate courses, at both introductory and more advanced levels, in which I have explained that it is wrong to think of learning as the *transmission* of a ready-made body of information, prior to its *application* in particular contexts of practice. On the contrary, we *learn by doing*, in the course of carrying out the tasks of life.[7] In this the contribution of our teachers is not literally to pass on their knowledge, in the form of a ready-made system of concepts and categories with which to give form to the supposedly inchoate material of sensory experience, but rather to establish the contexts or situations in which we can discover for ourselves much of what they already know, and also perhaps much that they do not. In a word, we grow *into* knowledge rather than having it handed down to us. This is what Jean Lave (1990) means when she says that learning is a matter of *understanding in practice* rather than *acquiring culture*.

Now if this is the way people learn in any society, then it must also be true of the way students learn in our own. Accordingly, the role of the student is not to take on board a corpus of authorised, propositional knowledge issuing from a superior source in the academy, but to collaborate in the shared pursuit of human understanding. Yet as Lave herself has pointed out, our institutions of education, at least in the western world, are largely premised on the theory that the classroom is a dedicated space for learning in which students are supposed to acquire the approved knowledge of society, which they can then take into the world outside and put into practice once their education is complete. As many of the more astute students taking my courses pointed out to me, there was a glaring inconsistency between *how* they were being taught, and *what* they were being taught about how learning actually occurs in the social world. Educators such as myself seemed to be the very last to practise what they preach.

This book

The challenge for me, then, was to find a way to teach as I had been taught. For if, as I have argued, the ultimate objective of anthropology is not documentary but transformational, it is surely incumbent on us to give to the future as we have received from the past. What value lies in transformations of the self if they end there, if selves do not go on reciprocally to transform others and the world? Had I gone to study with Rostropovich, I would have sought to transform the world through making music. By profession, however, I am not a musician but an anthropologist. I give lectures, not concerts. Yet my teaching – all teaching – would be worthless were it not transformational in intent. And conversely, my studies – all study – would be worthless if it did not lead us to teach with this intent. To teach is to honour our commitments by repaying what we owe the world for our formation. In short, teaching (and not ethnographic writing) is the other side of participant observation: there cannot be one without the other, and both are indispensable to the practice of anthropology as an art of inquiry. *To teach anthropology is to practise anthropology; to practise anthropology is to teach it*. This was the pedagogical principle at the heart of the course on the 4 As. And it also underpins this book. For me as much as for the students, the course was a journey upon which we were embarked together, with no knowing what we might discover, and in the following chapters I offer some of what I found along the ways the journey opened up: of what it means to make things, about materials and form, artefacts and buildings, the nature of design, landscapes and perception, animate life, personal knowledge and the work of the hand. But this is not a coursebook, let alone a textbook. So what kind of book is it?

Imagine that one night, whilst you are sleeping, an elfin trickster slips into your kitchen. Heading for the shelf where you keep your recipes, it removes your copy of *Katie Stewart's Cookbook* (Stewart 1983). Next it proceeds to your book-lined study, where it catches sight of *Outline of a Theory of Practice* (1977), by Pierre Bourdieu. With a mischievous glint in its eye, the elf silently removes the *Outline*, and inserts the *Cookbook* in its place. Then, returning to the kitchen, it slips the *Outline* into the place where the *Cookbook* had been. The following day you plan to cook a traditional Scottish dish – herrings in oatmeal – for dinner. You recall that Katie Stewart has the recipe, on page 78 of her book, and needing some tips to refresh your memory, you casually retrieve the book from its usual place on the shelf. Opening it up at the appropriate page, this is what you read: 'The habitus, the durably installed generative principle of regulated improvisations, produces practices which tend to reproduce the regularities immanent in the objective conditions of the production of their generative principle, while adjusting to the demands inscribed as objective potentialities in the situation, as defined by the cognitive and motivating structures making up the habitus.' Er, ... what? Who wrote this gibberish? How will it help you cook? Frustrated, you repair to your study to continue work on that academic paper for the journal *Anthropologica Theoretica*, which you have been trying to finish for weeks. There's a quote from Bourdieu you need: it is too long-winded to remember by heart. Better look it up! It's on page 78. Opening what you thought was the book, you find the following: 'Clean the herrings and cut off the heads. Place on a work surface and spread out flat, skin side up. Press along the back to loosen the bone, then turn each herring over and gently pull away the bone. Put the oatmeal on to a plate and season with salt and pepper. Coat the herrings by firmly pressing each side into the oatmeal.' What has that got to do with theory?

The trick the elf played, of course, was to mix up works normally belonging to contexts that you keep rigidly separate. There is a place for recipe books and manuals, in among the ingredients and utensils of a craft, be it cookery or anything else. Within the kitchen or the workshop, they may be a source not just of sound advice but of inspiration and insight. But in the study, such books appear as compendia of trivialities, without one ounce of intellectual substance. In her preface, Stewart writes: 'I have collected my best recipes as well as useful cookery hints and tips that I have discovered during the course of my work' (Stewart 1983: 7). In your study, however, the lifetime of experience distilled in the book counts for nothing. Not that Bourdieu fares any better in the kitchen. What is widely regarded as one of the most inspirational works of social and anthropological theory to have been written in the second half of the twentieth century is reduced to scholastic gobbledygook. Indeed the gap between practice and the theory of it – or, as we might say, *between herrings and habitus* – seems wider than ever. It has been my ambition all along to write a book that would close the gap, and somehow resolve the opposition between the theoretical and the practical. Such a book would reference the world, not just other books; its lines would mingle with the writing of the world, and its pages with the world's surfaces. Where, then, should it be housed? Where are you housed? While normally, Bourdieu stays in the study and Stewart in the kitchen, you are at home in both rooms and in any number of other places besides. So perhaps the book's place is with you, on your person, wherever you happen to be. Do not try to read it, as it will not inform you of what you need to know. You'll have to find that out for yourself. But do read *with* it. I hope, then, that it will guide you on your way.

2

THE MATERIALS OF LIFE

Touching objects, feeling materials

Let me begin by describing an experiment I have carried out along with the students in the very first week of the 4 As course. For this experiment, I asked them to gather a selection of objects that they found lying around the 'things' on which they had chosen to focus their projects. They arrived with a motley assortment of odds and ends: there were coins, paper clips, drinks cans, cigarette butts, a rubber ball, the feather of a seagull, and much else besides. First we deposited all the stuff they had brought in a heap in the middle of the floor (Figure 2.1). We looked at the heap, from which a spider scuttled out across the carpet. It had arrived as a passenger with some item, but no one knew from which. Or was it actually a *part* of the item? Picking up each object in turn, we examined it, investigated its form, interrogated the finder on where it was found and why it had caught his or her attention, and attempted to reconstruct the story of how it had fetched up at that particular place. The coins, for example, told of pockets and purses and of countless transpositions from hand to till and back. The paper clips once fastened the documents of a busy official, while the cans – previously filled with liquid – had been held to thirsty lips through which, only moments before, had been inhaled the smoke of smouldering tobacco. From the tooth marks on its surface, it was apparent that the rubber ball, recovered from a sandy beach, had been the plaything of a dog, while the feather had once graced a bird in flight, high in the air. All of these objects, in short, evidenced other lives – human, canine, avian. And yet in becoming objects they had broken off from these lives – like fallen twigs from a tree – and were left lifeless, as so much bric-a-brac stranded on the riverbank. Only the spider escaped.

In the following week I asked the students to return to their project sites and to bring along, this time, a selection of *materials* gathered from the environs of these sites. This time many of them came with containers full of stuff like sand, gravel, mud and leaf litter. Why containers? Because, as we found as soon as we emptied out the contents, materials do not, of themselves, stay in place or hold to the bounds of any form, and have an inherent tendency to run amok. We are all familiar with Mary

FIGURE 2.1 An assortment of objects on the floor: from the 4 As class

Douglas's (1966: 44) celebrated definition of dirt as matter out of place, and sure enough, we quickly got our hands very dirty. This offered an experience of tactility that could not have been more different from the clinical detachment with which we had examined the objects of the previous week. Then, it was as if we had worn protective gloves, to ensure that there should be absolutely no exchange of substance between the object and the hands that held it. Nor should it be bent, broken or squashed. Our concern had been exclusively with the stillness of form, and like detectives, we were at pains to handle every object delicately, so as not to tamper with the evidence or compromise its value as data. With materials, on the other hand, the experience of tactility was all about grain and texture, about the feeling of contact between malleable substance and sensitive skin, about dry sand cupped in the palm and running through the fingers, wet mud sticking and caking as it dries out, the rough abrasion of gravel, and so on.

I had myself come along with some materials, namely sheets of hardboard and a bucket of wallpaper paste. Having covered the boards with paste, everyone set to work mixing the materials they had brought and then smearing these mixtures, however they wished, onto the boards (Figure 2.2). The result was a rather astonishing series of artworks. I think what was most astonishing about them was the way in which they registered the traces of movement and flow: on the one hand the manual and bodily gestures of ourselves, as practitioners; on the other hand the particular flow patterns of the mixtures we had made. I suppose, in retrospect, that we should not have been so astonished by this; after all, it corresponds to our most commonplace experience in the kitchen. Next time you are making soup, pay attention to the way your stirring

FIGURE 2.2   Smearing materials onto boards covered with paste: from the 4 As class

gesture with the spoon both induces and responds to viscosities and currents of the mixed ingredients in the pan. What is odd is that studies of the material culture of kitchens have generally concentrated on pots and pans, and spoons, to the virtual exclusion of the soup. The focus, in short, has been on objects rather than materials. Yet on second thoughts, this is not a division between what we find in the kitchen: objects here; materials there. It is rather a difference of perspective. Householders might think of pots and pans as objects, at least until they start to cook, but for the dealer in scrap metal, they are lumps of material.

Likewise, we could return to the objects that the students brought in for our first session and ask: what would have happened if we had thought of all this stuff as materials? A coin: that's copper, and we could have sought to explore its properties by hammering it, or seeing what happens when you heat it up or put it in a flame (the flame would turn green). The paper clip: that's a length of wire, and we could unravel it and bend it to other purposes. The drinks can: that's aluminium; feel how light it is! The cigarette butt: well there is still some tobacco inside. Light it, and it will exude smoke, and the smoke makes trails in the air that bend this way and that in response to the fluxes and rhythms of our own breathing. The ball: that's made of rubber, and by applying pressure with the hands, we can feel its softness and springiness. We could even put it between our teeth and imagine what it feels like to be a dog. And of course, to think of the feather as a material is to recognise that it has grown along with the body of the bird of which it was once an integral part, mingling with the air in flight. In every case, by treating these erstwhile objects as materials we rescue them from the cul-de-sac into which they had been cast and restore them to the currents of life.

Making and growing

This chapter is about bringing things back to life. Its basic argument may be expressed by means of a simple diagram. Draw two lines: they need not be straight; indeed you can allow them to meander a little. However, they should proceed alongside one another, like the trails left by two people walking abreast. Each is a path of movement. Let one of these lines stand for the flow of consciousness, saturated as it is by light, sound and feeling. And let the other stand for the flow of materials as they circulate, mix and meld. Now imagine that each of these flows is momentarily stopped up. On the side of consciousness, this stoppage takes on the semblance of an *image*, like a fugitive suddenly caught in the glare of a spotlight. And on the side of materials it takes on the solid form of an *object*, like a boulder placed in the fugitive's path, blocking his passage. On our diagram we could depict both stoppages by a point or blob on each respective line. Now draw a double ended arrow connecting the two blobs. Unlike the original pair of lines, this arrow is not the trace of a movement; it is notional rather than phenomenal, and depicts a connection of some kind between image and object. Now that our diagram is complete (Figure 2.3), we can sum up the argument of this chapter, and indeed of the entire book. It is to switch our perspective from the endless shuttling back and forth from image to object and from object to image, that is such a pronounced feature of academic writing in the fields of anthropology, archaeology, art and architecture, to the material flows and currents of sensory awareness in which images and objects reciprocally take shape. In terms of our diagram, this entails a rotation of 90 degrees, from the lateral to the longitudinal.

We will find this rotation cropping up again and again, in various connections. Indeed we have already encountered it in the last chapter, in our distinction between ethnographic documentation (lateral) and anthropological transformation (longitudinal). With regard to perception, it underpins the distinction between an optical and a haptic relation to the world – a distinction that explains the quite different experiences of tactility described above, showing that the optical relation is by no means limited to a perception mediated by the eye (nor is the haptic relation limited to the hands). With regard to creativity, it distinguishes the improvisatory creativity of labour that works things out as it goes along from the attribution of creativity to the novelty of determinate ends conceived in advance. It underpins the distinctions spelled out in Chapter 7 between interaction and correspondence and in Chapter 8 between articulate and personal knowledge. Most fundamentally, however, it crops up in connection with the question of what it means to make things.

We are accustomed to think of making as a *project*. This is to start with an idea in mind, of what we want to achieve, and with a supply of the raw material needed to achieve it. And it is to finish at the moment when the material has taken on the intended form. At this point, we say, we have produced an *artefact*. A nodule of stone has become an axe, a lump of clay a pot, molten metal a sword. Axe, pot and sword are instances of what scholars call *material culture*, a phrase that perfectly captures this theory of making as the unification of stuff supplied by nature with the conceptual representations of a received cultural tradition. 'Material culture', as Julian Thomas (2007: 15) puts it, 'represents at once ideas that have been made material, and natural substance that has been rendered cultural.' In the literature, the theory is known as *hylomorphism*, from the Greek *hyle* (matter) and *morphe* (form). Whenever we read that in the making of

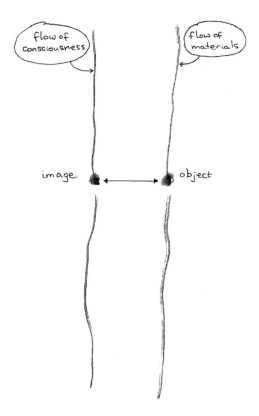

FIGURE 2.3   Consciousness, materials, image, object: the diagram

artefacts, practitioners impose forms internal to the mind upon a material world 'out there', hylomorphism is at work.

I want to think of making, instead, as a process of *growth*. This is to place the maker from the outset as a participant in amongst a world of active materials. These materials are what he has to work with, and in the process of making he 'joins forces' with them, bringing them together or splitting them apart, synthesising and distilling, in anticipation of what might emerge. The maker's ambitions, in this understanding, are altogether more humble than those implied by the hylomorphic model. Far from standing aloof, imposing his designs on a world that is ready and waiting to receive them, the most he can do is to intervene in worldly processes that are already going on, and which give rise to the forms of the living world that we see all around us – in plants and animals, in waves of water, snow and sand, in rocks and clouds – adding his own impetus to the forces and energies in play. The difference between a marble statue and a rock formation such as a stalagmite, for example, is not that one has been made and the other not. The difference is only this: that at some point in the formative history of this lump of marble, first a quarryman appeared on the scene who, with much force and with the assistance of hammers and wedges, wrested it from the bedrock, after which a sculptor set to work with a chisel in order, as he might put it, to release the form from the stone. But as every chip of the chisel contributes to the emergent form of the statue, so every drop of supersaturated solution from the roof of the cave contributes to the form of the stalagmite. When subsequently, the statue is worn down by rain, the form-generating process continues, but now without further human intervention.

To read making longitudinally, as a confluence of forces and materials, rather than laterally, as a transposition from image to object, is to regard it as such a form-generating – or *morphogenetic* – process. This is to soften any distinction we might draw between organism and artefact. For if organisms grow, so too do artefacts. And if artefacts are made, so too are organisms. What varies, among countless other things, is the extent of human involvement in the generation of form: but this variation is one of degree, not kind. This is not of course to deny that the maker may have an idea in mind of what he wants to make. He may even be seeking to copy a piece of work that already stands before him. Does this not distinguish the statue from the stalagmite, once and for all? Can we not speak, in a sense unique to artefacts, of their *design*? This is a question I will leave for later (see Chapter 5). Suffice it to say, at this point, that even if the maker has a form in mind, it is not this form that creates the work. It is the engagement with materials. And it is therefore to this engagement that we must attend if we are to understand how things are made. Time and again, scholars have written as though to have a design for a thing, you already have the thing itself. Some versions of conceptual art and architecture have taken this reasoning to such an extreme that the thing itself becomes superfluous. It is but a representation – a derivative copy – of the design that preceded it (Frascari 1991: 93). If everything about a form is prefigured in the design, then why bother to make it at all? But makers know better, and one of the purposes of this book is to bring them out of the shadows into which they have been cast by an uncritical application of the hylomorphic model, and to celebrate the creativity of their achievement.

Baskets in the sand

On a cold and windy day in February, the 4 As students and I were out on a sandy peninsula wedged between the beach and the estuary of the River Don, which flows into the sea on the northern flank of the city of Aberdeen. Patches of snow remained on the ground. We were learning to make baskets out of willow, under the direction of anthropologist and craftsperson Stephanie Bunn (see Bunn 2010: 49–50). To form a frame, an odd number of lengths of willow were stuck vertically into the ground, to form a rough circle, tied at the top. Horizontal pieces were then woven alternately in and out of the vertical frame so as gradually to build up a surface in the form of an inverted cone. Students worked at this either singly or in pairs (Figure 2.4). From the start, I think, many students were surprised by the recalcitrant nature of the material. In a finished basket, the willow seems to sit so naturally there, as if it had always been meant to fall into that shape and was merely fulfilling the role for which it was predestined. But the willow did not want to be bent into shape. Sometimes it put up a fight, springing back and striking the weaver in the face. One had to be careful and coaxing. Then we realised that it was actually this resistance, the friction set up by branches bent forcibly against each other, that held the whole construction together. The form was not imposed on the material from without, but was rather generated in this force field,

FIGURE 2.4 Making baskets in the sand, near Aberdeen beach in north-east Scotland. (Courtesy of Raymond Lucas.)

comprised by the relations between the weaver and the willow. Indeed as novices, we had little control over the precise form and proportions of our baskets. Kneeling on the ground, our weaving involved quite muscular movements of the entire body, or at least from the knees upwards, so that the dimensions of the basket related directly to such bodily dimensions as arm-reach and shoulder-height. Students discovered they had muscles in places they had never imagined, partly because after a while they began to ache. But other forces, too, entered into the formative process. One of these was the wind. A persistent, strengthening wind was bending all the verticals of the frame in one direction, with an inclination that increased with height. No wonder, then, that many baskets, especially those woven nearest to the shore, tilted over somewhat, in an elegant but wholly unintended curve (Figure 2.5).

We laboured for almost three hours, gradually developing a rhythm and a feel for the material. As the work progressed, however, we began to face another problem. How would we know when to stop? There is no obvious point when a basket is finished. The end dawned for us, not when the form came to match initial expectations, for we had none. It came rather with failing light and the imminent prospect of heavy rain, increasing chill and stiffness in the limbs, and the sense that each additional strand was becoming somehow superfluous. At that point it was time to insert a separately woven base and to cut the verticals at the height we had reached. At last, then, we could lift the woven construction from the ground, and turn it upside down to reveal that what we had made was indeed a basket. Each basket was different, uniquely reflecting the mood and

FIGURE 2.5 A near-complete basket. (Courtesy of Raymond Lucas.)

temperament, as well as the physical stature, of its maker. Finally the students straggled off into the gathering dusk, proudly bearing homeward the baskets they had made. Later they would tell me that they had learned more from that one afternoon than from any number of lectures and readings: above all about what it means to make things, about how form arises through movement, and about the dynamic properties of materials.

On matter and form

Perhaps it is unfair to use basketry as a way to criticise the hylomorphic model. The conclusion that the model does not work for weaving does not rule out the possibility that it might work perfectly well for branches of manufacture in which form is more ostensibly imposed on material. What about making bricks, for example? In forming the brick, prior to firing in the kiln, soft clay is pressed into a pre-prepared, rectangular mould. The mould, it seems, prescribes the form while the material – the clay – is initially formless. Surely, as the clay is pressed into the mould, form is united with material just as the logic of hylomorphism requires. But in a thesis entitled *L'individuation à la lumière des notions de Forme et d'Information*, the philosopher Gilbert Simondon shows that this is not so.[1] For one thing, the mould is no geometric abstraction but a solid construction that has first to be built from a specific material (traditionally, a hardwood such as beech). For another thing, the clay is not raw. Having been dug out from beneath the topsoil, it has first to be ground, sieved to remove stones and other impurities, and then exhaustively kneaded before it is ready for use. In the moulding of a brick, then, form is not united with material. Rather, there is a bringing together or unification of two 'transformational half-chains' (*demi-chaînes de transformations*) – respectively building the mould and preparing the clay – to a point at which they reach a certain compatibility: the clay can take to the mould and the mould can take the clay (Simondon 2005: 41–42). At the moment of encounter, when the brick maker 'dashes' a clot of clay into the mould, the expressive force of the maker's gesture, imparted to the clay, comes hard up against the compressive resistance of the hard wood of the mould's walls. Thus the brick, with its characteristic rectangular outline, results not from the *im*position of form onto matter but from the *contra*position of equal and opposed forces immanent in both the clay and the mould. In the field of forces, the form emerges as a more or less transitory equilibration. Perhaps bricks are not so different from baskets after all (Figure 2.6).

Simondon's central postulate of *individuation* holds that the generation of things should be understood as a process of morphogenesis in which form is ever emergent rather than given in advance. As Brian Massumi (2009: 37) explains, in a commentary on Simondon's text, this is to assert 'a primacy of processes of becoming over the states of being through which they pass'. Against the form-receiving passivity of matter posited by hylomorphism, Simondon took the essence of matter, or the material, to lie in *form-taking activity*. The hylomorphic model, Simondon (2005: 46) concludes, corresponds to the perspective of a man who stands outside the works and sees what goes in and what comes out but nothing of what happens in between, of the actual processes whereby materials of diverse kinds come to take on the forms they do. It is as though, in form and matter, he could grasp only the ends of two half-chains but not what brings them together, only a simple relation of moulding rather than the continuous modulation that goes on in the midst of form-taking activity, in the *becoming* of things.

In their 'treatise on nomadology', philosopher Gilles Deleuze and psychoanalyst Félix Guattari have taken up Simondon's crusade against hylomorphism, and, thanks to their influence, the issues it raises are beginning to percolate through to archaeology and anthropology. The trouble with the matter-form model, argue Deleuze and Guattari, is that in assuming 'a fixed form and a matter deemed homogeneous' it fails to acknowledge, on the one hand, the variability of matter – its tensions and elasticities, lines of flow and resistances – and, on the other hand, the conformations and deformations to which these modulations give rise. In reality, they insist, whenever we encounter matter 'it is matter in movement, in flux, in variation', with the consequence that 'this matter-flow can only be *followed*' (Deleuze and Guattari 2004: 450–451). Artisans or practitioners who follow the flow are, in effect, itinerants, wayfarers, whose task is to enter the grain of the world's becoming and bend it to an evolving purpose. Theirs is an 'intuition in action' (ibid.: 452).

Whereas Simondon took his key example from brick making, however, Deleuze and Guattari appeal to metallurgy. For them, metallurgy highlights a particular insufficiency of the hylomorphic model, namely that it can only conceive of technical operations as

The Brick Maker.

FIGURE 2.6 A brick maker at work under a thatched shelter, his wheelbarrow beside him. The engraving is by an unknown artist, dating from 1827. (Courtesy of Mary Evans Picture Library.)

sequences of discrete steps, with a clear threshold marking the termination of each step and the commencement of the next. But in metallurgy, these thresholds are precisely where the key operations take place. Thus, even as he beats out the form with hammer on anvil, the smith has periodically to return his iron to the fire: material variation spills over into the formative process and indeed continues beyond it, since it is only after forging that the iron is finally quenched. 'Matter and form have never seemed more rigid than in metallurgy', write Deleuze and Guattari, 'yet the succession of forms tends to be replaced by the form of a continous development, and the variability of matters tends to be replaced by the matter of a continous variation' (ibid.: 453). Instead of the concatenation of discrete operations to which analysts of techniques have given the name *chaîne opératoire*,[2] we have here something more like an unbroken, contrapuntal coupling of a gestural dance with a modulation of the material. Even iron flows, and the smith has to follow it.

The two faces of materiality

When scholars speak of the 'material world' or, more abstractly, of 'materiality', what do they mean? Put the question to students of material culture, and you are likely to get contradictory answers. Let me offer a few instances. The first comes from Christopher Tilley, on the topic of stone. Contemplating a stone in its 'brute materiality', Tilley perceives a formless lump of matter. Yet we need a concept of materiality, he thinks, in order to understand how particular pieces of stone are given form and meaning within specific social and historical contexts (Tilley 2007: 17). Andrew Jones (2004: 330), likewise, holds that the notion of materiality both encompasses 'the material or physical component of the environment' and 'emphasises how those material properties are enrolled in the life projects of humans'. Nicole Boivin (2008: 26) tells us that she uses the word materiality 'to emphasise the physicality of the material world', yet this physicality embraces the fact 'that it offers possibilities for the human agent'. Introducing a collection of essays on the theme of materiality, Paul Graves-Brown (2000: 1) asserts that their common focus is on the question of 'how the very material character of the world around us is appropriated by humanity'. And in almost identical terms, Joshua Pollard (2004: 48) explains that 'by materiality I mean how the material character of the world is comprehended, appropriated and involved in human projects'.

In every case, there seem to be two sides to materiality. On one side is the raw physicality of the world's 'material character'; on the other side is the socially and historically situated agency of human beings who, in appropriating this physicality for their purposes, are alleged to project upon it both design and meaning in the conversion of naturally given raw material into the finished forms of artefacts. This duplicity in the comprehension of the material world precisely mirrors that to be found in much older debates surrounding the concept of human nature, which could refer at once to the raw substrate of basic instinct that humans were alleged to share with the 'brutes', and to a suite of characters – including language, intelligence and the capacity for symbolic thought – by which they were said to be elevated to a level of being over and above that of all other creatures. The appeal, in these debates, to the '*human* nature of human nature' (Eisenberg 1972) did nothing to resolve this duplicity, but only served to reproduce it. Indeed the very notion of humanity, as we saw in the last chapter (p. 5), epitomises the predicament of a creature that can know itself and the world of which it is inextricably a part only by taking itself out of that world and re-inscribing itself on another level of being: mental rather than material; cultural rather than natural (Ingold 2010: 362–363). In just the same way, in the notion of materiality the world is presented both as the very bedrock of existence and as an externality that is open to comprehension and appropriation by a transcendent humanity. Materiality, like humanity, is Janus-faced.

Now it is not my intention, as archaeologist Bjørnar Olsen (2010: 16) alleges, to eliminate the word 'materiality' from our vocabulary or to ban its use. Just as with 'humanity', it would probably be difficult for us to manage without it. We do, however, need to be wary of the assumptions that it tends to bring in train, most particularly – as geographers Ben Anderson and John Wylie (2009: 319) warn – that the material world has by nature such properties of obduracy and consistency of shape as define the state of a *solid*. Olsen himself falls prey to this assumption when he appeals to the world's 'hard physicality' (Olsen 2003: 88). Why so hard, so solid? Consider, for example, an ordinary pot. In its time it has seen service in numerous campaigns, from when it was first made to when, cracked and discarded, it was returned to the earth, only to be uncovered thousands of years later in an archaeological excavation. Yet through all of that, has it not remained steadfastly what it was? Was not the pot, as the hard and physical thing it is, always a pot? Not so, answers archaeologist Cornelius Holtorf (2002: 54), in his 'Notes on the life history of a potsherd'. For the pot's materiality, he claims, is no more and no less than the ways in which, throughout its history, it was variably enrolled in human life-projects. It could, in principle, be anything anyone wanted it to be. But in this very claim, Holtorf lurches from one side of materiality to the other – from the physicality of matter to the forms of its social appropriation. This move does nothing to soften, liquefy or enliven the material. If the pot has a life history (and this could be either 'short' or 'long', depending on whether we count from the moment of manufacture to that of discard or to that of eventual recovery), it is not the history of a life intrinsic to the stuff of which it was made. It is of the human life that has surrounded it and given it meaning.

How about an artefact of flaked stone? Like the pot, the stone would also have had its moments – at least three, according to prehistorian Geoff Bailey (2007: 209): when it was acquired, when it was worked into the form of the artefact, and when the artefact was eventually discarded. To these could be added a fourth moment, when it was recovered by the archaeologist, a fifth when it was illustrated in a publication, and any number of possible moments thereafter. These moments are known to posterity only because they leave a material trace, and the artefact presents itself, according to Bailey, as an accumulation of such traces – for which he reserves the term 'palimpsest'. He even goes so far as to claim that the materiality of a thing such as a stone artefact is *by definition* that aspect by which it outlasts the active moments of its formation or inscription. It is a kind of negative imprint of the formative process. Yet this is to revert, once again, to the hylomorphic characterisation of materiality as form-receiving passivity rather than form-taking activity. In short, whether we find the history of things, with Holtorf, in the life that surrounds them or, with Bailey, in the traces that remain in them after life has moved on, it seems that in the appeal to materiality, the *becoming* of materials – their generative or regenerative potential, indeed their very life – has fallen through the cracks of an already solidified world.

The return to alchemy

What then is matter? What do we mean when we speak of materials? Are matter and materials the same or different? To understand the meaning of materials for those who work *with* them – be they artisans, craftsmen, painters or practitioners of other trades – I believe we need, as art historian James Elkins recommends, to take a 'short course in forgetting chemistry' (Elkins 2000: 9–39). Or more precisely, we have to remember how materials were understood in the days of alchemy. Elkins's point is that prior to the introduction of synthetic paints, the painter's knowledge of his materials was fundamentally alchemical. To paint was to bring together, into a single movement, a certain material mixture, loaded onto the brush, with a certain bodily gesture enacted through the hand that held it. But the science of chemistry can no more define the mixture than can the science of anatomy define the gesture. The chemist thinks of matter in terms of its invariant atomic or molecular constitution. Thus water is H_2O, and salt is sodium chloride. For the alchemist, by contrast, a material is known not by what it *is* but by what it *does*, specifically when mixed with other materials, treated in particular ways, or placed in particular situations (Conneller 2011: 19). Among innumerable other things, water gurgles down a spout, turns to steam when heated and to ice when cooled, and dissolves salt. And salt, inter alia, can be ground into fine white grains that pass through the hole of a dispenser, prevents the freezing of water on roads and pavements, and gives a distinctive flavour to food.

Chantal Conneller introduces her recent discussion of the archaeology of materials by comparing two definitions of gold. One comes from a chemistry textbook, the other from an eighth century Persian philosopher–alchemist. For the chemist, gold is one of the elements in the periodic table, and as such has an essential constitution that is given quite independently of the manifold forms and circumstances of its appearance or of human encounters with it. But for the alchemist, gold was yellowing and gleaming, and anything that yellowed and gleamed, and that would also shine ever brighter under water and could be hammered into thin leaf, would count as gold (Conneller 2011: 4). One way to accommodate these divergent understandings of what is ostensibly the 'same' material would be to argue, with the design theorist David Pye, for a distinction between the *properties* and *qualities* of materials. Properties, for Pye, are objective and scientifically measurable; qualities are subjective – they are ideas in people's heads that they project onto the material in question (Pye 1968: 47). But this would only be to reproduce the duplicity in our understanding of the material world – between its given physicality and its valorisation within human projects of making – that we are seeking to resolve (Ingold 2011a: 30). The experienced practitioner's knowledge of the properties of materials, like that of the alchemist, is not simply projected onto them but grows out of a lifetime of intimate gestural and sensory engagement in a particular craft or trade. As Conneller (2011: 5) argues, 'different understandings of materials are not simply "concepts" set apart from "real" properties; they are realised in terms of different practices that themselves have material effects'.

But precisely because these practices are so variable and have such different effects, Conneller warns, we should avoid the temptation to turn understandings drawn from one particular context of material–technical interaction into a meta-theory for everything else. Our task should rather be to describe and analyse every case in its ethnographic specificity. For this reason, whilst broadly sympathetic to attempts by scholars such as Simondon, Deleuze and Guattari, and even myself to overthrow the logic of hylomorphism, Conneller is also critical of their tendency to select just one field of practice as a lens through which to view all others. Thus where Simondon bases his argument on the operations of brick making, Deleuze and Guattari (2004: 454) feel equally free to generalise across the board from metallurgy: 'metal is coextensive to the whole of matter, and the whole of matter to metallurgy'. If even metal flows, then so – they say – do wood and clay, not to mention grass, water and herds. For my own part, I have drawn on the practices of basketry to advance a rather similar argument about how the forms of things – of all sorts – are generated in fields of force and circulations of materials that cut across any boundaries we might draw between practitioners, materials and the wider environment (Ingold 2000: 339–348). In a certain sense, then, we can say that the smith at his forge, or the carpenter at his bench, is actually weaving. Even the bricklayer may be said to weave as he knots bricks with mortar into the fabric of a wall to create a regular and repeating pattern (Frampton 1995: 6). This is not, *pace* Conneller, to pretend that there is no difference between the properties of willow, iron, wood and clay, or that the skills of the basket maker are no different from those of the smith, the carpenter and the mason. It is rather to focus on what it means to say of practice that it is skilled, or of materials that they are endowed with properties, whatever the field of practice or the materials involved may be.

The riddle of materials

Another case in point is the understanding of stone – a material that has been of particular interest to archaeologists, not least because of its alleged hardness, solidity and durability (Tilley 2004). Indeed, these properties have been so often highlighted as to make them seem all but universal (Conneller 2011: 82). If you want to build a monument that lasts, then hard stone is an appropriate material to choose. We cannot assume, however, that just because the stony elements of what is nowadays recognised as an archaeological monument have endured, while all the other materials that may have been used in the construction have long since rotted away, this is what the original builders intended, or the reason why they chose to incorporate stone into the construction in the first place. For all we know, stone may have been selected by people in the past not for its solidity and permanence but for their opposites – namely fluidity and mutability. No doubt the flint knappers of old, in the manufacture of stone tools, valued the hard edge. However, the alchemically informed painter values soft stone that can be ground to ochre for its colour. Some kinds of stone are heavy, others light; some are hard, others soft or crumbly; some separate into flat sheets, others can only be split into blocks. All things considered, Conneller (2011: 82) concludes, 'it is clear that there is no such thing as "stone"; there are many different types of stones with different properties and these stones become different through particular modes of engagement'.

It is not clear, however, whether this typological splitting of generic 'stone' into innumerable subtypes will take us any closer to a resolution of our initial question: what *is* a material? As the Swiss architect Peter Zumthor writes, 'material is endless':

> Take a stone: you can saw it, grind it, drill into it, or polish it – it will be a different thing each time. Then take tiny amounts of the same stone, or huge amounts, and it will turn into something else again. Then hold it up to the light – different again. There are a thousand different possibilities in one material alone.
>
> (Zumthor 2006: 25)

But if there are as many different kinds of stones as there are possible ways of engaging with them, then – as even Conneller is obliged to admit – no two stones can ever be quite the same. Taken to its logical conclusion, the project of classification would leave us with as many subtypes as there are stones in the world, and we would still not know what stoniness means! Indeed, any attempt to produce a classification of materials, in terms of their properties or attributes, is bound to fail for the simple reason that these properties are not fixed but continually emergent along with the materials themselves. 'The properties of materials', as I have argued elsewhere with specific reference to the stoniness of stone, 'are not attributes but histories' (Ingold 2011a: 32). Practitioners know them by knowing their stories: of what they do and what happens to them when treated in particular ways. Such stories are fundamentally resistant to any project of classification (ibid.: 156–164). Materials do not *exist*, in the manner of objects, as static entities with diagnostic attributes; they are not – in the words of Karen Barad – 'little bits of nature', awaiting the mark of an external force like culture or history for their completion. Rather, as substances-in-becoming they carry on or *perdure*, forever overtaking the formal destinations that, at one time or another, have been assigned to them, and undergoing continual modulation as they do so. Whatever the objective forms in which they are currently cast, materials are always and already on their ways to becoming something else – always, as Barad puts it, 'already an ongoing historicity' (Barad 2003: 821).

Materials are ineffable. They cannot be pinned down in terms of established concepts or categories. To describe any material is to pose a riddle, whose answer can be discovered only through observation and engagement with what is there.[3] The riddle gives the material a voice and allows it to tell its own story: it is up to us, then, to listen, and from the clues it offers, to discover what is speaking. To return to an earlier example: 'I yellow and gleam, and shine ever brighter under running water. What am I?' The answer is evident to the panner without his having to name it. For it lies there, glinting in the bed of the stream. Just as in the case of panning for gold, to know materials we have to follow them – to 'follow the matter-flow as pure productivity' – as artisans have always done (Deleuze and Guattari 2004: 454). Their every technical gesture is a question, to which the material responds according to its bent. In following their materials, practitioners do not so much *interact* as *correspond* with them (see Chapter 7, pp. 105–108). Making, then, is a process of correspondence: not the imposition of preconceived form on raw material substance, but the drawing out or bringing forth of potentials immanent in a world of becoming. In the phenomenal world, every material is such a becoming, one path or trajectory through a maze of trajectories.

In this sense we can agree with Deleuze and Guattari that materials evince a 'life proper to matter', albeit one that is hidden or rendered unrecognisable by the terms of the hylomorphic model, which reduce matter to inert substance. It is in this life, they argue – in 'the immanent power of corporeality in all matter, and … the esprit de corps accompanying it' – that the relation between making (as in basketry, brick making or metallurgy) and alchemy is to be found (Deleuze and Guattari 2004: 454). In the act of making the artisan couples his own movements and gestures – indeed his very life – with the becoming of his materials, joining with and following the forces and flows that bring his work to fruition. It is the artisan's desire to see what the material can *do*, by contrast to the scientist's desire to know what it *is*, that, as political theorist Jane Bennett explains (2010: 60), enables the former to discern a life in the material and thus, ultimately, to 'collaborate more productively' with it. Returning to the diagram with which I began (Figure 2.3), to see what the material will do, to collaborate with it or, in our terms, to correspond with it, is to read making longitudinally rather than laterally. In the following two chapters we will explore what this reading means in practice, first in the case of prehistoric stonework, second in the case of medieval architecture.

3

ON MAKING A HANDAXE

The Acheulean biface

One of the strangest enigmas of prehistory is a thing called a handaxe. I have before me, as I write, a replica made for me to order by the professional stone knapper, John Lord (Figures 3.1 and 3.2). It is a thing of great beauty, consummate craftsmanship and no obvious practical use at all. Of a size and shape that fits perfectly to the palm and outstretched fingers of an adult hand, I like just to hold it and feel its weight and texture. Wrought from a nodule of black flint, with some residual traces of white cortex, its form is of what prehistorians call a *biface*: that is, it has two convex faces, one bulging slightly more than the other, which meet around an edge that tapers from a thick butt towards a rounded tip. The two faces bear the scars of the technique by which it was made, involving the successive removal of flakes from an original core. This technique exploits the property of conchoidal fracture, that is, the tendency of flint to break off in slivers, issuing from a bulb-shaped cone at the point of impact, when struck at an oblique angle near a protruding edge. Since the ventral surface of each sliver is slightly convex, it leaves its mark on the core as an elongated concavity. Once the face is fully flaked, these concavities intersect to form an irregular pattern of well-defined ridges. The edge at which the two faces converge is surprisingly sharp, and has been trimmed through the addition of further serrations made by applying pressure through a punch of softer and less brittle material such as wood or antler.

That the thing is called a handaxe owes much to the circumstances surrounding the first substantial finds of prehistoric specimens, in the 1830s and 40s, at the site of Saint Acheul in northern France. Their discoverer was Jacques Boucher de Perthes, a customs officer from the nearby town of Abbeville. Believing them to be of great antiquity, de Perthes called them 'antediluvian axes' (*haches antediluviennes*). Ridiculed by his contemporaries, his claims subsequently found favour in a climate of thought that was growing increasingly accustomed to the idea that humankind had evolved over aeons of time. Thus it was that by the late nineteenth century, the site of Saint Acheul had come to stand for an entire epoch of prehistory, associated with the industry of making artefacts of just the kind that de Perthes had first uncovered there. In 1925, this industry

FIGURE 3.1 Replica Acheulean handaxe, made by John Lord, face up. (Courtesy of Susanna Ingold.)

FIGURE 3.2 The same handaxe, edge up. (Courtesy of Susanna Ingold.)

was officially labelled 'the Acheulean', and the label – along with the designation of its iconic artefacts as handaxes – has remained ever since. Yet far from being confined to France, or even to northern Europe, Acheulean handaxes were turning up all over the place: elsewhere in Europe, and in Africa, the Near East and South Asia. Not only have they been found across all three continents of the Old World; they have also been dated to periods spanning well over a million years. The oldest known handaxes, albeit rather crudely made, have been recovered from sites in East Africa dating around 1.7–1.6 million years ago. In Europe, artefacts of the same kind were still being made as late as 128,000 years ago. And although, comparing earlier and later specimens, there is some evidence of progressive refinement towards greater balance and symmetry, through all that time the overall form remained virtually unchanged (Schick and Toth 1993; Wynn 1995; Roche 2005).

There seems little reason to doubt that the handaxe is an outcome of purposive activity and that it is, in this sense, a thing that has been made. It is true that conchoidal fractures can occur accidentally, for example on the seashore when stones are knocked against one another in the surf. But no accident, or series of accidents, could generate the systematic, patterned flaking of the handaxe. It is also true that chimpanzees have been observed to crack open hard-shelled nuts using a technique that bears comparison with the way stones may be split, by placing them on a hard surface and delivering a percussive blow from above. Knappers still use this technique to obtain the cores from which they work.[1] Split-breaking, however, is quite different in both method and results from conchoidal fracture (Pelegrin 2005: 25). The latter requires a degree of bimanual dexterity and precision control that is beyond even the most rigorously trained ape, and that was equally beyond the capabilities of those ancestral hominins,[2] of two million and more years ago, which seem to have made extensive use of split stone but never to have flaked it. Thus the Acheulean is an industry that is genuinely without parallel in the animal kingdom. In the fossil record, the industry is generally associated with the remains of hominins of the kind long known as *Homo erectus*, and we may reasonably infer that the makers of handaxes were, in the main, individuals of this species. But if they made them for a purpose, we have no idea of what that purpose was. Explanations range from the plausible, such as that they were used for cutting and scraping animal hides or vegetable matter, to the bizarre, including one theory that hunters used the peculiar aerodynamic properties of the 'axe', when hurled with a spin, to stun or topple unsuspecting prey (Calvin 1993). All we know for sure is that the one use to which the thing *cannot* have been put is as an axe, since to have done so would have caused more injury to the user's hand than to whatever he or she might have been seeking to cut down.

For want of any better explanation, the majority of prehistorians have gone for the safe option of describing the artefact as a 'general purpose tool' (Wynn 1995: 14). The fundamental enigma of the handaxe, however, lies not in what it might have been used for, but in the stability of its form. To what can we ascribe this stability? When it comes to the tools of both contemporary and past human beings, it is commonly assumed that they are the products of intelligent design, as though their makers first 'saw', in their mind's eye, the form of the completed object, and then set to work to execute it in the material. When we contemplate the form of the Acheulean handaxe, reflecting on its regularity and balance, it is hard not to see it likewise as the realisation of deliberate, self-conscious design. The bifacial form does not appear to be in any way prefigured in the raw material – comprising naturally irregular lumps of stone – or in the knapper's relation to it. If the form is thus arbitrary, and imposed on the material, where could it reside save in the minds of makers, as part of a conceptually framed and socially transmitted tradition? Indeed, assertions to this effect are commonplace in archaeological writings. John Gowlett, for example, assures his readers that '*Homo erectus* of 700,000 years ago had a geometrically accurate sense of proportion and could impose this on stone in the external world' (Gowlett 1984: 185). Likewise, having himself attempted to master the skills of handaxe making, Jacques Pelegrin contends that the regularity and symmetry of the biface furnish the clearest evidence that its makers were guided by a 'pre-existing mental image … deserving of being termed a "concept"' (Pelegrin 1993: 310). In short, it is supposed that like any modern artisan, the Acheulean handaxe maker must have started work with a model or representation of some kind, in the imagination, of the things to be produced. 'The maker', as Brian Fagan asserts, 'had to envisage the shape of the artefact, which was to be produced from a mere lump of stone' (Fagan 1989: 138).

Instinct or intelligence

But if this is so – if the form is the expression of a design concept – then how can we possibly account for the stability of the concept over three continents and more than a million years? In the course of history, human beings have come up with an astonishing variety of designs, many of them of great ingenuity. Some have become lodged within well-established traditions and have persisted for many centuries, even millennia. But there is nothing in the record of ethnography, or in the last hundred thousand years of prehistory, even approaching the range and persistence of the biface form. To suggest, as Pelegrin does (1993: 312), that the form remained constant since progress 'at the level of mental images' was retarded by the 'inertia of tradition' merely begs the question of why such inertia should have exerted a stranglehold over innovation so much tighter during the heyday of *Homo erectus* than at any time since. If the handaxe makers had the intelligence to envisage forms in advance of their realisation, then, in principle, they should have been just as capable of devising alternative forms as are their latter-day descendants of the species *Homo sapiens*, among whom we would number ourselves. Could it be, then, that *Homo erectus* was not following the dictates of any mental model, traditional or otherwise, in their flaking of stone? In the constancy of its form, the biface seems almost like a prosthetic outgrowth of the hominin body, an adjunct of the skeleton that differs from teeth and nails only in that it is extra-somatic and detachable. After all, provided that they have opportunities to develop the necessary skills, birds build nests and beavers dams in ways peculiar and more or less invariant to their particular species, though responsive to the specific properties and qualities of available raw materials and environmental affordances. Why should it have been any different for *Homo erectus*? Could we go so far as to say that the making of handaxes was no more, and no less, than the expression of an instinct?

Precisely such an argument was advanced by one of the greatest and certainly most original minds of twentieth century archaeology, André Leroi-Gourhan, in his treatise of 1964, *Le Geste et la parole*.[3] In an idiosyncratic and now obsolete terminology, he called the handaxe makers 'Archanthropians'. Their tools, he tells us, 'were still, to a large extent, a direct emanation of species behaviour', each one 'a "secretion" of the anthropoid body and brain' (Leroi-Gourhan 1993: 91, 97). It is as if technical activity oozed from the Archanthropian body and congealed in the forms of the artefacts it brought into being. As closely bound to the body plan as the architecture of the skeleton, the forms of artefacts could change no faster than the skeletal morphology of the creatures that made them: both 'obeyed the rhythm of biological evolution' (ibid.: 106). Yet if anyone doubted this argument, or found it hard to believe, it was Leroi-Gourhan himself. Flatly repudiating his own assertions to the contrary, he insisted that the shape of the biface 'must be pre-existent in the maker's mind', whence it governs the choice of the stone from which it will be made, and the successive operations of flaking (ibid.: 97). Endowed with a complex intelligence, the Archanthropians were 'excellent artisans capable of visualising the future shape of their bifaces … in a lump of raw stone' (ibid.: 141). Why, then, could they not visualise alternative forms, or realise them in different materials? Though Leroi-Gourhan posed the question, he failed to answer it, weakly excusing his failure on the difficulty we all have, with our *Homo sapiens* brain, of understanding the intellectual life of a creature whose mind ran along lines very different from ours (ibid: 141).

Like so many prehistorians before and since, Leroi-Gourhan seems caught in a double bind. If, on the one hand, the form of the biface is tied to the body plan, then we can account for its constancy but not for the apparent intelligence of its design. If, on the other hand, we regard the biface as the product of a complex intelligence, then we can account for its design but not for the constancy of form. This is what leads Leroi-Gourhan at one moment to emphasise the intellectual prerequisites for Archanthropian technicity, only to deny, at the next moment, that it has any significant intellectual component at all. I do not believe, however, that the source of the problem lies in the limitations of the *Homo sapiens* brain. It rather lies in a constitutive dilemma underwriting our own collective self-definition as a species of nature that knows itself as such only through having uniquely crossed a threshold of being, into a domain that *surpasses* the natural. The roots of the dilemma run deep in the western philosophical tradition, through interminable arguments over the relation between the human body, understood as an integral part of the material world, and the soul that appears to bring to this world ideas and conceptions of its own. Ever since Aristotle, this distinction between body and soul has been taken as a specific instance of a more general division between matter and form. Any substantial thing, Aristotle had reasoned, is a compound of matter and form, which are brought together in the act of its creation.[4] Herein, as we saw in the last chapter (p. 20–21), lies the foundation of the hylomorphic model of making. In the subsequent history of western thought hylomorphic thinking became ever more entrenched. But it also became increasingly unbalanced. Form came to be seen as imposed by an agent with a particular design in mind, answering to his or her purpose, while matter – thus rendered passive and inert – became that which was imposed upon.

The finished artefact fallacy

When biological anthropologist Ralph Holloway, following a long line of predecessors, once more reclaimed culture as a distinctively *human* domain, defined by 'the imposition of arbitrary form upon the environment', we can clearly see this modern version of hylomorphism at work (Holloway 1969: 395). Culture furnishes the forms, nature the materials; in the superimposition of the one upon the other human beings create the artefacts with which, to an ever increasing extent, they surround themselves. Holloway was himself in no doubt that the Acheulean handaxe was an artefact in the strict sense of the word, and thus both an exemplary instance of material culture and an index of the essential humanity of its maker. At the time when his paper was published, over forty years ago, most archaeologists and anthropologists would have agreed. Whatever the differences may have been between *Homo erectus* and *Homo sapiens* – and these remain mired in controversy that hinges on the issue of speech production – the ability to envisage forms in advance of their realisation was widely taken to have been common to both.

However, at a conference convened in 1990 to address the connections, in human evolution, between toolmaking and cognition, and between both and the faculty of language, this consensus was shattered. In a paper co-authored with the psychologist William Noble, prehistoric archaeologist Iain Davidson presented a radically alternative argument to account for the formation of the handaxe. What if it had never been the intention of the maker to produce any such thing? Suppose that *Homo erectus* had frequent need for razor-sharp instruments that were small and disposable, and not blunted by use. What better than a flake, newly struck from a core? By carrying around a core and perhaps a hammer-stone, flakes could be detached on the spot, as and when required. Only once the core had been whittled down to the point where it could no longer be profitably flaked would it eventually have been discarded. What archaeologists have assumed to be purposefully manufactured artefacts, Davidson and Noble argued, are merely these residual cores. They are leftovers (Davidson and Noble 1993: 372).

At the conference, this argument was greeted with scepticism if not dismay, nor has it garnered much support since. Five years later another contributor to the conference, Thomas Wynn, published a comprehensive rebuttal (Wynn 1995). The bifacial symmetry of the handaxe, Wynn argued, is far greater than could result from any haphazard process of flake detachment. Furthermore the production of this symmetrical form involved the removal of many tiny, trimming flakes that were too small to have been of any conceivable use. Finally, the fact that it has been possible in some cases to reconstruct whole cores by refitting axes to the 'debitage' of surrounding flakes indicates that they were made in one sitting rather than left over from a series of dispersed episodes. Wynn's verdict is unequivocal:

> The handaxe was an idea that was imposed on the material world and also shared by many individuals. It was a true cultural category. Stone knappers set out to produce handaxes as final products. They may also have been cores, but the shape itself was clearly intentional, and therefore provides us with a glimpse into the mind of the knappers.
>
> (Wynn 1995: 12)

Jacques Pelegrin, combining his archaeological investigations with many years of practical experience in flint knapping, comes to much the same conclusions. The quality of work that is evident in a well-made handaxe, along with the regularity of shape, clearly indicates an intention on the part of the maker that was quite independent of the raw material. 'For palaeohominins such as *Homo erectus*', Pelegrin writes, 'their elaborated knapping methods provide evidence that hundreds of thousands of years ago they possessed not only accurate motor skills but that *mental templates* framed the entire knapping process. Technical actions were subordinate to, and structured by, *geometric intentions*' (Pelegrin 2005: 30, emphases added).

The evidence against the hypothesis that handaxe makers were mainly interested in producing flakes is indeed compelling.[5] In proposing this hypothesis, however, Davidson and Noble were really concerned to exemplify a more fundamental point of principle. This is that we should not be lulled into conflating the final form of an artefact, as it is recovered from an archaeological site, with the 'final form' as it might have been envisaged by its erstwhile maker. The lump of stone that the archaeologist recovers today and classifies as a biface is one that, many millennia before, had been cast aside by its maker-cum-user. It would have been discarded, however, not when it was newly made but when it was of no further use. A modern analogy might be drawn with the familiar, industrially produced pencil. I would not myself throw away a newly bought pencil in mint condition. As I use it, however, it has periodically to be re-sharpened, and with every sharpening some of the pencil is shaved and its length reduced, until eventually it is too short to hold. Only then do I throw it away. An archaeologist of the future who, having analysed the contents of early twenty-first century waste bins, came to the conclusion that things conventionally called 'pencils' could not actually have been made for drawing because they were too short (and perhaps had some ritual or symbolic function instead), would be committing what Davidson and Noble (1993: 365) call *the finished artefact fallacy*.

Indeed, in this regard, flint tools are not so very different from pencils. They wear in use and may have to be sharpened by further flaking until they too are reduced to a stub and discarded (Figure 3.3). Harold Dibble, for example, has shown how apparently different types of flaked stone implement belonging to the so-called Mousterian industry associated with Neanderthal humans (*Homo sapiens neandertalensis*) of some 40,000 years ago, and variously classified as points and scrapers, could just as well be understood as representing successive stages of flake reduction (Dibble 1987a). As for the Acheulean, even if we agree, with Wynn and others, that handaxe makers were primarily interested in shaping cores and not in producing flakes, the danger of the fallacy remains. We cannot assume that the shapes of recovered cores are those that their makers originally had in mind and sought to impose on the material, or even that anything equivalent to the 'mental templates' and 'geometric intentions' of which Pelegrin speaks was ever present in their minds at all.

Templates and geometry

Recall Wynn's assertion, to which I referred a moment ago, that 'stone knappers set out to produce handaxes as final products' (Wynn 1995: 12). How, then, do we know at what point the process of production ends? How can we tell a not-quite-finished axe from a finished one or, for that matter, from one that – having already crossed the finishing line – has already suffered the scars and abrasions of use? For a possible answer we can return to Holloway, who compares the fashioning of an axe to the construction of a sentence of language. To make a sentence we chain together words into a syntactically

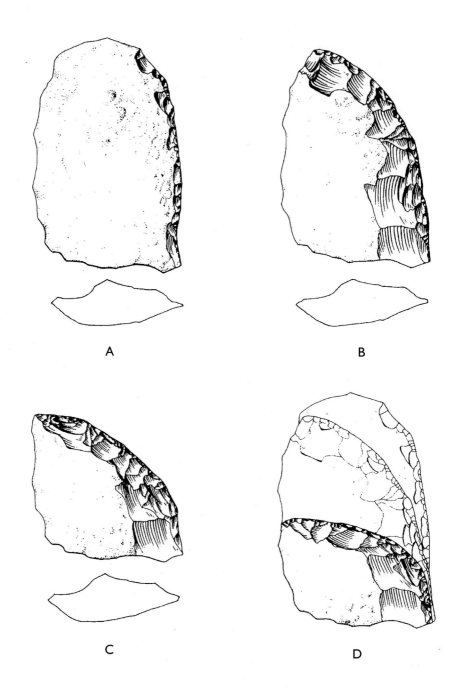

FIGURE 3.3 Successive stages (A–D) in the reduction of a flaked stone scraper, replicated by Harold L. Dibble. 'As reduction continues', Dibble observes, 'the retouch tends to get heavier, flake length and surface area decrease, and, typologically, the tool proceeds from a single-edged scraper to a transverse scraper' (Dibble 1987b: 112). Reproduced from *American Antiquity* 52(1), 1987. (Courtesy of the Society for American Archaeology.)

coherent whole; likewise, according to Holloway, 'the process of making a stone tool, such as an Acheulean handaxe, is a concatenated activity, hierarchically organised' (Holloway 1969: 402). Thus, an unfinished artefact is like an incomplete sentence. Try reading this last sentence with the final word, 'sentence', omitted. *An unfinished artefact is like an incomplete …* The effect is to reduce the remaining words to incoherence; they add up to nothing at all. So it is with the unfinished axe. To make it, the knapper has to deliver a number of blows, which differ in force and direction, and which alternate with other operations such as rotating the stone in the hands or turning it over so as to work on the other side. 'Taking each motor event alone', Holloway continues,

> … no one action is complete; each action requires a further one, and each is dependent in another way on the original plan. In other words, at each point of the action except the last, the piece is not 'satisfactory' in structure. Each unit action is meaningless by itself in the sense of the use of the tool; it is meaningful only in the context of the whole completed set of actions culminating in the final product. This exactly parallels language.
>
> (1969: 402)

Thus, in Holloway's understanding, the process of making has a clearly defined starting point, as well as an end point. The maker begins with both a plan and a finite set of component operations required to implement it. As the task proceeds, these components are assembled, bit by bit, to constitute a totality that corresponds precisely to the original design.[6] But only with the last operation – like dropping in the final piece of the jigsaw – does the artefact come into its own as a coherent whole.

There can, in short, be no final product without an initial design; no completion without an origin. For finality can only be judged in relation to a project of assembly that is already prefigured at the outset, albeit in virtual form, in the mind of the maker. That is why Wynn is able to speak of the handaxe, within the space of the short passage cited above, as both a 'final product' and 'an idea that was imposed on the material world' (Wynn 1995: 12). Like Holloway, Wynn is appealing here to the hylomorphic model of making in its modern incarnation, entailing the active imposition of cultural form upon materials supplied by nature. At the start of the process, the maker has, on the one hand, a design in mind, and on the other, a formless lump of stone. At the end, design and stone are united in the complete lithic artefact.

In the absence of a prior conception of form, however, not only is it impossible to answer the question of whether a thing is finished, it is meaningless even to ask it. To demonstrate the point, let me introduce, alongside the handaxe, another piece of stone that I have before me as I write. It was recovered from a shingle beach, not far from my home in the north-east of Scotland. Composed of granite, it is extremely hard, yet its form is so beautifully rounded that in outward appearance – and certainly by comparison to the scarred and serrated handaxe – it looks almost soft. To the touch it is perfectly smooth. Resting on the table its form is that of a slightly squashed sphere, presenting a near-circular outline when viewed from above and near-elliptical outline from the side (Figures 3.4 and 3.5). Indeed in terms of its geometry, this stone is no less symmetrical than the biface. True, the symmetry is not perfect, but then, nor is the symmetry of any handaxe. Not until I picked it up, however, at once appropriating it

FIGURE 3.4 A stone recovered from a beach in north-east Scotland, in broad profile. (Courtesy of Susanna Ingold.)

FIGURE 3.5 The same stone, in narrow profile. (Courtesy of Susanna Ingold.)

as a conclusion to my own project of collection (driven as it was by certain formal and aesthetic standards), was the stone in any sense 'finished'. Nor was it ever started. It was just *there*, forever subject to the continual grinding action, under the force of the waves, that has given rise to its current form.

Clearly, no geometric intentions or mental templates guided the formation of this stone. Nor, *on the strength of its symmetry alone*, are we any more entitled to impute design to the handaxe. I have, however, already observed that unlike my stone, the patterned flaking of the biface cannot be attributed to any ordinary process of erosion. It could only have come about through deliberate and highly skilled activity. Even this, however, does not entitle us to invoke prior intentions in the form of design concepts or assembly plans. For the intentionality of skilled practice inheres in the action itself, in its qualities of attentiveness and response, whether or not any prior intentions are affixed to it (Ingold 2000: 415). It is true, as we shall see in the next chapter (p. 54), that human craftsmen have often made extensive use of both templates and geometry. These templates are not in the mind, however, but are artefacts themselves, cut from materials and used alongside other tools of trade.[7] And the geometry is done at full scale, on site, using the body as a standard of measurement and string for drawing lines. As the art historian David Summers has shown, the apprehension of the measurable in terms of abstract geometries of ratio and proportion, in a virtual space of pure form detached from the materiality of things, is an accomplishment peculiar to the western tradition with specific roots in Aristotelian thinking (Summers 2003: 317). Rather than crediting *Homo erectus* with a cognitive style that is not even universal to human beings, let alone to hominins, and in the absence of evidence for the use of artefactual templates, it seems more reasonable to suggest that any templates or geometry guiding the making of handaxes were already built into the morphology and proportions of the bodies – and above all of the hands (Marzke 1997) – that made them. Indeed it is very easy to create a template for the handaxe, simply by placing the two hands together, palm to palm, and slightly cupped. The space enclosed between the palms almost perfectly matches the shape and volume of the biface. Yet I can form this space through a simple gesture, without having to call upon any mental imagery whatsoever.

Liquid stone

In short, Leroi-Gourhan may not have been so mistaken in tying the shape of the biface to the bodily conformation of the creatures he called Archanthropians, or in thinking of the handaxe as virtually an extension of the skeleton. There is no prima facie reason why the axe maker should have begun with a mental representation of any sort. As Davidson and Noble have shown, given the musculature and morphology of the hand, the gestural dynamics of flaking and the fracture properties of the material, it is almost inevitable that a handheld core, as it is reduced through the successive removal of flakes, will tend towards a bifacial form (Davidson and Noble 1993: 372). The form is not imposed on the material; it is rather an emergent outcome of the process of flake removal. Indeed, not only can the symmetry of the form be attributed to that of the body that made it; the same is true of its asymmetry, the cause of which lies in the difference between dominant and subdominant hands.

If this argument is accepted, however, then we have also to acknowledge that no handaxe can ever be truly finished save perhaps in the sense in which a pencil is finished, at the point of discard. Just as my stone, gathered from the beach, could only be considered complete in the context of my own project of collection, so also the handaxe can be regarded as a complete artefact only within the culture of collection of archaeologists, in which it can be shown to conform to one of a number of categorical types, namely the 'Acheulean'. But unlike modern experimental archaeologists, who deliberately set out to produce exemplary replicas of the type, the original handaxe makers knew nothing of this taxonomy, and were not guided by it. In relation to its maker, every handaxe was not a finished artefact, not the expression or realisation of a pre-existing cultural category (Wynn 1995: 12), but the crystallisation of an ongoing current of skilled activity that was carried through from one piece to the next. Every piece is testimony to a life of working with the material.

Recognising form as emergent rather than imposed at last provides us with an elegant solution to the enigma posed by the formal stability of the biface across a vast temporal span and geographical range. So long as we continue to regard making as the projection of cultural form upon raw material supplied by nature, both the handaxe and its makers are bound to appear anomalous. As Wynn admits, the handaxe 'does not fit easily into our understanding of what tools are, and its makers do not fit easily into our understanding of what humans are' (Wynn 1995: 21). Not human, yet not non-human, they come across to us in the writings of modern archaeologists and anthropologists not as the powerfully built, bimanually dextrous and supremely skilled creatures that they surely were, but as clumsy hybrids stuck for over a million years in the transition from nature to culture, credited either with minds already equipped with the cognitive capacities to generate design innovations but bodies too conservative to implement them or, conversely, with bodies motorically capable of implementing alternative designs but minds unable to plan out or to conceptualise the necessary technical operations. Yet as Tetsushi Nonaka, Blandine Bril and Robert Rein show in a recent experimental study with modern stone knappers of varying levels of ability, the skill of controlled flaking is reducible neither to mental capacities nor to bodily biomechanics. For the evaluation of stones and planning of action entail exploratory bodily movements such as dynamic touch, while the control of movements in flaking depends on a perceptual awareness of what can be done with hammer-stone and core that continues for the duration of the task (Nonaka, Bril and Rein 2010: 165).

In making an axe, the detachment of every flake is the outcome of a complex interplay of forces, both internal and external to the material. There are muscular forces, imparted through one hand that delivers the hammer blow and the other that anchors the core. And there are forces of compression, locked into the material in the course of its geologic deposition, whose release yields the characteristic pattern of fracture. Thus the form of the handaxe is constrained neither by cognition nor by biomechanics but by the developmental potentials inherent in the field of forces established by way of the lifelong engagement of practitioners with their lithic materials, and cutting across the interface between them (Ingold 2000: 345). To understand the form as emergent is to recognise that it is generated in the very unfolding of this force field. As should now be evident, the enigma of the handaxe has its source in the hylomorphic model of making, and to resolve it we have had to challenge the model at its very foundations. Quite clearly, the properties of the material are directly implicated in the form-generating process. The distinction between form and matter, upon which the entire philosophy of hylomorphism rests, is therefore unsustainable.

Our investigation into the curious case of the Acheulean biface draws us inexorably to the conclusion that the essential relation in a world in formation (as distinct from a world that we look back on, as though it were completed long ago), is not between form and matter but between *forces* and *materials*. In this, I once more take my cue from Deleuze and Guattari (2004), for whom – as we saw in the last chapter – the refutation of the hylomorphic model has been a centrepiece of their intellectual project. One example they adduce in order to demonstrate the inadequacy of the model is the operation of splitting timber with an axe: not an Acheulean handaxe, of course, but one that can actually be used for the purpose. The practised woodsman brings down the axe so that its blade enters the grain and follows a path already incorporated into the timber through its previous history of growth, when it was part of a living tree. As it finds its way through the wood, splitting it as it goes, the axe is guided – as Deleuze and Guattari say – by 'the variable undulations and torsions of the fibres'. This is not an imposition of form on matter but a bringing out of forms, more topological than geometrical, that are latent in the variations of the material itself, in its energetic lines of tension and compression. With due allowance for the very different properties of flint, as compared with timber, the point could have been exemplified just as well by the practice of flaking stone with a hammer as by that of splitting timber with an axe. In both cases, to borrow the words of Deleuze and Guattari once again, it is a question of 'surrendering' to the material and then 'following where it leads' (Deleuze and Guattari 2004: 450–451).

This leaves us with a picture of making altogether different from the 'construction kit' view proposed by Holloway and others, according to which the maker begins with a plan or template and a finite set of parts, and ends when the final piece is put in place. In this view, the process of making is a concatenation of separate steps that follow one another like beads on string.[8] In the view we propose, by contrast, the process of making is not so much an *assembly* as a *procession*, not a building *up* from discrete parts into a hierarchically organised totality but a carrying *on* – a passage along a path in which every step grows from the one before and into the one following, on an itinerary that always overshoots its destinations. Once again to adopt a helpful distinction from Deleuze and Guattari (2004: 410), this is not an *iteration* of steps but an *itineration*: making is a journey; the maker a journeyman. And the essential characteristic of his activity is not that it is concatenated but that it *flows*. In the hands of the skilled knapper, brittle flint becomes liquid, and is revealed as a maelstrom of currents in which every potential bulb of percussion is a vortex from which fracture surfaces ripple out like waves. The knapper follows these currents in the rhythmically percussive movement of detaching flakes. If there is regularity in the form of the artefact, it comes from the fluent rhythmicity of the movements that gave rise to it: 'rhythms', as Leroi-Gourhan observes, 'are the creators of forms' (Leroi-Gourhan 1993: 309). This is a point to which we will return (Chapter 8, p. 115). Our next step, however, is to turn from the field of archaeology to that of architecture, and from making to building, where we shall find that many of the same considerations apply.

4

ON BUILDING A HOUSE

The idea of architecture

Much can ride, in English, on the indefinite article. Building is an activity; it is what builders do. Add the article, however, and the activity is brought to a close. Movement is stilled, and where people had once laboured with tools and materials, there now stands a structure – *a* building – that shows every sign of permanence and solidity. Instead, attention shifts to what goes on *in* the building, to the activities – such as cooking, eating, sleeping and socialising, and perhaps worship – that are conducted under its roof. It is conventional, at least in western societies, to describe the people who engage in these activities as the *residents* of the building. This is to suppose, however, that their occupation is a matter of taking up, for their own use, a space that has already been constructed. Thus, even if they have put up the building with their own hands, the activities of residence are categorically distinguished from those that led to its erection in the first place. Residence begins when building ends, much as the use of an artefact follows from its making. We have already seen, however, that in the case of the artefact, to draw a line between making and using means marking a point in the career of a thing at which it can be said to be finished, and moreover that this point of completion can only be determined in relation to a totality that already exists, in virtual form, at the outset – that is, in relation to a *design*. It is precisely the same with the building. If the activities of residence are truly distinct from, and consequential upon, those of building, then there must be some determinate point at which the building is finished – when building yields *a* building – which means, in turn, that its form must be judged as the realisation of a pre-existent design. This is precisely the judgement that is entailed in regarding the building as an instance of *architecture*.

It has, of course, long been the conceit of the architectural profession that all the creative work that goes into the fashioning of a building is concentrated in the process of design, and that the subsequent phase of construction adds up to little more than its realisation in the proverbial 'bricks and mortar' of the built environment. The architect would like to think that the complete building stands as the crystallisation of an original design concept, with all its components finally fixed in their proper places. As with the jigsaw puzzle, should any components be added, or taken away, the entire structure would be reduced to incoherence. In the ideal case, once it is finished the building should hold for all eternity to the form the architect intended for it. 'The whole idea of architecture', writes the inventor and designer Stewart Brand (1994: 2), 'is permanence.' Yet buildings are part of the world, and the world will not stop still but ceaselessly unfolds along its innumerable paths of growth, decay and regeneration, regardless of the most concerted of human attempts to nail it down, or to cast it in fixed and final forms. There is inevitably a 'kink', as Brand calls it, between the world and our idea of it: 'the idea is crystalline, the fact fluid' (loc. cit.). Builders, in practice if not in principle, inhabit this kink, and so do residents. For both, it is the process that claims their energy and attention, more than the product. Builders know all too well that operations seldom if ever go according to plan. Working in a fickle and inconstant environment, they have continually to improvise solutions to problems that could not have been anticipated, and to wrestle with materials that are not necessarily disposed to fall, let alone to remain, in the shapes required of them. Completion is, at best, a legal fiction. The reality, as Brand (1994: 64) wryly observes, is that 'finishing is never finished'.

Nor does the handover of the never-quite-finished building to its legally appointed residents bring the process any nearer to a conclusion. Only then, according to the distinguished Portuguese architect Alvaro Siza, does the serious work of building actually begin, as residents embark on their daily struggle to limit the damage inflicted by invasions of insects and rodents, the rot brought with fungal infestation and the corrosive effects of the elements. Rainwater drips through the roof where the wind has blown off a tile, feeding a mould that threatens to decompose the timbers, the gutters are full of rotten leaves, and if that were not enough, moans Siza, 'legions of ants invade the thresholds of doors, there are always the dead bodies of birds and mice and cats' (Siza 1997: 47). Indeed nothing better exemplifies the mismatch between the perceptions of the architect–designer and those of the resident–builder than their respective attitudes to rainfall. Within the formal world of the architectural design, rain is simply unimaginable. Falling raindrops, and the rivulets of running water to which they give rise when they impact upon surfaces, cannot be part of any plan. Nor is the geometric purity of the modern architect's conception to be clouded by prospects of stormy weather. But with its clean lines, sharp angles and flat surfaces, any building constructed in accordance with this conception is almost bound to leak. Brand notes that in the 1980s, some 80 per cent of post-construction claims against architects were for leaks (Brand 1994: 58). To clients who complained of leaking roofs, the celebrated American architect, Frank Lloyd Wright, is alleged to have retorted 'That's how you can tell it's a roof.' His most famous building, Fallingwater in Pennsylvania, was affectionately known by its original owner as 'Rising Mildew', and as a 'seven-bucket building'. A makeshift solution to an endemic problem, the bucket – put in to catch the drips – perfectly epitomises the kink between the architect's crystalline conception and a fluid reality, which it is the occupant's singular misfortune to have to iron out.

The architect and the carpenter

Yet five centuries before Fallingwater was built, in the first treatise since Graeco-Roman Antiquity to be written on the theory and practice of architecture, Leon Battista Alberti had warned explicitly against the dangers of rain and exhorted the architect to take special care in designing the roofs of buildings so as to ensure adequate protection and runoff. 'For rain', Alberti wrote, 'is always prepared to wreak mischief, and never fails to exploit even the least opening to do some harm: by its subtlety it infiltrates, by softening it corrupts, and by its persistence it undermines the whole strength of the building, until it eventually brings ruin and destruction on the entire work' (Alberti 1988: 27). Completed around 1450, Alberti's treatise *On the Art of Building in Ten Books* is indeed remarkable for its combination of practical wisdom and design ambition, the former based on profound respect for traditional and local knowledge, the latter on a concern to raise the status of the architect to a place of honour and recognition well above that of the humble craftsman. On the one hand, for example, Alberti (1988: 63) recommends that in choosing the ground on which to build, advice should always be sought from local residents whose daily experience both with existing buildings and with constructing new ones will have yielded a reliable understanding of the nature and quality of the soil. Yet on the other hand, he paints an unashamedly self-aggrandising portrait of the architect as a man of 'learned intellect and imagination', who is able 'to project whole forms in mind without any recourse to the material' (ibid.: 7). As one of the founding figures of the European Renaissance, Alberti can be seen in retrospect to stand at a pivotal juncture in the process that ultimately led to the professionalisation of architecture as a discipline devoted exclusively to design as opposed to implementation. His treatise both looks back to the time of his predecessors, the master builders of the past, and looks forward to a time when the architect would prescribe only the formal outlines of the building, leaving its actual construction in the skilled and capable hands of workmen.

In the prologue to the *Ten Books*, Alberti (1988: 5) is at pains to explain what he means by an architect. He does so by telling us precisely what the architect is *not*. Specifically, he is not a carpenter. 'For it is no carpenter that I would have you compare to the greatest exponents of other disciplines: the carpenter is but an instrument in the hands of the architect.' But why should Alberti have chosen the carpenter, of all people, as the architect's alter-ego? To find the answer, we can return to the importance that Alberti attaches to ensuring that the building has a well-made roof. Traditionally fashioned from wooden beams, the construction of the roof would have been the carpenter's responsibility. But by a curious twist of fate, the carpenters of Alberti's day had commonly come to be known as architects. The designation can be traced back to an ecclesiastical document from the year 945. It appears that the author of the document had mistaken the verb *architector* for a compound of the Latin *arcus* (arch) and *tectum* (roof), jumping to the conclusion that the architect must be a specialist in the making and repair of vaulted roofs! Over the ensuing centuries other writers followed this example, until in time the usage became a matter of convention (Pevsner 1942: 557). Nowadays, if your roof leaks, you might want to blame the architect for defective design. But in the Middle Ages, you would have called him in to fix the problem. If the roof was wooden, you would need a carpenter, but if it was supported by arches of stone you might also need a mason. Indeed the architect, in medieval times, was as commonly a mason as a carpenter: there were many similarities in their respective working methods (Pacey 2007: 87), and the skills of masonry and carpentry were not infrequently combined in one and the same person. In an influential statement, the seventh century scholar Isidore of Seville had identified the architect as a mason (*masionem*), a word that he derived, in turn, from the Latin *machina*, meaning the hoist that is required to lift heavy materials in constructing the high walls and roof.

Significantly, however, he was also regarded as one who lays out the foundations for the building (Carruthers 1998: 22, 284 fn. 40). In this latter regard, Isidore was following the precedent of the Apostle St Paul, in the first of his Letters to the Corinthians. Describing himself as a 'wise masterbuilder', Paul declares: 'I have laid the foundation, and another buildeth thereon' (*Corinthians I*, III: 10). The notion that the architect, however skilled he may be, is no mere mason or carpenter but rather one who lays the foundations on which others build, conforms more closely to the conventions of Graeco-Roman Antiquity than to those of the Middle Ages. Etymologically, the term 'architect' is of Greek rather than Latin origin, and translates quite literally as master-builder (from *arkhi-*, chief, and *tekton*, maker).[1] In Greece, Plato had insisted that the architect 'is not himself a workman, but a ruler of workmen', and in his *Ten Books on Architecture* the Roman author Vitruvius, writing in the first century BC, likewise emphasised the need for the architect to have a thorough knowledge of both theory and practice, and to combine manual skill with sound scholarship (Vitruvius 1914: 5). As Nikolaus Pevsner (1942: 549) has pointed out, Vitruvius was undoubtedly thinking not of masons or carpenters but of learned, literate men of high social standing. It is no surprise, then, that Alberti, seeking to restore the architects of his own time to similar standing, should have modelled his own *Ten Books* on the Vitruvian precedent.[2] Nor is it surprising that he sought to distinguish the architect from the carpenter, for in doing so he wanted to lay to rest, once and for all, the medieval idea of the architect as a lay craftsman, and to replace this figure on the pedestal on which he had formerly stood in antiquity.[3] What he also drew from antiquity, however, was an unequivocal commitment to the hylomorphic model of making, as a bringing together of form and matter. 'The building', he observes, 'consists of lineaments and matter, the one the product of thought, the other of Nature, the one requiring the mind and the power of reason, the other dependent on preparation and selection; but ... neither on its own would suffice without the hand of the skilled workman to fashion the material according to lineaments' (Alberti 1988: 5). What Alberti here calls 'lineaments' (*lineamenta*) comprise a precise and complete specification of the form and appearance of the building, as conceived by the intellect, independently and in advance of the work of construction (*structura*). Just as for Vitruvius, theory (*ratiocinatio*) precedes and underwrites practice (*opus*), so for Alberti, *lineamenta* precede and underwrite *structura* (Rykwert *et al.*, in Alberti 1988: 422; see also Vitruvius 1914:11).

Practical geometry

On paper, the lineaments would have been inscribed as drawn lines, which could be either straight or curved, and which meet or intersect at certain angles. This was drawing, however, understood not as the trace of a gesture but as the geometric projection of a conceptual image. It was in this sense that in a number of European languages, the word for drawing came to be the same as that for design: in French *dessin*, in Italian *disegno*, in Spanish *dibujar*. In each case, whether as design or drawing, the connotations were of pattern and intent rather than of movement or process (Maynard 2005: 66–67). As long ago as 1568, Giorgio Vasari wrote, in this vein, that *disegno* 'is nothing but a visual expression and clarification of that concept which one has in the intellect, and that which one imagines in the mind and builds up in the idea' (cited in Panofsky 1968: 62). Indeed Alberti's lines have their source in the formal geometry of Euclid. 'The straight line', he explains, 'is the shortest possible line that may be drawn between two points', while 'the curved line is part of a circle' (Alberti 1988: 19). What art historian Jean-François Billeter writes of the line of Euclidean geometry applies with equal force to the Albertian lineament: it 'has neither body nor colour nor texture, nor any other tangible quality: its nature is abstract, conceptual, rational' (Billeter 1990: 47). The space thus delineated on paper, as Bruno Latour and Albena Yaneva (2008: 82) have observed, is a world apart from that in which real buildings are built and inhabited.

Now the masons and carpenters of the medieval period also drew lines, and made use of a certain geometry in doing so (Pacey 2007: 59–86). They even appealed to Euclid. But theirs was a geometry informed by a tactile and sensuous knowledge of line and surface rather than by an eye for abstract, conceptual form. And their Euclid was a legendary figure very different from the real Euclid of Alexandria whom we remember today as the author of the *Elements*. A story recounted of Euclid by an unknown cleric from the late fourteenth century, and incorporated into the English 'Constitutions of Masonry', offers a clue to the difference. According to this story, Euclid had learned his geometry from the biblical Abraham, for whom he had worked as a clerk during the latter's stay in Egypt. At that time, the waters of the Nile flooded the land to such an extent that people could not dwell along it, but Euclid taught the people how to build walls and ditches to keep the water out, and by means of geometry he measured out and partitioned the land. And so, the story continues, the Egyptians 'took their sons to Euclid to govern them at his own will and he taught to them the craft of masonry and gave it the name of Geometry because of the parting of the ground that he had taught to the people' (in Harvey 1972: 197). On the evidence of this account, as the architectural historian Lon Shelby (1972: 396–397) remarks, 'for mediaeval masons Euclid had virtually become the eponymous hero of a craft, and the word geometry had become synonymous with masonry … That is to say, neither "Euclid" nor "geometry" may have meant to mediaeval masons what today we mean by Euclidean geometry'. So what did geometry mean to the craftsmen of the Middle Ages?

It was, in the first place, an essentially practical pursuit, rather than a matter of theory. Already in the twelfth century, the Parisian philosopher–theologian Hugh of St Victor had divided the discipline of geometry into two branches: the theoretical and the practical, though his idea of practical geometry was limited to what we would now call surveying (Shelby 1972: 401–402). Evidently influenced by Hugh, his near contemporary, the Spanish philosopher and translator Dominicus Gundissalinus, explained that in geometry, the purpose of theory is to teach, by way of formal demonstration and proof, whereas the purpose of practice is to achieve results. For Gundissalinus, however, practical geometers were of two kinds: besides surveyors, there were also craftsmen. The latter, he tells us, are those who exert themselves by working in the constructive or mechanical arts – such as the carpenter in wood, the smith in iron, the mason in clay and stones… Each indeed forms lines, surfaces, squares, circles, etc., in material bodies in the manner appropriate to his art. These many kinds of craftsmen are distinguished according to the different materials in which and out of which they work. Any one of these thus has his proper materials and instruments. The instruments … of the carpenters are the axe, adze, broadaxe, string and many others. Those of the smith are the anvil, shears, hammer, and many others. Those of the masons are the string, trowel, plumb, bob, and many others…

(cited in Shelby 1972: 403)

Now it is very unlikely that any medieval mason or carpenter would have had access to the teachings of theoretical geometry, which were mainly confined to the universities, that had little to offer them, and to books they could ill afford (Shelby 1970: 14–15). Already in possession of a corpus of traditional geometrical knowledge adequate to his purpose, the craftsman would have had no need for academic book-learning (Harvey 1972: 114). His knowledge would have been largely acquired 'on the job', through apprenticeship to a master. It was a matter of learning by doing, rather than acquiring theoretical precepts for subsequent application in practice. The craftsman operated not with theorems but with rules of thumb, valued not for their mathematical correctness or logical consistency but for their guidance in getting the job done. The geometry of masons and carpenters, as Gundissalinus explains, was carried out on site with the tools of their trades, including axes and chisels of all kinds, trowel, plumb line and string, along with three crucial instruments that he does not mention, namely, pre-cut templates, straight edge and square (Shelby 1971: 142).

Precisely because this knowledge was both learned and passed on as a living tradition, in the spoken words and manifest deeds of practitioners, it has left little documentary trace. A rare exception is the sketchbook, with accompanying instructions, bequeathed by the French master mason, Villard de Honnecourt. Writing in the thirteenth century, Villard hopes that those who peruse his book will find in it 'sound advice on the great techniques of masonry and on the devices of carpentry … as the discipline of geometry requires and instructs' (in Barnes 2009: 35). One page from the sketchbook gives a good idea of what this geometric art entailed (Figure 4.1).[4] The upper two rows give instructions, among other things, for measuring the diameter of a cylindrical shaft (rest the shaft against a wall, and rest a square with its short side on the shaft and its long side against the wall), for cutting the keystones and voussoirs for an arch, and for raising the spire of a tower. Below are three more drawings. The one on the left tells how to cut the voussoirs for a hanging arch. During construction, the pendant of the arch is temporarily supported by a tree trunk. Fix a nail on the trunk halfway from the base to the crown of the wall and tie a string to the nail. Stretching the string to points along the arch gives the angles of cut. The drawing in the middle shows how to obtain two pillars of the same height without the use of plumb line or level. Place a hinged post halfway between the two pillars so that it touches the top of one of them. Then swing it across to check the height of the other. On the right of the page is a drawing of a tower. To determine the height of the tower, set an instrument shaped as a right-angled isosceles triangle on the ground such that when you look up along

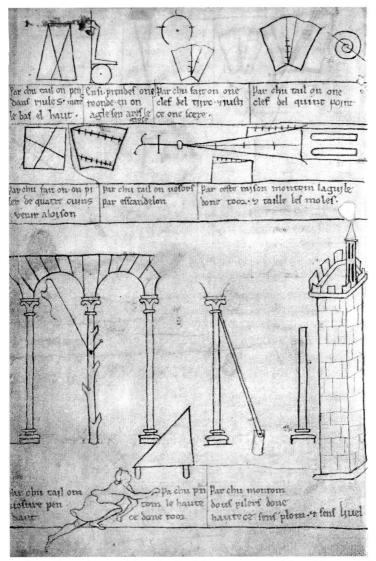

FIGURE 4.1 A page from the portfolio of Villard de Honnecourt (sheet 20, verso). (Courtesy of the Bibliothèque nationale de France.)

the hypotenuse, from ground level, your line of sight strikes the top of the tower. The distance along the ground from the tip of the triangle to the base of the tower then equals the height (Barnes 2009: 140–145, see also Shelby1972: 409–410; Bucher 1979: 122–124). What is striking about these procedures is not just their simplicity but their sheer physicality. In the practice of their geometry, masons and carpenters did not project onto stone and wood forms that had already been deduced through the power of abstract reason and rational calculation. They solved design problems as they went along, through the manipulation of the instruments and materials at their disposal, and drawing on a fund of 'tricks of the trade' – such as those illustrated by Villard – picked up on the way.

Plans in stone

In that sense, as Shelby (1972: 409) shows, their geometry was not just practical but, more precisely, *constructive*. Their straight lines were not the notional point-to-point connectors of Euclid, but actual lengths of cord pegged out on site and at full scale (Pacey 2007: 63). Their points were nails or stakes, hammered into wood or ground. And the figures of their geometry were not empty outlines but solid, weighty pieces with tangible surfaces and edges, cut and shaped from wood or stone. And among these shapes, by far the most important were the templates or 'moulds' that were used as guides to stone cutting.[5] These templates were usually made from thick planks of wood, though they were sometimes cut from canvas or parchment, or occasionally sheets of lead (Shelby 1971: 142–143; Pacey 2007: 35). The master mason would draw designs onto planks, and the carpenter would cut them out, after which they would be passed to the workmen on site, with the task of actually cutting the stone.

The art of cutting solids into pieces that fit together tightly is known technically as *stereotomy* – from the classical Greek *stereo*, solid, and *tomia*, to cut (Sanabria 1989: 266; Frampton 1995: 5). It is simple enough to build a wall of rectangular blocks, but in the construction of complex buildings with arches, vaults and pinnacles, medieval masons faced formidable stereotomical challenges. These challenges were not solved, however, through exact pre-calculation and precision cutting. They were rather solved through a combination of rule of thumb and creative extemporisation, leaving ample scope, as Shelby (1971: 154) notes, 'for individual differences and the play of personal choice'. Although the constructive geometry of the masons laid down carefully prescribed steps that apprentices were taught to follow, none was so constraining as actually to preordain the course of action, nor were the rules they observed any substitute for the skill and inventiveness, born of long experience, on which the success of their enterprise finally depended (Shelby 1972: 420). 'Rules of art can be useful', observes philosopher Michael Polanyi (1958: 50), 'but they do not determine the practice of an art; they are maxims, which can serve as a guide to an art only if they can be integrated into the practical knowledge of the art. They cannot replace this knowledge.' The masons' rules were maxims in this sense: they comprised resources for action, but did not determine it (see also Suchman 1987: 52; Ingold 2000: 35–36).

If masons were restricted in what they could do it was not, then, because the stereotomical puzzle of assembling a building from elementary solids admitted only one, mathematically correct solution. Though it might seem so to our modern eyes, great medieval buildings were not assembled like puzzles from pre-cut pieces, nor were they finished when the last piece was slotted into place. A better analogy, suggested by John Harvey (1974: 33), might be with the patchwork quilt. As patches are sewn into the quilt, so stones are added to the building piecemeal, each shaped and, if necessary, reshaped so as to fit the space prepared for it by previous ones, and in turn preparing the spaces for those that follow.[6] Here is Hugh of St Victor once again, in his *Didascalicon* of 1127, describing the mason at work:

> Take a look at what the mason does. When the foundation has been laid, he stretches out his string in a straight line, he drops his perpendicular, and then, one by one, he lays the diligently polished stones in a row. Then he asks for other stones, and still others, and if by chance he finds some that do not fit with the

fixed course he has laid, he takes his file, smooths off the protruding parts, files down the rough spots, and the places that do not fit, reduces to form, and so at last joins them to the rest of the stones set into the row.

(Hugh of St Victor 1961: 140)

It seems from this account that the lineaments of the structure, far from being imposed upon the material, emerge from the process of building itself. But if that is so, then what need, if any, did the medieval mason have for designs or plans? Did there have to be, as Alberti (1988: 7) was later to insist, a 'precise and correct outline, conceived in the mind, made up of lines and angles', before the work of building could even begin?

The question of whether there existed plans or project drawings for complex medieval buildings such as cathedrals remains unresolved, and expert opinion is sharply divided. The architectural historian Francis Andrews, in an essay penned in 1925, answers definitively in the negative:

No church or other work was just the outcome of the mind of any single man who had sat down and deliberately designed it and having drawn it up then got up and supervised its execution... Such a man was not necessary... What was wanted and what was supplied was the man who would work earnestly and honourably and leave, so to speak, the designing to take care of itself. Hence there was no architect to make a design.

(Andrews 1974: 8–9)

Taking precisely the opposite view, Harvey finds it inconceivable that even the simplest building can be put up without its having first been designed, and without that design having been committed to a surface of some kind. In medieval architecture, Harvey (1972: 101) argues, drawings were as essential for the transmission of ideas from the designer to the workmen as is musical notation to the performance of complex polyphonic music.[7] Shelby, for his part, does not deny the existence of working drawings, but argues that templates, rather than drawings per se, were the primary means by which master masons transmitted architectural forms to the workmen who executed them (Shelby 1971: 142). Following a comprehensive review of the available evidence, historian of science and technology Arnold Pacey (2007: 161, 228) concludes that masons were making detail drawings of window tracery from around the beginning of the thirteenth century, but that drawings of other parts of buildings rarely appear until much later, and only from the end of the sixteenth century did masons begin to make drawings of entire structures at less than full scale.

There does seem little doubt that medieval builders drew. What is doubtful is that any of their drawings can be understood as plans, in the strict sense of a full geometrical pre-specification of the intended work. For medieval builders, drawing was not the visual projection of an idea already fashioned in the intellect – as implied by the synonymy of drawing and design in *disegno* – but a craft of weaving with lines. As architectural design theorist Lars Spuybroek (2011: 18) has argued, it was in this regard more *descriptive* than *prescriptive*. Today's architectural drawings, complete with front and side views and cross sections depicted at various scales, precisely specify the final form of the whole structure. Medieval builders, by contrast, would draw, say, the tracery for a window at full scale, on a stone tracing floor, as a way of working out particular details preparatory to their actual carving in stone. There was no radical division here between drawing and building, as though the former were exclusively on the side of abstract design and the latter on the side of material execution; rather, both were integral to the craft itself: whereas the draughtsman '*draws as if he is weaving*', the stonemason '*carves as if he is drawing*' (Spuybroek 2011: 40). In short, design was neither placed before the work, as Harvey contends, nor left to take care of itself, as does Andrews. For it was in the very course of 'taking care' – in the intelligence of skilled craftsmanship – that medieval buildings were designed. Of the masons who built them, we can say that they both designed as they drew, and drew as they designed. But their designing, like their drawing, was a process of work, not a project of the mind.

The cathedral and the laboratory

Recently, the whole issue of whether or in what sense medieval buildings can be said to have been planned has been revisited in a strikingly original contribution by sociologist of science David Turnbull (1993, see also Turnbull 2000: 53–87). His focus is on the building of the magnificent Gothic cathedral of Chartres. Rebuilt, following a fire, between the years 1194 and 1230, the cathedral has a spire of 345 feet, and has stood for nearly eight centuries. Yet if the building ever had an architectural designer, his identity is unknown; nor are any plans extant. It is of course impossible to prove beyond doubt that no prior designs or plans existed for Chartres, nor does Turnbull make any attempt to do so. There are all sorts of reasons why plans, had they existed, might not have survived: clearly – as Pacey (2007: 59) notes – a plan marked out at full size 'would occupy as much space on the ground as the actual building', and would simply be swallowed up by the construction. Turnbull's critique is rather directed at those, such as Harvey (1972: 101), who assume on grounds of logic and principle that plans *had* to exist, since without them no complex structure could ever get built.[8] 'To the modern mind', Turnbull (1993: 319–320) writes, 'the design argument in architecture seems self-evident.' Yet to attribute all form to a prior design specification, he maintains, 'explains too little and too much'.

On the one hand, designs do not magically transmute into the forms they specify. Their fulfilment calls for workmanship, and in the case of a building like Chartres Cathedral, it was clearly workmanship of a very high order. Even Alberti recognised that 'the hand of the skilled workman' is needed to fashion a structure according to lineaments. The argument from design explains too little because it does not account for workmanship. But to make up for the deficit it pretends that all skilled practice can ultimately be factored as the sequential output of a codified system of rules and algorithms. It is in this respect that the argument explains too much, for as Turnbull (1993: 320) remarks, it 'attributes powers to rules they cannot have'. As we have already seen, the rules followed by medieval cathedral builders could not and did not prescribe their practice in every detail, but instead allowed scope for action to be precisely fine-tuned in relation to the exigencies of the situation at hand.

In an audacious move, Turnbull invites us to compare the work of building a cathedral, in medieval times, to what goes on in a large-scale research laboratory, in our own day. In the laboratory, teams of researchers are beavering away at the task of advancing knowledge in some branch of science. Each team operates more or less autonomously, under the direction of research leaders who come and go, while nevertheless keeping in touch with all the others, exchanging information about protocols and procedures, methods and equipment, experimental results and the new ideas and thinking that flow from them. Out of all this activity, there emerges an edifice of a kind, recognisable as a body of knowledge. But this body is not the brainchild of a lone genius, born fully formed from his superior intellect, nor is the work of the laboratory single-mindedly dedicated to its empirical substantiation. It is rather a composite of many parts, imperfectly integrated, every part conditioned by ways of doing things peculiar to each of the teams that have contributed to its development, and patched together thanks to communicative exchanges between them.

Likewise, a great medieval building, as John James (1985: 123) writes of the cathedral of Chartres, 'was the *ad hoc* accumulation of the work of many men'. According to James, the work of rebuilding Chartres was carried out by teams of labourers under the direction of no fewer than nine master masons, in some thirty separate, short-term campaigns over a period of more than three decades (ibid.: 25, 60). And the result, despite its exterior magnificence and apparent harmony, is revealed on closer inspection to be a patchwork of irregularly disposed and imperfectly matched architectural elements (Figure 4.2). Just as there is no master plan for constructing the edifice of scientific knowledge, so, too, the building of Chartres did not bring to glorious completion the speculative vision of an unknown architect. No one could have predicted, while the work was underway, exactly how it would turn out, what complications would arise in the process, or what means would be devised to deal with them. Yet despite the episodic character of the work, and frequent changes of leadership, a degree of continuity was assured through the traffic of communication not only between master masons and workers on site, but also between the master and other masons, and between them and the ecclesiastical patrons who commissioned the work (Turnbull 1993: 320). And in this communication, no single item played a larger part than the template.

Chartres remains unfinished. As with every other surviving structure of its kind, the work of building and rebuilding continues to this day, albeit motivated by a characteristically modernist desire to preserve in perpetuity what is imagined to have been a historically completed form, the perfect realisation of an original design. This one building, then, stands as an embodiment both of the geometric craftsmanship of the thirteenth century and of the architectural conceits of the twentieth, and gives us a bridge across which we can return from the building practices of medieval times to the contemporary understanding of the building, from which I began this chapter, as the timeless expression of the architect's vision. Turnbull's objective is to lay to rest the idea that any 'great divide' separates the sites of technoscientific activity of the past, such as the cathedral works, and those of the present, such as the laboratory. 'Technoscience then and now', he claims, 'results from site-specific, contingent and messy practices' (Turnbull 1993: 332). But if this is true of the modern laboratory, then it is surely equally true of the sites of contemporary building. Just as science, however, has invested heavily in the distinction between speculative theory and experimental practice, so has architecture invested in that between design and construction. Thus in a recent, authoritative statement, Simon Unwin defines architecture as 'the determination

FIGURE 4.2 Spot the difference! The west facade of Chartres Cathedral. Redrawn from Plate 407 of G. Dehio and G. von Bezold, *Die kirchliche Baukunst des Abendlandes: historisch und systematisch dargestellt*. From the collection of the University of Pittsburgh Digital Library, courtesy of Alison Stones.

by which a mind gives intellectual structure to a building', whereas building is 'the performance of physical realization', of which '*a* building' is the product (Unwin 2007: 102). The architect, then, conceives the lineaments of the structure, while the builder's task is to unite the structure with the material.

These definitions, however, belie the creativity of the 'messy practices' that give rise to *real* buildings. Whether of sketching, tracing, modelling, staking out, digging, cutting, laying, fixing or joining, all involve care, judgement and aforethought, and are carried on within worldly fields of forces and relations. None can be placed unequivocally on one side or the other of any distinction of fundamental ontological import, such as between intellectual conception and mechanical execution. On what grounds then, if at all, can architecture be distinguished from building or, more generally, design from making? This is our topic for the next chapter.

5

THE SIGHTED WATCHMAKER

Designs and traps

Let me begin this chapter as you probably begin your day, by sitting down to breakfast. Here you are, seated on a chair, before a table that is covered with a cloth. On the cloth, more or less under your nose, is placed a bowl, and to the right of the bowl, a spoon. A little further away, a jug contains milk, and a cardboard box contains your favourite cereal. You pick up the box to pour some cereal into a bowl. The action is about to commence.

But what a hazardous performance this is! Pouring cereal from a box in the right amount is hard enough. Many people attempt to solve it by pinching the inner, paper lining of the box to make a kind of funnel, which helps to channel the cereal into the bowl. To the consternation of visitors who consider it unclean, I have developed the habit of plunging my bare hand directly into the box and extracting a handful of cereal, which is just about the right amount. But having achieved this without tipping over the box and depositing its contents on the floor, your problems have scarcely begun. Next you have to add the milk. Now the milk jug is altogether superior to the cereal box. It has a handle that helps you pick it up and hold it securely, and a lip which channels the flow of milk when you tip it to pour. But when, having done so, a drop remains on the lip nothing prevents it running down the outward side of the jug where it eventually reaches your clean tablecloth. The cloth is soiled. The real challenge begins, however, when you begin to eat. For this you need the spoon. Taking up one end between thumb and both fore and middle fingers, you dip the other end, with its oval concavity, into the bowl, and bring it up again, brimming with milk and filled with a precariously poised heap of cereal flakes. Somehow this unstable mass has to be raised from bowl level to that of your open mouth without spillage. This means keeping the spoon's concavity perfectly horizontal throughout the entire trajectory. Even the most dextrous of eaters rarely succeed in this entirely, and some spillage on the cloth is almost inevitable. Then finally, as you withdraw the spoon, your lips must close on it to make sure that nothing dribbles out, and to clean it off, ready for the next dip.

The breakfast table, in short, is nothing if not an obstacle course. Yet everything on it has, at one time or another, been designed: the box, the jug, the bowl, the spoon, the cloth. So, too, have the table and the chair. But tables, at least of the kinds to which we are accustomed, are awkward things. They are always either too big or too small, or too high or too low; they get in the way when you want to move around, their surfaces are vulnerable (which is why we cover the breakfast table with a cloth) and their legs have a habit of hitting the shins or snagging the toes of unsuspecting sitters or passers-by. As the design theorist and renowned furniture maker David Pye (1978: 14) once remarked, in some despair, a dining table that was properly fit for purpose 'ought to be variable in size and height, removable altogether, impervious to scratches, self-cleaning, and having no legs'. As for the chair, since sitting is not a posture that comes readily to the human body, there is no chair that does not impose a degree of discomfort to which sitters have to adjust as best they can. I often deal with this by tipping forward on my chair so as to straighten my back and balance it better. The effect, however, is to raise the chair's rear legs off the ground, leaving them perfectly poised to trip up anyone walking behind. Restaurant waiters beware!

All of this leaves us with a conundrum of the following kind. Surely as individuals, we have certain needs and desires that we wish to have fulfilled. We would like to live comfortable, healthy lives. We want things to be easy, not difficult. Is it not the purpose of design, then, to make them so? 'A major role of new technology', writes psychologist Donald Norman (1988: 191), 'should be to make tasks simpler.' It would take the optimism of a Dr Pangloss to allow that it has succeeded in such a purpose. No doubt this master of bogus philosophy, the target of Voltaire's famous satire in his novella *Candide*, would have been able to come up with a host of reasons why body-contorting chairs, toe-snagging table legs, milk-spilling jugs, overturning boxes and overflowing spoons are 'all for the best' in this 'best of all possible worlds'. But such reasons, as Voltaire wanted us to see, are invariably spurious. If design, then, has failed – and failed so spectacularly – in making everything for the best, should we conclude that its real purpose is quite the reverse: to set obstacles in our path that we are challenged through our own skill and ingenuity to overcome? Perhaps, far from specifying solutions, it is design that sets the rules of the game.

In a strikingly original essay, the design philosopher Vilém Flusser (1995) offers a clue to how this conundrum might be resolved. By way of an enquiry into the etymology of the word 'design' – along with a range of other words with which it is associated such as 'machine', 'technique' and 'artifice' – Flusser concludes that it is fundamentally about trickery and deception. 'A designer', he writes, 'is someone who is artful or wily, a plotter setting traps' (Flusser 1995: 50). Every object of design sets a trap by presenting a problem in the form of what appears to be its solution. Thus we are deceived into thinking of the spoon as a solution to the problem of how to transport food from bowl to mouth, when in fact it is the spoon that determines that we should do so rather than, say, holding the bowl directly to our lips. We are fooled into supposing that chairs afford the possibility to sit down, when it is the chair that dictates that we should sit rather than, say, squat. And we imagine that the table is the solution to providing support for box, jug, bowl and spoon, when it is only because of the table that we are expected to place things at such a height, rather than at ground level. Manipulating spoons, sitting on chairs and eating from tables are bodily skills that take years to acquire. They do not make things any easier for us.

Contrivance and imperfection

As a creator or inventor of things, then, the designer is a trickster. Far from striving after perfection, his field is the management of imperfection. His path, like that of the mythical Daedalus, is always labyrinthine, never straight. It is hard to see, indeed, how it could be otherwise. How could there be design in a perfect world? If all ends are satisfied, what need have we of means; if nothing defective, why look for remedies? According to a rather literal reading of the biblical story of origin, God created the world, and all the creatures that inhabit it. But when you consider the intricate complexity of living things, you wonder why He should have put Himself to so much trouble. For centuries, for example, naturalists have marvelled at the structure and workings of the eye. Many have taken the eye as living proof that any organism so endowed must have been designed by some transcendent or divine intelligence, for how could an apparatus so well attuned to the achievement of vision have emerged of its own accord? One of the most celebrated of arguments along these lines was presented in 1802 by the noted theologian and philosopher, William Paley, in a treatise entitled *Natural Theology; or, Evidences of the Existence and Attributes of the Deity, Collected from the Appearances of Nature*. He, too, thought that the eye must have been designed by God to enable its bearer to see. Yet he was shrewd enough to notice that this designer-God had not only solved the riddle of vision, but had posed it as well (Paley 2006).

If an omnipotent Creator had determined that His creatures should be endowed with the capacity to perceive objects at a distance, beyond the range of touch, then presumably He could have simply willed it upon them rather than going through a circuitous route involving the reflection of light from the opaque surfaces of objects to be perceived and its refraction through transparent substances, so as to stimulate an inner membrane in communication with the brain. Likewise, He could perfectly well have bestowed on his creatures a faculty of hearing without having to design such a complicated instrument as an ear. 'Wherefore all this?' Paley wonders, and continues: 'Why make the difficulty in order only to surmount it? … Why resort to contrivance, where power is omnipotent? Contrivance, by its very definition and nature, is the refuge of imperfection. To have recourse to expedients, implies difficulty, impediment, restraint, defect of power' (Paley 2006: 26). Paley's answer was that by both setting up and resolving His own puzzles, and by revealing these solutions in the design of living things, God testifies to us the power of rational intelligence in order that we may emulate it. Or to put it another way, God created Nature as a theatre in which to put on a virtuosic display of intelligence for our benefit. In effect, to be an observer of nature is to attend a masterclass in the exercise of reason and thus to fashion ourselves, in God's image, as rational beings.

As a student at Christ's College Cambridge in the late 1820s, the young Charles Darwin read Paley's work and was, by his own admission, deeply impressed by it. In his autobiography, Darwin (2008: 14) wrote that Paley's *Natural Theology* gave him as much delight as did his reading of Euclid, and that it was indeed one of the few books on his list of required reading that was of the slightest use. 'I did not at that time trouble myself about Paley's premises', he recalled, 'and taking these on trust I was charmed and convinced of the long line of argumentation.' Darwin took from Paley a deep appreciation of the manifold ways in which organisms adapt to their conditions of life, and of the contrivances by means of which they do so. Yet in a story too well known to bear repeating here, Darwin would eventually overthrow the very assumption that first he had taken on trust, and from which Paley's entire line of argument followed, namely that there can be no design without a designer. Living organisms, Darwin admitted, have all the design properties that we might assign to manufactured artefacts, and more. But they have no designer. No mortal being, nor any divine intelligence, intended their creation. Rather, they evolved. I shall return in a moment to this alleged distinction between organism and artefact. Before doing so, however, let me first recapitulate the steps of Paley's argument. For while his proof of the existence of God, based on the evidence of life forms, may have been refuted, the assumptions about the nature of design that underwrite it have not.

Suppose, began Paley, that in walking across a heath you happened to stub your foot against a stone. Wondering how it came to be there, you might simply answer that it had lain there forever or perhaps that its presence was the fortuitous outcome of perpetual processes of erosion. Maybe, already loosened from its matrix in the soil by passing feet, it had been kicked up by the boot of a preceding walker. But now suppose that you find, lying on the path, an old, discarded watch. Someone, you think, must have dropped it. Exposed to the elements, and trodden on by unheeding passers by, it might be broken beyond repair. Not being an expert in timepieces yourself, you might not be sure what all the parts are for, or how they work together. Yet on inspection, you can be in no doubt that this object, unlike the stone, was made for a purpose, and hence that there must have existed, sometime and somewhere, a person or persons who – with this purpose in mind – designed it as a means to that end. 'There cannot be design without a designer', declared Paley, nor can there be 'contrivance without a contriver; order without choice; arrangement, without any thing capable of arranging; subserviency and relation to a purpose, without that which could intend a purpose; means suitable to an end, and executing their office in accomplishing that end, without the end ever having been contemplated, or the means accommodated to it.' And all of these, Paley (2006: 12) reasoned, 'imply the presence of intelligence and mind.' A watch may be lost or broken by accident, but no series of accidents could conceivably have thrown it together.

The watch and the earwig

Let us now suppose, rather more improbably, that on further examination the watch you have found turns out to incorporate a mechanism that, even as it moves the hands upon the dial, also fashions another watch identical to the first. Might we not say of the second watch that, while it has all the properties of its antecedent, it was the product not of intelligent design but of a purely mechanical operation? Paley moves at once to refute any such suggestion. It makes no difference, he contends, whether the watch we examine is the first, tenth, hundredth or thousandth, or indeed whether the series is finite or infinite, for every single object in the series ultimately depends on the original design – a design that is all the more remarkable in that it now includes an additional mechanism that allows each watch to turn out replicas of itself. The sense in which the artificer 'makes' the first watch is thus entirely different from that in which the first 'makes' the second, the second the third, and so on in the series, for the former is by intelligent design, whereas the latter is by mechanical execution. We might say, in a more formal idiom, that while the *proximate* cause of the *n*'th watch is watch *(n – 1)*, its *ultimate* cause is watch *0*, the design that governed the making of watch *1*. Thus the discovery that the watch, in the course of its operation, fabricates a likeness of itself, far from cancelling out our initial inference that it must be a product of intelligent design, only compounds it further. The argument from design, Paley concludes (2006: 14–15), is only strengthened rather than undermined.

It is obvious where Paley is going with his self-replicating watches! For we see their equivalents all around us in living creatures. Suppose, then, that it was not a watch that we found in our path but an earwig. Close examination reveals it to be a thing of wondrous precision, possessed of all the properties assigned to the self-replicating watch, and more. As Paley went on to testify (2006: 16), 'every indication of contrivance, every manifestation of design, which existed in the watch, exists in the works of nature; with the difference, on the side of nature, of being greater and more, and that in a degree that exceeds all computation'. What further proof, then, is needed that in living things, the wisdom of the Deity is at work? Even if we admit that our particular earwig is the output of a mechanism of replication installed in its immediate precursor that in turn was fashioned likewise – even if, as we might say, 'it is earwigs all the way down' – the entire series could not be supported were it not for the originary conception that set it in train.

It was on precisely this point that Darwin eventually took leave of Paley's line of argument. What he showed was that in living nature the process of 'contrivance' – with which, on Paley's account, the Deity teases us as a way of manifesting his power, and which is completed *in advance* of the series of perfectly self-replicating objects of His creation – is actually spun out indefinitely along the entire series, as generation follows generation, each differing ever so slightly from its predecessor. Moreover it is precisely because the mechanics of replication are *not* quite perfect, leading to the possibility of variation and recombination in the elements of transmitted design, that this evolution can occur. It does so because in a finite and therefore competitive environment, design elements that tend to favour the reproduction of the organisms that carry them will be proportionally better represented in future generations than elements that do not. This is what is meant by natural selection.

In the science of today, few commentators have been more outspoken in their advocacy of Darwinian evolutionary theory than Richard Dawkins, and in one of many books extolling the explanatory power of the theory, Dawkins returns to Paley's image of the watch. The book is entitled *The Blind Watchmaker* (Dawkins 1986). Declaring himself, like Darwin, to be an admirer of Paley's *Natural Theology*, Dawkins nevertheless holds the analogy between the watch and the living organism to be false. This is not because no watch yet devised can actually produce replicas of itself, for after all, Paley asks us – purely as a thought experiment – to imagine one that can. Thus if living organisms can reproduce, so can Paley's watch. Nor is it because the watch is a machine, for Dawkins is convinced that living organisms are machines too. A bat, for example, is a machine 'whose internal electronics are so wired up that its wing muscles cause it to home in on insects, as an unconscious guided missile homes in on an aeroplane' (Dawkins 1986: 37). The analogy is false for one reason alone: the watch had a designer, the bat did not.

A true watchmaker has foresight: he designs his cogs and springs, and plans their interconnections, with a future purpose in his mind's eye. Natural selection, the blind, unconscious, automatic process which Darwin discovered, and which we now know is the explanation for the existence and apparently purposeful form of all life, has no purpose in mind. It has no mind and no mind's eye. It does not plan for the future. It has no vision, no foresight, no sight at all. If it can be said to play the role of the watchmaker in nature, it is the *blind* watchmaker.

(Dawkins 1986: 5)

Let us put the blind watchmaker to one side for the moment, and focus on his sighted counterpart. The one thing, then, that is immediately apparent from Dawkins's account is that the sighted watchmaker neither sees nor makes watches. He only designs them, configuring the arrangement of their parts in his allegorical mind's eye. Sight, here, has nothing to do with the actual workings of the eye, which Dawkins describes in some detail (1986: 15–17), nor with optics. It has to do with foresight, with the ability to form a plan or representation in mind in advance of its material realisation. Indeed it seems that so far as Dawkins is concerned, once the watch has been designed, it is as good as made. In this, he is in accord with Paley, who likewise asks only how the watch was designed, but has nothing to say about how it might have been put together, or about the craftsmanship and dexterity involved in doing so. And so it is, too, on the side of living nature. Paley's earwig appears on the scene ready-made, with all its instruments or 'contrivances' prepared for use. Likewise for Dawkins, once you have a design for a bat, you effectively have a bat. The evolution of the design for a creature, albeit guided by natural selection rather than divine intelligence, *is* the evolution of the creature, for the creature and its design are one and the same.

The argument from design

But where, exactly, *is* this design? To return to Paley's scenario, when you stubbed your foot against a stone, it was the stone you encountered, not a design for a stone. Indeed you can be pretty sure that there was never any such design, since the stone seems to have no regularity of form and to answer to no purpose. With the discarded watch, of course, it is quite otherwise, for you feel sure that it must once have had a maker who, as Paley (2006: 8) put it, 'comprehended its construction, and designed its use'. Yet as with the stone, what you found was the watch itself, not a design for a watch. We only *infer* that the design once existed, in the mind of the maker. It is on the basis of this inference that we judge the watch, unlike the stone, to be an artefact. But now consider the earwig, or the bat. When we encounter an earwig on the forest path, or a bat in the rafters, it is the creature itself that we observe, not a design for the creature. That it has a design is, again, an inference we make, it is not observably present in the living thing that stands before us. Where, then, can this design be, if not in the mind of an omnipotent Creator?

There can be only one answer to this question. It lies in the imagination of the observing scientist. The design for a bat, for example, exists in the mind's eye of a Dawkins. Rather than having been conceived in advance of the bat's appearance in the world, it is derived, *ex post facto*, from systematic observations of the creature's behaviour. This is how it is done. Look for the regularities that underwrite any differences attributable to the particularities of local environmental conditions; from these regularities build an algorithm that models how the bat would behave under any circumstances it might conceivably encounter. There's your design. Now suppose that this design is inserted into the heart of the organism itself, as if it were encoded in its DNA. Observe how the organism behaves as it develops in a particular environment and hey presto! The behaviour appears to be generated from that very design. What was a model *of* behaviour has become an explanation *for* it. The circularity of this procedure requires no further elaboration, and is largely responsible for the hold it continues to exercise over our thinking. Only a hair's breadth, then, separates the so-called 'intelligent design' of divine creation from that which science attributes to natural selection. For in the principle of natural selection, science sees its own rationality perfectly reflected in the mirror of nature. Rather than fashioning ourselves as rational beings in the image of God's creation, it seems to be nature itself that is fashioned in the image of scientific reason.

I am not of course suggesting that any scientist ever designed a bat, in the sense that an engineer might design an electronically guided missile system. Without design engineers, there would certainly be no missiles. Bats, on the other hand, would be around and would have evolved, without any scientists to observe them. *Designs for bats*, however, would not. And when a scientist like Dawkins claims that such a design is coded into the animal's DNA, whence it controls its behaviour just as already wired-in electronics guide the missile, he is advancing an argument from design just as strong as any to be found in Paley's natural theology. Indeed as David Turnbull has pointed out, and as we already saw in the last chapter, to the modern mind this argument seems so self-evident that it is barely questioned. Turnbull (1993: 319) summarises it thus: 'the world is a very complex place, full of intricate mechanisms like the eye; therefore it had to have a designer'. The attribution of ultimate responsibility for the design to natural selection rather than God does not in the least affect the logic of the argument, namely that there can be no functional complexity without prior design.[1] Turnbull's concern, however, is with the design not of life forms but of architectures. And among architectural theorists just as among evolutionary biologists, the argument from design remains largely implicit, deeply embedded in the premises of their own enquiry.

It is true that some theorists, in their analyses of architectural design, have suggested a move analogous to the Darwinian move in biology. What if the forms of vernacular architecture, for example, could be understood as outcomes of the variation and selection of intergenerationally transmitted, recombinant elements? Design theorist Philip Steadman, for one, has drawn attention to the manifestly fallacious consequences of such a move. For the effect would be to erase altogether the creative contribution of traditional artisans to the forms they build. They would be reduced to mere intermediaries, destined to implement designs carried unknowingly in their heads. Their sole purpose, Steadman argues (1979: 188–189), would be to assist like midwives at the rebirth of the inherited design, introducing small, accidental errors – analogous to mutations – as they do so. But even though the effect of a literal application of the Darwinian analogy to the architectural arts would be to eliminate the creative agency of the human builder, it would still present us with an argument from design. That is to say, it is still assumed that forms issue from designs, albeit ones that their builders had

FIGURE 5.1 The watchmaker at work. This photograph, which appeared in the in-house publication of the Elgin National Watch Company, *Watch Word*, in September 1949, shows company employee Les Linder making final adjustments to the movement of a railroad watch. I am grateful to librarian Betsy Vera and collections services manager William R. Blohm, of Gail Borden Public Library in Elgin, Illinois, for tracking down the photo and providing a copy.

no hand in shaping, of which they have no conscious awareness and that analytically trained design theorists are alone capable of articulating.

We have already seen in the last chapter (p. 56), by way of Turnbull's example of building the great Gothic cathedral of Chartres, how this argument both fails to account for workmanship and attributes powers to rules they cannot have. But the same counter-argument could be applied just as well, on a miniature rather than monumental scale, to the case of watchmaking. Picture for a moment the real watchmaker at work (Figure 5.1). There he is, in his workshop, delicately fitting together tiny cogs and springs, along with other components, under a close and observant eye. He may well have to use a magnifying glass to see well enough what he is doing. Before that, he may have had to manufacture the individual components, a task that calls for an equally close-up engagement with metal and precious stones. A watchmaker who was truly blind, but whose intellectual faculties were unimpaired, could in principle *design* a watch. He could, as Dawkins intimates, design the cogs and springs, and plan their interconnections. Yet the foresight that Dawkins attributes to the watchmaker will not *make* a watch. For that you also need skilled vision and manual dexterity. And just as medieval cathedral builders had to work things out as they went along, following flexible rules of thumb rather than procedures precisely laid down in advance, so too did the watchmakers of Paley's day, else they would not have had to pay such close attention to what they were doing.

The design of everyday life

In this regard, the foresight required of the watchmaker is of a very different kind from that which the argument from design attributes to the designer. It lies not in the cogitation that literally comes *before sight* but in the very activity of *seeing forward*, not in *preconception* but in what the sociologist Richard Sennett, in his study of the work of the craftsman, calls *anticipation*: being 'always one step ahead of the material' (Sennett 2008: 175). The philosopher Jacques Derrida has resort to the same idea in reference to the art of drawing in which, he claims, the inscribing hand continually overtakes the cogitations of the head. To anticipate, he says, is 'to take the initiative, to be out in front, to take (*capere*) in advance (*ante*)' (Derrida 1993: 4). 'If the mind wants to be involved in the process of making', writes design theorist Lars Spuybroek (2011: 160), 'it must not only be open but forward-looking, in the direction of as-yet-unknown creation.' This is a matter not of predetermining the final forms of things and all the steps needed to get there, but of opening up a path and improvising a passage. To foresee, in this sense, is to see *into* the future, not to project a future state of affairs in the present; it is to look where you are going, not to fix an end point. Such foresight is about prophecy, not prediction. And it is precisely what enables practitioners to carry on.

To make a watch takes time. This time is not incidental, or collapsible into an instant or series of instants. It is rather a time of growth or formation, of ontogenesis. Thus the designing of the watch continues into its making – in the ways the pieces assembled there answer to one another in the generation of internal coherence. What the maker has to hand, to begin with, are cogs and springs, among other minute pieces. These pieces do not belong together, in preordained positions, by dint of some external necessity. They are no more parts of a watch than are twigs on the forest floor parts of a bird's nest. Rather, as with the nest, pieces become parts only as the assembly proceeds and tends increasingly to cohere. They gradually acquire a feel for each other, they *settle*, holding each other in place ever more tightly as the work advances asymptotically towards closure without ever absolutely reaching it. The task of the maker is to bring the pieces into a sympathetic engagement with one another, so that they can begin – as I would say – to *correspond*. Peering through his eyeglass (Figure 5.1), the watchmaker inhabits a realm *in among* the pieces, rather than *above and beyond* them, adjusting each in relation to the others, and serving as a kind of go-between in their correspondence. Only as the work nears completion can the pieces be judged, with reasonable confidence, to be the parts of a whole.

On these grounds, Spuybroek (2011: 67) maintains that Paley *could not have been more wrong* in his inference that the watch, accidentally encountered on the heath, attests to an intelligent design that preceded its manufacture, 'as if things resembled wholes with predefined parts, each restricted to a single act'. No more are cut and carved stones the predefined parts of a building, and we would be equally mistaken – as we have already seen – to infer the precedence of architectural design from such a complex structure as a cathedral. Design extends into making as the builder, in among the stones, brings them into correspondence. Our models for art and design, Spuybroek (2011: 243) suggests, should ideally be drawn not from horology or architecture but from gardening and cooking. 'A great gardener or chef', he observes, 'not only sees the state of things but senses where they are going' (ibid.: 240). I have called this sensing anticipatory foresight: a foresight that does not so much connect a preconceived idea to a final object as *go between*, in a direction orthogonal to their connection, following and reconciling the inclinations of alternately pliable and recalcitrant materials. You do not have to be a gardener or chef of distinction, however, in order to design in this sense, for it answers to our most everyday experience, for example at the breakfast table, from where we begin each day and whence I began this chapter. Let us briefly revisit it, before moving on.

I suggested earlier that the table is tantamount to an obstacle course, on and around which every designed object is a hurdle to be overcome. Yet it is really not that hard, except perhaps for infants who still have to master the manipulation of the spoon, and whose physical size is not matched to the adult proportions of the furniture. It is not hard because in their enrolment in a fluent and skilful performance, box, jug, bowl, spoon and cloth, as well as table and chair, are not encountered as finished objects answering to a design that preceded and underwrote their manufacture. Indeed, as will become clear in the next chapter, they are not really encountered as objects at all, but as things. These things are not finished but are carried on in their use even as you carry on with your own life as you sit down to eat. What Norman (1988) calls 'the design of everyday things' does not, then, achieve its ends with their manufacture. For them to be things at all, and not objects, requires that they be brought into a relation with one another – into a correspondence – that is itself defined by a narrative of anticipated use. Everyday design catches the narrative and pins it down, establishing a kind of choreography for the ensuing performance that allows it to proceed from the moment when you sit down to eat. In such a straightforward task as laying the table – in enrolling into your relation bowl and spoon, milk jug and cereal box – you are designing breakfast. In amongst the furniture and tableware, your role is to act as a go-between. Not until the table is already laid can we say with assurance what any particular item is *for*. And this gives the lie to the mantra of 'user-centred' design, which casts practitioners as the mere consumers of objects designed *for* them, and not *by* them, in order to satisfy predetermined 'needs'.

Breaking trail and catching dreams

What, then, can design possibly *mean*, if not to set up a plan in advance of its implementation? If things are never finished – if the world is perpetually under construction by way of the activities of its inhabitants, who are tasked with keeping life going rather than bringing to completion projects specified at the outset – then can design any longer be distinguished from making? Are design and making merely two words for the same thing? We have already noted (Chapter 4, pp. 50–51) that in some

European languages, the word for design is the same as that for drawing. Their original synonymy, however, rested on the idea of the drawing as the outline of a mental image, geometrically projected onto a plane surface. In the writings of such Renaissance figures as Alberti and Vasari, for example, the Italian word *disegno* signified both the idea and its visual expression. Here, design and drawing figure as two sides of the same coin, with one side in the mind and the other on paper. But what if we were to think of drawing in another way: not as the projection of a ready-made image but as the inscriptive trace of a movement or gesture comparable to weaving with threads or carving in stone?

The artist Paul Klee (1961: 105) famously described drawing as taking a line for a walk. The line that goes for a walk does not represent or prefigure anything. Quite unlike the straight line of Euclidean geometry, it does not connect predetermined points. On paper, it is the trace of a movement rather than a statement of intent (Maynard 2005: 66–67). As we have already said of the anticipatory foresight of the skilled practitioner, it breaks a trail, continually launching forth from its tip and tracing a path as it goes. If design is to be the other side of drawing in this sense, then it would have to be about anticipating the future. Far from seeking finality and closure, it would be open-ended, dealing in hopes and dreams rather than plans and predictions. As the Finnish architect Juhani Pallasmaa (2009: 110–111) writes, 'design is always a search for something that is unknown in advance'. It is precisely this inner uncertainty, according to Pallasmaa, expressed in the hesitancy of his drawing, which drives the creative process. Unlike material bodies, however, hopes and dreams can fly: they are not bound to the spatio-temporal limits of earthly life. The difficulty is that in taking flight they can all too easily be lost. It is the task of design to go after them and bring them back. Travelling light, unencumbered by the dead weight of heavy materials, the line of the designer seeks to give chase to the phantasms of a fugitive imagination and to rein them in before they can get away, setting them down as signposts in the field of practice that makers and builders can track at their own, more laboured and ponderous pace.

Picture for example a composer, at work on a symphony. The music flies ahead in his imagination like a bird on the wing. It is all he can do to catch it and get it down before it is lost beyond the horizon of his recollection. With so many staves, each for an instrument of the orchestra, it can take many hours of painstaking work to notate a passage that in performance would last barely a minute. Composing would be easy, were it not for music's propensity to outpace its material inscription. Nor is this a problem confined to musical composition. The performer, writes the philosopher Maurice Merleau-Ponty (1968: 151), who feels that the music 'sings through him', finds that he 'must "dash his bow" to follow it'. The architect Alvaro Siza compares the task of designing a building to tracking a character, or rather a host of characters, who are always slipping away from him. His predicament, he says, is not unlike that of the novelist, whose characters have a way of outrunning his capacity to write them down. It is vital not to lose them (Siza 1997: 51). In writing as in drawing, notes Serge Tisseron (1994: 36), thought 'darts out like an unruly horse, which is later led back and tamed, bound to the line which the hand holds fast upon the paper'. Or in another image, the writer or draughtsman is like a man swept away by a wave from a ship: the line is the rope from which he is hanging on (Tisseron 1994: 37). Even painters are challenged to rein in their fleeting visions of an evanescent world before they escape. 'It is the fear of not going fast enough', wrote Charles Baudelaire, 'of letting the phantom escape before the synthesis has been extracted and pinned down; it is that terrible fear that takes possession of all great artists and gives them such a passionate desire to become masters of every means of expression so that the orders of the brain may never be perverted by the hesitations of the hand' (in Baudelaire 1986: 17). While the frenzy of creation that Baudelaire evokes so vividly sweeps practitioners ever forward as though on a wave crest, the hesitancy of the body and the weight of materials perpetually hold them back. It seems that composer, performer, architect, writer, draughtsman and painter alike are continually caught between the anticipatory reach of imaginative foresight and the tensile or frictional drag of material abrasion – whether of pen on paper, bow on strings, or brush on canvas.

The trick, then, is to be able to hold the foresight that pierces the distance like an arrow in check with the close-up, even myopic engagement that is necessary for working with materials. Recently, anthropologist Rane Willerslev (2006) has argued that one of the singular properties of vision, by which it is distinguished from other sensory modalities (including hearing and touch), is that it brings foresight and the close-up together, to the extent of making the former a *condition* for the latter. The inspiration for this move comes from Merleau-Ponty's claim that 'to see is *to have at a distance*' (Merleau-Ponty 1964: 166). With hearing and touch, if you come close to something, then the boundary between yourself and the thing begins to blur and eventually dissolves altogether. You merge with it. In vision, by contrast, if you are too close to something, you cannot see it. To see, at least with binocular vision, you must take a certain distance. And in this distantiation lies the possibility for a kind of reflexive self-awareness. You do not just see but see yourself seeing. It is this self-awareness, then, that makes it possible to come close to another thing or being, and hence to engage with it materially, without actually merging with it. This is a prerequisite for hunting, for example. To succeed, the hunter must identify with his prey, but were he to merge with it the consequences would be fatal. Likewise the artist painting a landscape must immerse himself in the sensory environment, whilst remaining afar from it. It is difficult, Willerslev (2006: 41) concludes, to see how this could be pulled off without vision.

I am not so sure, however. For one thing, if vision is a condition for self-awareness, then this leaves us wondering how human beings with visual impairments can be aware of themselves – as they manifestly are – or why non-human animals (even those endowed with binocular vision) apparently are not. For another thing, anyone who has had to make their way in pitch darkness, relying on tactile and aural perception alone, knows that touch and hearing, too, can induce a sense of distance, just like vision. You may be startled by sounds, and recoil from what is touched. Be that as it may, the general point that a designerly process of making is one whose close-up engagements are guided by foresight is a powerful one. It has been said that painters cannot see what they are painting, since they are too close to it, and likewise that composers cannot hear – even that writers cannot remember what they are writing about (Deleuze and Guattari 2004: 544). But it would probably be closer to the mark to say that the particular skill of painters, composers and writers lies in their practised ability to keep their distance whilst in the thick of the labours of proximity. The parallel with hunting, as Willerslev intimates, is precise. Hunters often dream of animals before they encounter them. Artists, architects, composers and writers are likewise bent upon capturing the insights of an imagination always inclined to shoot off into the distance, and on bringing them back into the immediacy of material engagement. *Like hunters, they too are dream catchers*. Human endeavours, it seems, are forever poised between catching dreams and coaxing materials. In this tension, between the pull of hopes and dreams and the drag of material constraint, and not in any opposition between cognitive intellection and mechanical execution, lies the relation between design and making. It is precisely where the reach of the imagination meets the friction of materials, or where the forces of ambition rub up against the rough edges of the world, that human life is lived.

6

ROUND MOUND AND EARTH SKY

Becoming earth

If you heap stuff up over a period of time, always adding to the top of the pile and allowing it to settle of its own accord, it will generally form a mound, roughly circular in plan and conical or bell-shaped in elevation. On a miniature scale, we can observe this process of mound formation in the sand of an hourglass. On a gigantic scale, it can be witnessed in the formation of volcanic cones. From molehills to ants' nests, mounds are among the commonest forms in nature. They often result from human activities too – think of shell middens, stone cairns, sandcastles, and heaps of compost, refuse and slag. In every case, the roundness of the form emerges spontaneously, due to the way in which the pressure of material added from above displaces material already deposited, equally in all directions. One could say that the mound builds up precisely because the material of which it is made is continually falling down. Each and every particle, as it falls, eventually finds its own more or less enduring place of rest. The Brazilian artist Laura Vinci has brought this process to life in a work that simultaneously demonstrates the dynamics of mound production – as a conveyor belt continually transports fine-ground marble from one heap to another – and comments on the environmental impact of industrial mining in the state of Minas Gerais. The work, entitled *Máquina do Mundo* ('Machine of the World'), is described by the artist herself as an 'anti-machine' that overturns the values of permanence, solidity and timelessness associated with classical architecture and statuary by using the very material that epitomises these values – white marble – to enact the contrary principles of perdurance, transformation and the passage of time (Figure 6.1).

From a distance, the growing mound looks like a perfectly formed cone. Look closely at the surface, however, and it is awash with movement as every particle finds its way, jostling under the impact of all the others. Close examination of the surface of a growing ants' nest likewise reveals it to be a hive of activity (Figure 6.2). In this respect the mound is the very opposite of the edifice. If Vinci's *Máquina* is in reality an anti-machine, then the mound is truly an anti-building. In Chapter 4 I introduced the classical idea of the architect as one who lays the foundations on which others

FIGURE 6.1 'The Machine of the World' (*Máquina do Mundo*), an installation by the artist Laura Vinci. Photo by Denise Adams, reproduced by courtesy of the artist.

build (p. 50). In the construction of an architectural edifice each successive piece is carefully laid to rest upon the last in such a way that a static equilibrium is maintained. The permanence and integrity of the structure depend on the way in which additional material is locked into position through its abutment to what has already been set down, without causing further movement or displacement in the latter. In building a tower of stone blocks, for example, every layer of blocks has to be added so that it bears down precisely on the preceding layer, which bears in turn upon the layer before that, and so on right down to the foundations. Without fixed and solid foundations, the entire building process could not even begin. Ultimately, therefore, every edifice must rest upon foundations set in the earth. If the foundations give way, whether due to subsidence or tremors, the entire structure can come crashing down. If and when it does, the result will likely be a mound of stones!

But the mound has no foundations. Nor is it ever complete. One can always carry on adding new material. The growth of the mound, as Vinci's *Máquina* demonstrates, is never-ending. As it rises in height, it also expands at the base. But although every particle of the mound comes to rest on other particles, the mound as a whole does not rest upon the earth. In this regard, Vinci's installation is a little misleading. For the purposes of display, it is placed on the pre-prepared floor of an interior gallery. One has little difficulty, then, in distinguishing the material of the floor, with its flat, solid and homogeneous surface, from the material of the mound that is ever-forming upon it. Outside this rather artificial situation, however, one cannot say with any assurance where the mound ends and the earth on which it rests begins. For the mound is as

FIGURE 6.2 Becoming earth: a nest of forest ants, photographed on the shore of Lake Pielinen in eastern Finland. (Courtesy of Susanna Ingold.)

much *of* the earth as *on* it. Indeed its emergent form bears witness to the continual process wherein the accretion of material converts deposition into burial. Today's deposit becomes tomorrow's substrate, buried under later sediment. Like the compost heap or the ants' nest, the mound, we could say, is *becoming earth* (Figure 6.2). Indeed, the mound forces us to acknowledge that the earth itself is not the solid and pre-existing substrate that the edifice builder takes it to be. It is rather the source of all life and growth. Plants grow in the earth, not on it, and from these, animals – including human beings – draw their subsistence. Metabolised and decomposed by the processes of life, materials drawn from the earth are eventually returned to it, fuelling further growth. In this sense, the earth is perpetually growing over, which is why archaeologists have to dig to discover evidence of past lives (Ingold 2008a: 31). Formed in the process of life becoming earth, the mound could be regarded as a growth or swelling, manifested as a bump on the ground surface. But it is not an edifice erected upon it.

Now in many regions of the world, the earth is peppered with such bumps of a scale, location and composition that lead prehistorians to believe – not without reason – that they are the results of past human activity, although precisely what that activity may have entailed, or what its purpose could have been, often remain a mystery (Leary, Darvill and Field 2010). Yet most prehistorians, convinced that any kind of making or building involves the projection of form onto the material world, are predisposed to think of the mound as a sculptured earthwork, answering to the specifications of a preconceived design. It is as though the mound builders, as they piled up earth and stones, had an idea of how the work would finally look, and kept on piling until the height, diameter and contours of the accumulated material matched their expectations. As a thought experiment, let us imagine that we are equipped with a time machine that enables us to revisit the folk who, in the distant past, were living in and around those places where now there are round mounds.[1] Let us ask them what they are doing. They may perhaps answer that they are burying their dead, or that they are meeting to resolve their affairs. They might say that they are conducting ceremonies to restore the fertility of the land. They might even claim to be depositing their rubbish, or simply building and rebuilding – as countless generations have done before – on the same spot.

The one answer, however, that they would be most unlikely to give would be 'building a mound'. Rather, the mound that confronts us today is the cumulative by-product of all kinds of activities, carried on over long periods of time and not only by human beings. Burrowing animals, from worms to rabbits, have played their part in its evolution. The roots of trees, bushes and grasses, threading through its volume, have helped to fix it. The weather, and above all the rain, has shaped it internally and externally, in the creation of patterns of drainage and run-off. Crucially, these organic and hydrological processes continue in the present as they have always done in the past. To observe the mound today is to witness their going on. The mound, we could say, exists in its *mounding*. This is to think of it not as a finished object, standing on foundations and set over and against its surroundings, but as a locus of growth and regeneration where materials welling up from the earth mix and mingle with the fluxes of the weather in the ongoing production of life. The mound has not turned its back on us, as we might suppose, hiding secrets within its dark, enclosed interior that we can discover only by tunnelling in. On the contrary, it is open to the world. As the ever-emergent outcome of the interplay of cosmic forces and vital materials, the mound is not built but grows (Figure 6.3).

Mound and monument

In the conventions of prehistory, round mounds are commonly classified and conserved as ancient monuments. This is to make two assumptions: first, that they were designed and built to last in perpetuity as a testimony to the endeavour of those who constructed or commissioned them; secondly, that having been built at a particular historical moment, they can be granted a certain antiquity. In other words we can, in principle, tell how old they are. Both assumptions, it seems to me, are false. Let me deal with each in turn: the first in this section; the second in the next.

History is littered with the products of monumental attempts to put an end to it. Countless edifices, intended by their architects to seal their immortality, lie buried and forgotten, lost in the mists of time. Others, rediscovered and excavated by archaeologists in the service of the modern project of nation building, have been given a new lease of life, in an idiom that nevertheless consigns the past to a bygone if heroic age. Indeed the paradox of monuments is that they can serve as memorials only because they have failed in the objective set for them by the powers that originally intended their construction. Had they succeeded – if, that is, their architects had managed, in the words of anthropologist Vincent Crapanzano (2004: 169), to 'close memory to its beyond' and thereby to render themselves eternal – then there would be no future generations to look back on them and marvel at how they had come to be built.[2] Impressive in

FIGURE 6.3 The mound mounding. The round mound of Pitnacree in Perthshire, viewed from the south. © Courtesy of Royal Commission on the Ancient and Historical Monuments of Scotland (J. M. Coles and D. D. A. Simpson). Licensor www.rcahms.gov.uk.

their permanence and solidity, monumental structures intended by their makers to confer everlasting life provide irrefutable evidence, to those who subsequently come across them, that the past is dead, over and done with. Like beached whales, they seem to have been left stranded on the shores of history, while time moves on. As it does so, the gap between a lost past and the vivid present grows ever wider. For while the monument speaks *for* itself, calling out the names or preserving the likenesses of those whom it commemorates, it also speaks *to* itself in the idiom and language of its time. To visit a monument is to eavesdrop on past conversations that we can no longer fully understand, or that are comprehensible only to specialist antiquarians. They were then, we are now.

This is not to deny that the monument may hold memories for us. Perhaps it stands in a place we have often visited, and that generations of our families have visited previously. We might have old photographs to prove it, and looking longingly at the figures in the photos, we exclaim that 'they are us!' This kind of memory-work allows us to tell stories that flow as seamlessly from past to present as our own lives. Throughout, the monument stands as a focus. Yet what it records, if anything, is incidental to the stories we tell. We remember that we visited, as did others before us. It is the latter, and not the persons immortalised in the monument, that we draw into our conversations. 'It is a common mistake', as the historian Mary Carruthers (1998: 40) notes, 'to confuse the activity of remembering with the "things" humans may use to locate and cue their memories.' Carruthers is concerned with the liturgical processions of early medieval pilgrims as they went from site to site. For these pilgrims, it mattered little whether any physical record remained at each site of the personages or events with which it was associated. What was real and authentic about the sites, for them, lay not in the objects to be found there, but in 'the *memory-work*, the thinking to which they gave clues' (1998: 42). Sites of pilgrimage are places where the work of memory is carried on, not capsules in which to preserve its more durable relics. Conversely, as the fate of so many monuments reveals, the encapsulation of the past in such relics holds no guarantee that it will be remembered.

Now without doubt, round mounds are and have long been places of memory. The remembering goes on in the very activities that we – like our predecessors – carry on around them, in walking, cultivating, excavating and so on. Like sites of pilgrimage, many are known to have been holy places, often situated along lines of travel that have been in use from time immemorial. Yet most are so inconspicuous that they can scarcely be discerned today, and it often takes a trained or locally knowledgeable eye to see them. Their most extraordinary quality, as the historical geographer Kenneth Olwig observes with reference to the mounds that crop up all over the countryside of Jutland, in what is now Denmark, lies in 'their unmarked anonymity and the absence of monumental signs' (Olwig 2008). Convinced, however, that they must be monuments, and thus capsules for the past, generations of archaeologists have been impelled by a relentless search for some inner secret – a kernel of meaning that the original mound builders left inside as an enduring record of their lives and deeds. If only something spectacular could be found at the heart of the mound, we would at last know who built them and why! More often than not, however, excavation has been unrewarded by discovery. Though mounds might draw attention to themselves as places to dig, they often turn up no more than would be uncovered by digging anywhere else. For the archaeologists of today it is precisely in the finding, and not in what (if anything) is found, that the work of memory lies. This must have been equally true for people in the past. Perhaps it was in the very process of trying to find things, or alternatively of trying to get rid of them, that – over the millennia – mounds were formed.

The antiquity of things

Thus while the architectural monument, originally designed and built to last for all eternity, eventually sinks into the sands of time, the round mound – quietly and inconspicuously – just carries on mounding. That is to say, it *perdures*. And this brings us to our second assumption. Of a monument, it is surely straightforward to ask how old it is. We would respond that it dates from that defining moment when a form, which until then had been present only as an idea, was unified with hitherto formless raw material, so as to create a finished work of architecture. It might require some archaeological detective work to discover when this moment was, but we do not doubt that it existed. But what if we were to ask this question of a mountain? How can we possibly date it, even in principle? For the mountain was neither made nor built. Rather, it took shape, gradually and – to ordinary mortals – imperceptibly, over great aeons of geological time, through processes of deposition, compression, uplift and erosion that are still going on now much as they have always done. At no singular point in time did these processes begin, nor have they come to an end. The mountain is not, and never will be, completed. Thus, no amount of detective work on the part of the geologist will suffice to determine its age or antiquity. It is a question that cannot even be sensibly asked of the mountain, let alone answered. Monuments can be ancient, but mountains cannot.

What, then, of the mound? Can we say how old it is? Apparently more artificial than a mountain, but more natural than a monument, the mound seems to lie halfway between the two. Yet this very distinction between the natural and the artificial, and with it the question of antiquity, rests on the axiom of the hylomorphic model of making, namely that it is the imposition of pure form that raises naturally given raw material to an artificial state. The phenomenon of the mound obliges us, however, to reject this axiom. The mound certainly differs from the mountain in that it is of a more human scale, and its formation undoubtedly owes more than that of the mountain to the labour of human beings and other living creatures. Yet like the mountain, its form is ever-emergent through the play of forces and materials. Moreover, once we turn this argument back on the monument, the question of its antiquity, which had initially seemed so simple, begins to look a good deal more complex. Why should we date a monument from the moment it was built? Is this not just one, relatively arbitrary point in the life of a thing, and of its constituent materials? Suppose, for example, that the monument is built of stone. Even before the stones were laid, they had first to be quarried and cut, and even after the masons' work was done, the structure has remained subject to weathering, erosion and wear and tear, calling for periodic restorative intervention. In building, as we observed in Chapter 4, finishing is never finished. How, then, can originating ever have an origin? Do we not rather have to conclude of things made or built, as much as of things grown, that they are originating all the time?

Why, in the face of these questions, does archaeology remain so committed to the unequivocal determination of the antiquity of things? The answer, I think, lies in its concern to treat these things as comprising a *record* of times long past. For an entity of any kind to become part of the archaeological record, it must hold fast to a point of origin, receding ever further from the horizon of the present as the rest of the world moves on. Conversely, things that carry on, that undergo continuous generation or, in a word, that *grow* cannot be part of the record. Are they, then, of no further archaeological interest? Of course not. They are of principal interest, however, to an archaeology that is concerned with what Cornelius Holtorf (2009: 37) has called the 'pastness' of things rather than their antiquity, or with what we would rather call their perdurance. What matters, in the archaeology of perdurance, is not the determination of dates but the ability to follow things through in their temporal trajectories from past to present. Everything there is, according to geographer Torsten Hägerstrand (1976: 332), from living organisms through tools to stones, has its trajectory; each is a strand in 'the big tapestry of Nature that history is weaving'. Thus the handaxe has its trajectory; so do the watch and the cathedral, and so does the round mound: each of these things carries on in its own way, and each has – or rather *is* – its own record, of the processes and occurrences that went into its formation.

Indeed the very word 'record' suggests a *cord* (strand, string) that is *re*-covered or *re*-wound. To recover or rewind the thing is to pick up one line of Hägerstrand's 'big tapestry' and to pull it through to the present. But to turn these things, these *re-cords*, into objects *in* the record is to cut the very cords that carry on, and to let them fall like cuttings to the floor. The record is a collection of such cuttings: it is the scrapbook of history. At full scale and in three dimensions, these scrapbooks are our museums. Inside the museum, dated and cured, things grow older with every passing day, yet their ageing is artificially arrested. But out in the open, the mound keeps mounding, ageing all the while without, however, growing any older.

The shape of the land

We will return to the record (Chapter 8, pp. 120–121), in connection with an experiment in making string. For now, let us revisit the round mound. Imagine a traveller, making his way towards the mound along one of the many time-worn tracks that lead there. Stretching out before and around him is a vista, with the earth below and the sky above, divided along the line of the horizon. In his sights, the mound appears on this line as a rather inconspicuous bump. Now as I have already shown, the mound is not an edifice. It does not stand erect on solid foundations. On the contrary, it lies down. Like a collapsed, dormant figure, it is both *on* and *of* the earth. Let us suppose that the traveller, having come to the mound, follows suit, and lies down with it. At once, the horizon disappears beyond the periphery of his visual awareness, which merges with the shimmering luminosity of the sky, while his body is wrapped in the embrace of the damp earth. Thus earth and sky, far from being divided along the line of the distant horizon, are unified at the very centre of the traveller's emplaced being. What had been a tiny speck in the distance opens up from the inside to reveal the unbounded immensity of what I shall henceforth call the *earth-sky world*. Such would be the experience of the mound itself, were it gifted with sensory awareness, as indeed it would be of any body or bodies buried beneath. Many – though by no means all – round mounds do incorporate burials, and from the perspective of the deceased they were evidently laid to rest in an earth-sky world. There they are still, at least until disinterred by archaeologists, buried in the earth, but looking up into the sky.

Thus the switch in perspective from moving towards an empty place on the horizon to merging with it in the world of earth and sky is associated with the transition from life to death. Yet in another sense, the round mound epitomises the mystery of life itself, comparable to that associated in Indo-European cosmology with the number zero, signifying the unknowable nothing from which everything comes. Likewise, as Olwig observes (2008: 33), from the 'womblike hollowness' of the mound there unfolds an entire cosmos. The significance of the mound, however, is – or at least was – not only cosmological but also political. In Jutland as throughout southern Scandinavia, many mounds bear the name *Tinghøj* ('Thing Hill'). Well into medieval times the *ting* continued as a place of assembly, to which the inhabitants of the surrounding *landskap* would come to resolve their affairs. Literally meaning 'land shaped' (from Old English *sceppan* or *skyppan*, 'to shape'), the *landskap* referred in the usage of the time to an imprecisely delimited expanse of land bound into the customary practices and subject to the unwritten laws of those who would gather at the same *ting*. Thus from earliest times, there was an intrinsic connection between landscape and thing. On the one hand as a gathering, a knotting together of life courses and paths of activity, the thing *enfolds* the landscape. On the other hand as a source of law, the thing *unfolds into* the landscape – in the practices guided by it, of dwelling and habitation, and of tilling the soil.

In this relation of enfolding and unfolding, the mound once again differs from the monument. 'At the *Ting*', Olwig writes (2008: 33), 'law was committed to living memory, whereas the monument literally chisels memory into dead stone.' In the mound, the past is assembled as a matrix for the ongoing continuation of life; in the monument the past is cast aside and survives only as a relic. Where the mound-thing welcomes us in, as participants in its mounding, the monument shuts us out. It is closed, finished. Standing before us as a fait accompli, it presents only its congealed outer surfaces to our inspection. Many erstwhile thing-places, of course, have now been designated as ancient monuments, and are assiduously preserved in what are imagined to have been their final forms. For visitors to leave marks or traces of their presence in such places is then no longer to contribute to their formation but to threaten their preservation. A cairn, for example, is just a pile of stones that grows as every traveller, passing by a particular place, adds a stone picked up along the way as a memento of the trip. But a cairn that has been designated for preservation as a monument should remain untouched: to add or remove any stone would be to commit an act of despoliation.

It is precisely this shift from an ever-evolving mound-thing to the already completed monument that differentiates the shaping of the land, in its modern sense, from its medieval precursor. In medieval times, the *landskap* was shaped by work in fields and forests, according to the law of the *ting*. The modern sense of shaping the land, by contrast, has its roots not in agrarian practice but in architecture. We have already seen (Chapter 4, p. 50) how in distinguishing the architect from the carpenter, Leon Battista Alberti sought to distance the idea of architecture from the practical craftsmanship of the journeyman, and to think of it instead as the form that the intellect contributes to the building, independently and in advance of the work of construction. Subsequently, the concept of landscape would undergo an equivalent transformation: from the land-shaping labours of farmers and woodsmen to the scenographic projections of artists and architects. In the vocabulary of post-Renaissance aesthetics, landscape served as both stage and scenery, furnishing not only the solid foundation on which the monument is erected but also the scenic backdrop against which it may be displayed or 'set off' to best advantage. Together, the monument and its landscape were understood to comprise a totality that was complete and fully formed. Here, following the precepts of the hylomorphic model, land is to scape as material substance to abstract form, and the land is shaped by their unification.

Through the doorway

It is with these precepts that historian Simon Schama opens his magnum opus on *Landscape and Memory*. The scenery, he tells us, 'is built up as much from strata of memory as from layers of rock … it is our shaping perception that makes the difference between raw matter and landscape' (Schama 1995: 7, 10). Perhaps you would care to join the students taking the 4 As course and me, as we leave the classroom to take a walk outside, in the open air. We wanted to test for ourselves the idea, so clearly articulated for our times by Schama, that it is perception that lends shape and form to the world around us. Our walk began from the foot of the hill of Bennachie, not far from the city of Aberdeen. With its steep sides and knobbly peak, and rising from relatively flat farmland, the hill is a prominent feature of the Aberdeenshire skyline, and is popular with walkers who can wander along forest trails at lower levels or climb the paths to the open, heather-covered top that is ringed by an impressive prehistoric earthwork or 'hill fort'.

Before setting out, we had been reading an article by the archaeologists Christopher Tilley, Sue Hamilton and Barbara Bender. They had been working on Leskernick Hill, one of a number of hills comprising Bodmin Moor in the county of Cornwall. Strewn across one flank of the hill are the remnants of a village settlement that was evidently inhabited until around 2,500 years ago, but had since been abandoned and gone to ruin. A visitor walking over the moor today would encounter a host of stones, of all shapes and sizes, their surfaces scoured and textured by millennia of weathering. To the contemporary eye it is as though these stones had already found their fixed and final resting places, in a land already shaped. This is not, however, how the landscape would have been experienced by its erstwhile inhabitants, who incorporated many of the stones into the fabric of their houses and into the walls surrounding their fields. For them, stone would have been a vital material in a land they were actively shaping through the arduous physical labour of house building and cultivation. Tilley and his colleagues were keen to gain a sense of what the landscape would have felt like for these prehistoric land shapers. Their aim, they say, was 'to perceive Leskernick Hill from within, not from looking at it as if in a painting' (Tilley, Hamilton and Bender 2000: 60).

One of their experiments was to spend time looking out from what was left of the doorways of the original houses. They wanted to know how a villager would have seen the landscape from his front door. But since only the foundations of the houses remained, up to a height of about one metre, this was hard to record. To make it easier, they built a 'doorway' in the form of a light, rectangular wooden frame. Carrying the frame from house to house, they recorded the landscape features visible through the frame in each location. According to their report, however, this procedure had a dramatic and unintended effect on their way of seeing. Limiting, controlling and defining the field of vision, the frame turned the landscape into a picture. Quite contrary to their original intention, they found that they were looking at it in the manner of traditional landscape art (Tilley, Hamilton and Bender 2000: 53–55).

Returning to our walk on the hill of Bennachie, we wanted to try this experiment for ourselves. Not far up the slopes of the hill lie the remains of a small crofting colony. Throughout the latter decades of the nineteenth century changes in land tenure had made life increasingly difficult for the crofters, and the settlement had gradually declined. The last of the colonists still dwelling on the hill died in 1939, and their tiny cottages, built from local stone taken from a nearby quarry, now lie in ruins (Vergunst 2012). Stopping by one ruin, we made a flimsy frame from light wooden battens that we had brought with us, and set it up in the space where a gap in the walls, now reduced to rubble, indicated that the door once stood. The frame, we found, did not turn the landscape into a picture. On the contrary, it had the remarkable effect of turning the ruin back into a cottage. It was easy to cross the walls of the building, simply by straddling the stones, at any point. The frame, however, invited us to enter. Hunching our shoulders and bending our heads a little as we passed, as if through a low and narrow door of the kind the cottage would originally have had, we found ourselves literally on the 'inside'. Although the present ruin is open to the elements, the very movement of entry yielded a sense of the cottage as the interior space that it once was for its inhabitants. Conversely, retracing our steps through our improvised frame returned us to the open.

As this little exercise proved, for there to be an interior and an exterior one must go in and come out, rather than crossing from side to side. The spaces of dwelling are not already given, in the layout of the building, but are created in movement. That is to say, they are *performed*. 'In a kind of double movement', David Turnbull writes, 'people perform objects of all kinds, but especially buildings, by moving through and around them but buildings also perform people by constraining their movements and by making likely certain kinds of encounters between them and others' (Turnbull 2002: 135). It follows that our most fundamental architectural experiences are verbal rather than nominal in form. They consist, according to Juhani Pallasmaa, not of encounters with objects – the façade, door frame, window and fireplace – but of acts of approaching and entering, looking in or out, and soaking up the warmth of the hearth. 'The doorhandle', Pallasmaa (1996: 40, 45) affirms, 'is the handshake of the building.' It bids us welcome. In just the same way, we have found that the mound comes into its own, in its mounding, through the movement of lying down with it, soaking up the dampness of the earth while mingling with the immensity of the sky. And in this the mound – like the building – is no longer encountered as an object but experienced as a thing.

In his celebrated essay on *The Thing*, the philosopher Martin Heidegger was at pains to figure out what makes a thing different from an object (Harman 2005). The object, he argued, is complete in itself, defined by its confrontational 'over-againstness' – face to face or surface to surface – in relation to the setting in which it is placed (Heidegger 1971: 167). We may look *at* it or even touch it, but we cannot join *with* it in the process of its formation. However metrically close our interaction with the object may be, it remains affectively distant. But if objects are *against* us, things are *with* us. Every thing, for Heidegger, is a coming together of materials in movement. To touch it, or to observe it, is to bring the movements of our own being into close and affective correspondence with those of its constituent materials. In lying down with the mound, in adding a stone we have picked up along the way to a cairn, in turning the handle of the door and hunching our shoulders to enter through the wooden frame, we experience mound, cairn and cottage as things. To reinforce the point, Heidegger made much of the etymological derivation of 'thing' from *ting* (or its Germanic equivalents). And it was above all the sense of the thing as a *gathering* that he drew from the word's earlier usages (ibid.: 177). To witness a thing is not to be locked out but to be invited in to the gathering. The round mound, as we have seen, is a thing, a gathering place, in a landscape of things. So too are cottage and cairn. And so, writes Heidegger, are tree, pond, brook and hill. As the mound persists in its mounding, so do cottage, cairn, tree, pond, brook, hill, each carrying on, or 'thinging', in its own particular way and, in so doing, issuing forth from a world that is itself 'worlding'. To join the gathering, as Heidegger puts it in his inimitable style, is to correspond with the thing 'in its thinging from out of the worlding world' (ibid.: 181–182). To convert any of these things into a monument, however, or into a feature of its landscape setting, is to bring the correspondence abruptly to a halt. The thing that once had beckoned us on becomes an object that blocks our path (Flusser 1999: 58).

The eye of the wind

Having satisfied ourselves with the results of our experiments with the ruined cottage, we proceeded to the summit of the hill, carrying our wooden battens with us. The summit, known locally as Mither Tap, afforded a panoramic view of the surrounding countryside. Far below, we saw a patchwork of fields and forests. What would happen, we wondered, if we observed the scene through a frame? Would it, this time, turn the landscape into a picture? Once again, we arranged our battens into a rectangle, now with the longer sides horizontal rather than vertical, more like a window than a doorway. While two volunteers held up the rectangular construction, the rest of us took it in turns to have a look. We all agreed that apart from minimally obstructing the view, the frame made no difference whatever! What could be seen on the inside of the frame was no more pictorial than what could be seen on the outside. When, however, we subsequently printed out the photographs we had taken of the experiment, we were surprised to discover that the difference was striking (Figure 6.4). Beyond the rectangular outline the photo was of a landscape, but within it the photo was of what could itself have been a picture of a landscape. We concluded that it was not the frame that had turned the landscape into a picture, but rather the pictorialisation of the landscape, on the plane surface of the photographic print, that had turned our frame into a *picture* frame, thus leading us to perceive what it enclosed as a representation, as opposed to the reality beyond its borders.

Of someone who is so caught up in the minutiae of life that they are unable to comprehend the overall picture, it is often said that they cannot tell the wood for the trees. To see the wood, it seems, you have to get out from among the trees and take a long view from a bare hilltop, or even from the air. Seen thus from afar, the wood appears to be laid like a mosaic over the contoured surface of the land. This was how the woods appeared to us from the summit of Mither Tap. But suppose that you rejoin us now, as we descend from the heights and re-enter the wood. Are we, once again, overwhelmed by minutiae? Do we see only individual trees rather than the wood as a whole? Not a bit of it! To enter the wood, and to find ourselves surrounded on all sides by trunks and branches, is not just to undergo a change of focus, from distant to close-up, but to experience a radically different perception of the world. In this perception, the wood ceases to appear as an aggregate of individual trees. Perhaps the Oxford English Dictionary gets closer to the mark when it defines the wood as 'trees collectively *growing together*' (Figure 6.5). In the twisting, turning, gnarling, knotting and branching of its roots, trunk and limbs, each tree bears testimony to a process of growth that is continually responsive to that of its neighbours, as well as to rainfall, wind and light, and the passage of the seasons. To perceive the wood from within is to become immersed in these ongoing entanglements of life. It is to see every tree not as a discrete, bounded individual but as something more like a bundle of fibrous threads, tightly wound along the trunk but splaying out above ground in

FIGURE 6.4 A window on the landscape. Looking through a rectangular frame from the summit of Mither Tap, Aberdeenshire. In the foreground are the reconstructed walls of the ancient hill fort.

the canopy and below in the roots. And it is to see the wood no longer as a mosaic of individual pieces but as a labyrinth of thread lines.

So entangled are these lines that it is scarcely possible to say with any certainty where any particular tree ends and the rest of the world begins. Is the bark a part of the tree? If so, then what of the insects which burrow in it, or the lichens that hang from it? And if insects are part of the tree, then why should we not also include the bird that nests there? Or even the wind, which causes the branches to wave and the leaves to rustle in characteristic ways? When seeds and leaves drop to the ground, do they not continue the life stories of the trees from which they fell? Thus the ground, too, is no mere surface, upon which trees stand like an army of soldiers on parade. To walk in the woods is to find your footing, at every step, in a morass of shrubs and foliage, fallen twigs and leaf litter, soil and stones. You seem always to be treading either on growing vegetation or on stuff that has been deposited, whether by the wind, the

FIGURE 6.5 Trees growing together: a wind's eye view of the wood. Photo taken in rural Aberdeenshire by Cristina Saez, reproduced by courtesy of the artist.

action of rainwater or simply having dropped from the trees above. The very ground underfoot, in short, is a tissue of lines of growth, erosion and decomposition. Far from separating the earth below from the sky above, the ground is a zone in which earth and sky intermingle in the perpetual generation of life.

It is, paradoxically, in the depths of the woods that the world opens up most fully to our perception, for it forces us to cast aside the illusion, to which people in high places are prone, that the world we inhabit is spread out like a mosaic beneath our feet, with its forms and patterns already impressed upon the physical substrate of nature. As the philosopher Henri Lefebvre has written, this means abandoning the pretence that we are witnessing a scene that is given all at once, as a spectacle. 'Go deeper', Lefebvre advises, 'be like the wind that shakes these trees' (Lefebvre 2004: 80). This is to gain what we could call a wind's-eye view of the woods. The eyes of the wind do not look *at* trees but roam *among* them, setting them ever so slightly in motion, tickling their surfaces and watching them come alive to the visual touch (Figure 6.5). They are the very same eyes as those that Pallasmaa calls 'the eyes of the skin': eyes that stroke the surfaces, contours and edges of things (Pallasmaa 1996: 29). These are eyes tuned not to the discrimination and identification of individual objects but to the registration of subtle variations of light and shade, and of the surface textures they reveal. Indeed, the environment they disclose is not one of objects at all. It is rather an environment of things, including swellings like mounds, growths like trees, outcrops like the tors of Bodmin Moor and the rocky peak of Mither Tap, and buildings such as those of the colony of Bennachie or the settlement on Leskernick Hill. Though we may *occupy* a world of objects, to the occupant the contents of the world appear already locked into their final forms, as though they had turned their backs on us. To *inhabit* the world, by contrast, is to join in the processes of formation. It is to participate in a dynamic world of energies, forces and flows. Such, I contend, is the world of earth and sky.

7

BODIES ON THE RUN

Being alive

In 1953, the British sculptor Henry Moore began work on a piece entitled *Warrior with Shield* (Figure 7.1). The idea for it, he said, came from finding a pebble on the seashore that reminded him of the stump of a leg, amputated at the hip. First he added the body, leg and one arm, to make a reclining, wounded warrior. Then he added a shield, altering the pose to make a seated figure, with a head that – in his own words – 'has a blunted and bull-like power but also a dumb animal acceptance and forbearance of pain' (in James 1966: 250). A year later, under somewhat controversial circumstances, Moore's *Warrior* was purchased by the Toronto Art Gallery. Subsequently, in the mid-1980s, an apparently quite unconnected event occurred. A new species of zebra mussels (*Dreissena polymorpha*) was accidentally introduced into Lake St Clair, on the US/Canadian border, by way of bilge water from one or more transoceanic trading ships originating from ports along the Black Sea. The species found the plankton-rich waters of Lake St Clair and the adjoining Lake Erie much to their liking, and multiplied rapidly. Within a few years they had colonised virtually every firm surface in Lake Erie, to a density of up to 70,000 mussels per square metre, and by 1992 they had already spread via Lake Michigan to the Mississippi basin. It was an intervention by the artist Simon Starling, in 2006, that forged a link between these two events. Starling created a full-scale replica of Moore's *Warrior* in steel, and then had it submerged in the waters of Lake Ontario. It remained there, on the lake bottom, until early in 2008, when it was raised from the depths. The surface of the figure was encrusted all over with mussels. The work was subsequently exhibited, under the title *Infestation Piece (Musselled Moore)*, at Toronto's Power Plant Gallery of Contemporary Art (Figure 7.2).[1]

For me, this piece makes a powerful statement about what it means for a body to be alive. The original *Warrior* is monumental in the strict sense of the term: closed in on itself, immobilised, presenting only its bronze-hard outer surfaces to our sight. Thrusting out its shield to the front, it tells us in no uncertain terms to back off. As Moore himself acknowledged, the figure has sunk into the solitude and paralysis of its

FIGURE 7.1 *Warrior with Shield* by Henry Moore (1953–1954, bronze, height 155 cm). © The Henry Moore Foundation. All Rights Reserved, DACS 2012 / www.henry-moore.org. Reproduced by permission.

own pain, solidly impervious to its environs. It belongs to another place and another time, as though caught in a battle fought thousands of years ago, or overcome by a volcanic eruption. Staring hollow-eyed at a world it neither knows nor even recognises, it will not respond to us, nor can we respond to it. On the lake bed, however, the figure has effectively been turned inside out. Under water, the surface in which it was once encased has become a substrate for life and growth, which in turn has been made possible by way of the continual exchange of substance with a nutrient-rich medium. Through the mussels that infest the surface, the figure seems to extrude itself into the surroundings, literally oozing from every pore, as though opened up from the inside. It has become a real living organism, albeit one sorely afflicted. Like a person whose body is covered in scabs, weals or boils, perhaps due to some acute infection, the musselled figure may be repulsive to look *at*, but we can at least look *with* it and feel some sympathy for its plight. It is of our time and place. Indeed it has become, in many ways, more

FIGURE 7.2 Simon Starling, *Infestation Piece (Musselled Moore)*, 2007/8 (bronze, mussels, variable dimensions). Installation view, The Power Plant, Toronto, 2008. (Courtesy of Steve Payne.)

mound-like than monumental, formed from a process of encrustation that carried on right up to the moment of its recovery from the water.

Every living organism, like the musselled Moore, is itself a site of infestation: a seething colony of lively, jostling materials alternately compressed into blobs and stretched into filaments that twist and coil around one another to form configurations of extraordinary complexity. The organism may look outwardly composed. Lift the lid, however, and you find something more like a compost heap than the formal architecture that anatomists and psychologists like to imagine. Indeed as a gathering together of materials in movement, the organism fully qualifies as a thing in the sense outlined in the last chapter. But it is not a thing that moves; it is rather composed (or better, composted) in movement. This is to say that it is fundamentally *animate*. Yet for just this reason, it would be wrong to describe it as embodied. It would be hard to imagine a figure more embodied, for example, than Moore's *Warrior*. The figure is so completely wrapped up in itself that any residue of animate life has been stilled. Starling's *Infestation Piece*, to the contrary, is animate precisely to the extent that its surfaces have opened up to the surrounding medium. Comparison of the two pieces vividly demonstrates how animacy and embodiment pull in opposite directions: where the former is a movement of opening, the latter is bent on closure. For the living, animate beings we are, argues dance philosopher Maxine Sheets-Johnstone, the term 'embodiment' is simply not experientially apposite. We do not, she insists, experience ourselves and one another as 'packaged' but as moving and moved, in ongoing response – that is in *correspondence* – with the things around us (Sheets-Johnstone 1998: 359; Ingold 2011b: 10). Of course we have bodies – indeed we *are* our bodies. But we are not wrapped up in them. The body is not a package, nor – to invoke another common analogy – a sink into which movements settle like sediment in a ditch.[2] It is rather a tumult of unfolding activity. As such, according to dance anthropologist Brenda Farnell, it is something to think *from* rather than *about* (Farnell 2000: 413).

The change of perspective entailed here precisely parallels our earlier injunction, taken from Gilles Deleuze and Félix Guattari, to 'follow the materials' (Chapter 2, p. 25). To think from materials, they say, is to find 'the consciousness or thought of the matter-flow' (Deleuze and Guattari 2004: 454). As the artisan thinks *from* materials, so the dancer thinks *from* the body. In the living, dynamically composed body, person and organism are one. The body *is* the organism–person. But as noted above, the body is also a thing. Thus we should no longer speak of relations between people and things, because *people are things too*. To highlight the overlap between personhood and thinghood, as Jane Bennett observes (2010: 4), is to acknowledge 'the extent to which the us and the it slip-slide into each other'. Or as the title of a recent article by archaeologists Timothy Webmoor and Christopher Witmore declares, 'Things are us!' (Webmoor and Witmore 2008). This is not to treat persons as anything less than what they are, let alone to compare them to objects rather than subjects. It is rather to find a way beyond this troublesome dichotomy. Objects and subjects can exist only in a world already thrown, already cast in fixed and final forms; things, by contrast, are in the throwing – they do not exist so much as carry on. And as the things they are, people too are 'processes, brought into being through production, embroiled in ongoing social projects, and requiring attentive engagement' (Pollard 2004: 60).

In this regard, persons are just like pots (Figure 7.3). In a study of ceramics from Northwest Argentina dating from the first millennium AD, Benjamin Alberti argues that it would be a mistake to assume that the pot is a fixed and stable object, bearing the imprint of cultural form upon the 'obdurate' matter of the physical world (Alberti 2007: 211, see also Alberti and Marshall 2009: 354). On the contrary, evidence suggests that pots were treated like bodies, and with the same concern: namely, to counteract chronic instability, to shore up vessels for life against the ever-present susceptibility to discharge that threatens their dissolution or metamorphosis. The living body, likewise, is only sustained thanks to continually taking in materials from its surroundings, and in turn discharging into them, in the processes of respiration and metabolism. Yet as with pots, the same processes that keep it alive also render it forever vulnerable to dissolution. That is why constant attention is necessary, and also why bodies and other things are poor containers. Left to themselves, materials can run riot. Pots crumble; bodies disintegrate. It takes effort and vigilance to hold things together, whether pots or people.

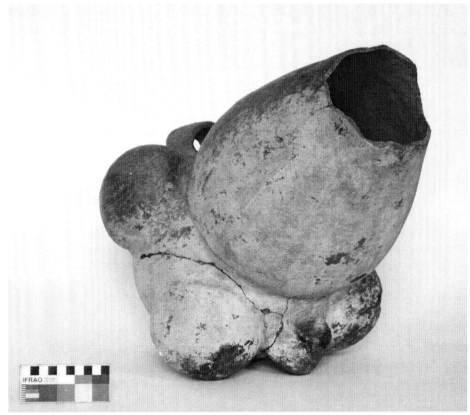

FIGURE 7.3 La Candelaria-style ceramic vessel showing biomorphic 'protrusions', Northwest Argentina, first millennium AD, from the collection of the Museo de La Universidad Nacional de Tucumán. Photo by Benjamin Alberti, reproduced with permission.

Much ado about agency

We may conclude that things can exist and persist only because they *leak*: that is, because of the interchange of materials across the surfaces by which they differentiate themselves from the surrounding medium. The bodies of organisms and other things leak continually, indeed their lives depend on it. Now this propensity of things to leak, and for material flows to override or seep through their surfaces, bears crucially on the question of material agency. This question has been discussed ad nauseam, and it is beyond the scope of this chapter to review the literature that has amassed around it in any depth (for wide-ranging treatments, see Knappett and Malafouris 2008; Jones and Boivin 2010; Johannsen 2012) save to venture that it is largely beside the point. The question only arises on account of the reduction of things to objects consequent upon the application of the hylomorphic model. Cut off from the life-support system comprising the flux of vital materials, things suffer the fate of Moore's *Warrior*. They suffocate and die. It is no wonder that theorists have been compelled to invoke a concept of object agency in a futile effort to resuscitate them! The appeal to agency, in other words, is a corollary of the logic of embodiment, of turning things in on themselves. To undo this logic is, once and for all, to exorcise the spectre of embodied agency and to bring things back to animate life. As a bundle of potentials in an ever-unfolding field of forces and energies, the body moves and is moved not because it is driven by some internal agency, wrapped up in the package, but because as fast as it is gathering or winding itself up, it is forever unravelling or unwinding, alternately breathing in and out.

Nowhere is the dead hand of objectification more clearly at work than in the essay that launched much of the current debate, Alfred Gell's *Art and Agency* (1998). Here, the question is explicitly posed as one about the ascription of agency to what Gell does not hesitate to call 'art objects'. The presumption is that in the making of such objects, intentions initially framed within the mind of the artist are projected onto the material: thus the intention is the cause, the artwork the effect. And the viewer, subsequently observing the work, is supposed to look through the work to the agency within and behind it (Knappett 2005: 128). But as we saw from Simondon's example of making bricks, introduced in Chapter 2 (pp. 24–25), this scenario focuses on an arbitrary starting point (the image in the artist's mind) and an equally arbitrary end point (the allegedly finished work), while missing out all that goes on in between. The living work of art, however, is not an object but a thing, and the role of the artist is not to give effect to a preconceived idea but to follow the forces and flows of material that bring the work into being. To view the work is to join the artist as a fellow traveller, to look *with* it as it unfolds in the world, rather than *behind* it to an originating intention of which it is the final product (Ingold 2011a: 216). The vitality of the work of art, then, lies in its materials, and it is precisely because no work is ever truly 'finished' (except in the eyes of curators and purchasers, who require it to be so) that it remains alive.

Indeed the entire question of agency rests on a false premise. Assuming that persons are capable of acting because they possess an agency, the question was one of how objects in the vicinity of these persons could nevertheless 'act back', causing them to do what they otherwise might not. The facile answer was to say that the objects, too, possess agency. The speed bump, for example, is credited with an agency that causes the driver to slow down (Latour 1999: 186–190). Yet the causal attribution of action to an 'agency', of which that action is the effect, is perverse, even for human beings. Take a thinker like Jane Bennett, who is convinced – as we are – that materials are inherently lively, but who remains so spellbound by the grammar of agency that she cannot bring herself to renounce it. 'Why speak of the agency of assemblages?' she asks herself. Why indeed? 'No one really knows', she goes on to admit, 'what human agency is, or what humans are doing when they are said to perform as agents.' It remains 'something of a mystery' (Bennett 2010: 34). In a curiously backhanded argument, however, she professes that since we have no idea what agency is or how it works for humans, we have no a priori reason to deny agency to non-humans. But if our aim, like Bennett's, is to counter human exceptionalism, why not argue to the contrary, that there is absolutely no reason to credit humans with agency in the first place? Would it not make more sense to remove the wool from over our own eyes than to wrap the rest of the world up in it?

That all living beings, humans included, are forever 'immersed in action' – as the philosopher Alfred North Whitehead once put it – from the moment of birth if not before, is not in doubt (Whitehead 1938: 217). All are at sea in the tumult. However, to attribute this action to an agency, of which it is supposed to be the effect, seems like putting everything back to front. For only in the retrospective reconstruction of action already undertaken – in tracing it *back* to a putative point of origin – can we derive the agency that is supposed to have given rise to it. Otherwise put: humans do not *possess* agency; nor, for that matter, do non-humans. They are rather possessed by action. Karen Barad admits as much when she argues that agency 'is an enactment, not something that someone or something has' (Barad 2003: 826–827). Taking up the same theme, Andrew Jones and Nicole Boivin allow that 'causality does not lie with human agents… Instead it is the reiterative quality of performance that produces agency and causality' (Jones and Boivin 2010: 351). However, to read into action, a priori, what we have read off from it, a posteriori, is manifestly circular. Agency becomes the cause and effect of itself (Alberti and Marshall 2009: 346). Here's Bennett again, valiantly trying to decide whether to use the term 'agents' or 'agencies' for her vital non-humans. 'As I struggle to choose the right term', she confesses, 'I confront a profound ambiguity in both terms regarding wherein lies the cause and wherein the effect' (Bennett 2010: 108, 151 fn. 37). This ambiguity, however, and the convolutions to which it gives rise are no more than the results of trying (and failing) to express processes of growth and becoming in a language of causation that is wholly unsuited to them. As we have seen, the generativity of action is that of animate life itself, and lies in the vitality of its materials. We need a theory not of agency but of life, and this theory must be one – as Barad puts it – 'that allows matter its due as an active participant of the world's becoming' (Barad 2003: 803).

Running flying thinking

Traditionally, of course, this due has been accorded to mind rather than matter. Where, then, does our emphasis on the flow of materials leave the mind? Should we, as archaeologist Chris Gosden urges, do away with the concept of mind altogether (Gosden 2010)? Or can we retain an ecology of mind, as Gregory Bateson thought, alongside and complementing an ecology of substance, the first dealing with information, the second with the exchange and circulations of energy and materials (Bateson 1973)? Drawing inspiration from Bateson, cognitive theorist Andy Clark has charted just such a way forward in his theory of the 'extended mind' (Clark 1997, 2001; Clark and Chalmers 1998). In a nutshell, the theory postulates that the mind, far from being coextensive with the brain, routinely spills out into the environment, enlisting all manner of extra-somatic objects and artefacts in the conduct of its operations. The artefactual world then becomes a kind of 'wideware' (Clark 1998) or 'distributed mind' (Jones 2007: 225). For many archaeologists the theory was a godsend, since it implied that in their studies of material culture they could claim to contribute directly to understanding the cognitive processes of people in the past (Malafouris and Renfrew 2010). As Lambros Malafouris argues, if we acknowledge (with Clark 1997: 98) that cognition is fundamentally a way of engaging with the world – if, in that sense, cognition is indissociable from action – *'then material culture is consubstantial with mind'* (Malafouris 2004: 58).

For Malafouris, the mind is not a mirror on the world. It is not there to represent what is or could be 'out there' but rather emerges in practice, from the synergistic conjunction of brains, bodies and things. There is, however, a catch in the argument. For in identifying things with 'material culture', Malafouris inadvertently reproduces the very division between mind and world that he hopes to erase. For material things to be enrolled in cognitive processes, must they already have been rendered in cultural forms? Why should people think with artefacts alone? Why not also with the air, the ground, mountains and streams, and other living beings? Why not with materials? And if cognition is indeed enacted, as Malafouris claims (2004: 59), then how does it differ from life itself? Does thought lie in the *interactions* between brains, bodies and objects in the world, or in the *correspondences* of material flows and sensory awareness wherein consciousness, to recall the words of Deleuze and Guattari, is the 'thought of the matter-flow' and material 'the correlate of this consciousness' (Deleuze and Guattari 2004: 454)?

It was in an attempt to answer this latter question that the students and I, in our investigations of the 4 As, embarked on another experiment. This time, it was to make and fly kites. Fashioned quickly and simply from thin card, matchstick bamboo (for the struts), strips of newspaper (for the streamers) and twine (for the harness), and held together with glue and sticky tape, it had seemed to us that the kites we had made would qualify under any conventional definition as artefacts. They would not be out of place in any catalogue of objects of material culture. As soon as we took our creations out of doors, however, something odd happened. The kites began to leap around (Figure 7.4). And we ran! The more we ran, the more they leapt, higher and higher into the air, straining at the nylon threads by which we held them, just as fast as we could pay them out. Now of course there is a simple aerodynamic explanation for the kites' behaviour. They rose because as they were dragged through the air, with their noses tilted upwards at a slight angle to the horizontal, a pressure differential was set up between the air beneath and above the planar surface, which was enough to countervail the force of gravity. But a purely mechanical account of this kind will only take us so far. For the aerial gymnastics of the kites were not only outwardly visible, as linear trajectories of object displacement that could in principle be measured and plotted just like the path of a cannonball. They were also inwardly felt. We were aware of the kites' flying in the same way that we were aware of our running, through the bodily sense we had of our own movement, or in a word, through *kinaesthesia*.

Mindful of what we were doing, and improvising as we went along, our kite-flying could be reckoned as an instance of what Sheets-Johnstone calls 'thinking in movement'. This is not to think *by means of* movement, or to have our thoughts *transcribed into* movement. Rather, the thinking *is* the movement: 'To think is to be caught up in a dynamic flow; thinking is, by its very nature, kinetic' (Sheets-Johnstone 1998: 486). In the context to which I have just referred, Sheets-Johnstone is speaking of improvisation in dance. Might we suggest, then, that flying a kite is also a kind of dance? Philosopher and sociologist of science Andrew Pickering would certainly agree, having coined the expression 'dance of agency' to describe the kinds of back-and-forth engagements with the material world in which humans and non-humans alternately take the upper hand, not just in the conduct of scientific investigations but quite generally (Pickering 2010: 194–195, see Pickering 1995). Let us, then, make a provisional attempt at analysing the situation along the lines that Pickering proposes.

Here we have a person running; and there a kite flying. They are connected by a thread. So we have an interaction between a human being and a material object. At one moment the flyer makes the running while the kite is dragged along behind, but

FIGURE 7.4 The kite in flight. The string can be seen on the left, harnessed to the main body of the kite, from which attached streamers, cut from strips of newspaper, flutter towards the right. (Courtesy of Susanna Ingold.)

at the next it is the kite that pulls at the hand of the flyer, as if struggling to get away. This certainly seems to fit Pickering's description of the dance as one 'in which activity and passivity on both sides are reciprocally intertwined' (2010: 195). But that cannot be the whole story. For if the kite is to act on the human flyer as well as the flyer to act on the kite – if, that is, the kite-object is to join the dance – then it must be endowed with some kind of agency. So where did this come from? So long as the kite remained indoors, it had been limp and lethargic. By what magic, then, was the power of agency contrived to jump into the kite at the moment it was carried out of doors? The answer, of course, hangs in the air. Because the air is invisible, we had temporarily forgotten about it. But now, all becomes clear. The kite's flying is surely the combined effect of the flyer, the kite *and the air*. The dance of agency, it turns out, is a threesome in which each partner acts upon, and is in turn acted upon by, the other two (Figure 7.5). Take away any one partner, and the performance will fail. Even in the air, a kite will not fly without a flyer; even with a flyer, the kite will only fly in the air; even if the flyer is out in the air, there will be no flying without a kite. The air, then, was the missing link that activated the kite, allowing an action potential that was already immanent within it – in its very construction – to be expressed in motion.

In his efforts to show how mind emerges from practitioners' engagements with the stuff of the material world, Malafouris also toys with the idea of the dance of agency. His key example is pottery. At the potter's wheel, he writes, 'brain, body, wheel and clay relate and interact with one another throughout the different stages of this activity' (Malafouris 2008: 19). But does the potter dance with the wheel or with the clay, or with both at once? Curiously, when Malafouris (2004: 59) first introduces the idea, he has the potter dancing with the wheel, which may at one moment 'subsume the plans of the potter and define the contours of activity', but at another, 'serve as a passive instrument for his or her manufacturing purposes'. Otherwise put, the wheel alternately governs and is governed by what the potter does. In a subsequent elaboration of the argument, however, the potter is dancing not with the wheel but with the clay. Noting that at any time, either potter or clay may take the lead, Malafouris nevertheless insists that the dance 'is between equal partners' (2008: 25). It is enacted, for example, in the grasping and fingering movements of the potter's hands in the initial task of centring a lump of clay on the wheel. These movements may indeed be compared to

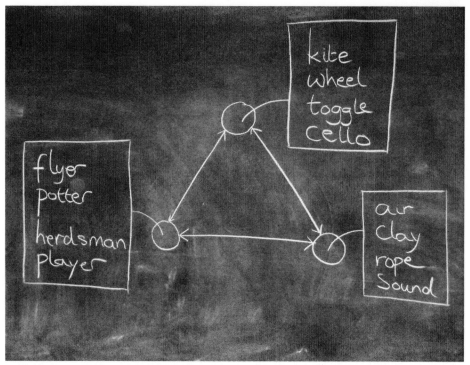

FIGURE 7.5   The dance of agency, understood as a threesome in which the partners may be flyer–kite–air, potter–wheel–clay, herdsman–toggle–rope, or player–cello–sound. Chalk on blackboard. (Courtesy of Susanna Ingold.)

dance. They observe a certain choreography. And as we saw in the comparable instance of metallurgy discussed in Chapter 2 (pp. 25–26), this gestural dance is coupled with a modulation in the material. But is it a dance of *agency*? Do potter, wheel and clay, as indicated in Figure 7.5, make up a threesome analogous to that comprising flyer, kite and air?

The dance of animacy

Let me return for a moment to the example of kite-flying.[3] Following Pickering, we had assumed that what we were witnessing was an interaction between a person (the flyer) and an artefact (the kite). The question, then, was how the kite could exert any kind of agency, and in order to explain this we had to bring in the air. Our conclusion was that you cannot dance with a kite without introducing the air as a 'third party'. There is, however, a snag in this argument. For how can air possibly be regarded as an agent? The very idea of agency, as we have seen, is the corollary of a logic of embodiment, of closing things up in themselves. But air cannot be closed. More than any other element, as the philosopher Luce Irigaray reminds us, air is 'opening itself' (Irigaray 1999: 8). The flow of air – the wind (*anemos*), the breath of life – is the very antithesis of embodied agency. But if the air cannot be closed upon itself, then no more, as we have seen, can the organism–person that lives and breathes. Thus even if we allow that in flying a kite, the flyer dances with the air, it cannot be a dance of

FIGURE 7.6 Lasso and toggle. (Courtesy of Susanna Ingold.)

agency. It can only be a *dance of animacy*. And in this dance, flyer and air do not so much interact as correspond. The kite, in effect, sets up a correspondence between the animate movements of the flyer and the currents of the aerial medium in which he or she is immersed. It is not that you need air to interact with a kite; rather, you need a kite to correspond with the air.

A moment's reflection, moreover, indicates that the same is true of what happens at the potter's wheel. This is not, as we have seen in the parallel case of brick making (Chapter 2, p. 25), an imposition of form on matter but a contraposition of equal and opposed forces immanent respectively in gesturing hands and wet clay, set up thanks to the rotations of the wheel. You do not, then, need clay to interact with the wheel, but you do need a wheel to correspond with the clay. In both cases, of pottery and kite-flying, the mindful or attentive bodily movements of the practitioner, on the one hand, and the flows and resistances of the material, on the other, respond to one another in counterpoint. As with any dance, this should be read not laterally, back and forth, but longitudinally as a movement in which partners take it in turns to lead and be led or – in musical terms – to play the melody and its refrain. In the dance of animacy, bodily kinaesthesia interweaves contrapuntally with the flux of materials within an encompassing, morphogenetic field of forces.

The kite puts me in mind of another example, familiar to me from my fieldwork among reindeer herdsmen in Finnish Lapland. This is the lasso (Ingold 1993). The operative component of the lasso is the toggle. You often find toggles, expertly crafted and sometimes beautifully decorated, in collections or exhibited in museums of Saami material culture. Traditionally carved from antler, the toggle has two holes: one small, the other larger. The small hole secures the end of a long rope that is looped through the larger one (Figure 7.6). In operation, of course, the toggle is nothing without the rope, and indeed without the herdsman for whom the manual-gestural skill of casting the lasso, requiring years of practice, is one of the most highly prized of the herding repertoire. It is a task that calls for intense concentration. But in the mindfulness of casting the lasso, do we witness an interaction between a person (the herdsman) and an artefact (the toggle) that has been endowed with agency thanks to the rope? Of course not! To argue along these lines would be as absurd as claiming that pottery entails an interaction between potter and wheel made possible by the intervention of clay. Rather, just as it is the wheel that allows the potter's gestures to be carried over into the evolving contours of the clay, so the toggle allows the skilled gestures of the herdsman to be cast into the ever-emergent form of a flying noose.

Here is one more example to clinch the point. Apart from my ham-fisted attempts to throw a lasso, I also play the cello. There is a close parallel between the two (Ingold 2000: 413–414). Both call for finely honed manual-gestural skills; both carry forward a mindfulness that is immanent in the action itself, in its attentiveness to surrounding movements (of the conductor and other instrumentalists; of the throng of animals in the round-up enclosure); and both create sinuous forms – whether of the musical phrase or the flying noose – that are suspended in the current of ongoing activity. Moreover like the toggle for the herdsman, the cello is an artefact, a thing of great beauty that requires immense craftsmanship to make. But to perform music is not – or at least not just – to interact with a cello. It is to correspond with sound. In the performance, the player's gestures describe a melodic line. What part, then, does the cello play in this? What does it do? And what, for that matter, does the toggle do? Or the kite? Or the potter's wheel?

Transduction and perdurance

The answer is the same in every case. In the dance of animacy, cello, toggle, kite and wheel are all examples of what we could call *transducers*.[4] That is to say, they convert the *ductus* – the kinetic quality of the gesture, its flow or movement – from one register, of bodily kinaesthesia, to another, of material flux. In the vibration of bowed strings, amplified by a soundbox, the cellist's manual gesture is rendered audible, as melody. In the sliding of the toggle, the herdsman's throw is cast as a loop of rope. In the rotation of the wheel, the potter's hand and finger movements are registered in the contours of soft clay. And finally, in the kite, slicing the air like an axe through wood (see Chapter 3, p.45), following its undulations and torsions, the running of the flyer becomes a line of flight. In each case, the transducer slides along the thread of time, like a toggle on a rope, ever present on the threshold of emergence of things. It is this ever-presence that lends it an aura of immutability (Figure 7.7).

Consider the following, offered by Bjørnar Olsen as simple statements of the obvious: 'Things are more persistent than thought. They evidently last longer than speech or gestures. Things are concrete and offer stability…' (Olsen 2010: 158). Of transducers, all three statements may be broadly true. They are still there, changed but little after the performances they have mediated have come to a close. The toggle, for example, outlasts the throw of the lasso; the cello outlasts the concert. But the work of art lies not in the transducer but in what issues from it, and of such a work the question of its duration is not so easily answered. Let us return to the potter at the

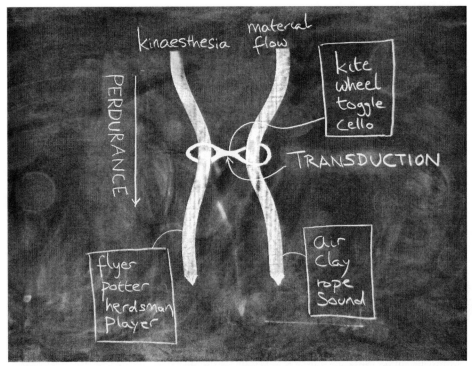

FIGURE 7.7 Transduction and perdurance. The movement of kinaesthetic awareness (respectively of the flyer, the potter, the herdsman and the player) is converted by way of a transducer (respectively kite, wheel, toggle and cello) into a corresponding flow of material (respectively of air, clay, rope and sound). In terms of this diagram, the perdurance – or 'carrying on' – of awareness and materials runs downwards, while transduction couples across. Chalk on blackboard. (Courtesy of Susanna Ingold.)

wheel. It is not just because it is made of the material stuff of clay that the pot lasts longer than the gestures which helped to shape it. The pot retains its form only because it has been fixed by subsequent processes of drying and firing (Ingold 2000: 418). In an installation by the artist Clare Twomey, tables were laid with rows of clay pots that had been thrown on the wheel but not yet fired. The pots were filled with water from a jug. Before the eyes of the viewer, they were seen to buckle, crack and collapse, as if in slow motion, discharging their contents over tabletops and floor to the accompaniment of the quiet tinkling of running water, while new ones were continually added in their place (Figure 7.8). In this enactment, every pot had become a living thing, not so much the fixed and final realisation of a prior design as the passing envoy of ever-replenished but ultimately forlorn hope.

As this example shows, we cannot assume that pots are stable simply on account of some aspect of their 'materiality'. Alberti's study of ceramics from prehistoric Northwest Argentina has already taught us that despite the assertions of Olsen (2003: 88) and many others to the contrary, there is nothing intrinsically *hard* about the world of materials. Indeed for the people who originally made and used them, Alberti suggests, ceramics 'may have been considered less stable and reliable even than other forms of discourse' (Alberti 2007: 219). How long then, compared with these other discursive

FIGURE 7.8 'Is it madness. Is it beauty.' Close-up of installation by artist Clare Twomey. In the performance of this work, according to the artist's statement, 'the repetitive action of continually filling unfired ceramic bowls with water, that then collapse, isolates the notion of action and continued hope within the human condition'. Reproduced by courtesy of the artist.

modalities – dialogical, gestural, verbal – do pots last? How long do bodies last? Which lasts longer, Moore's *Warrior* or its mussel-infested double? If longevity be judged by the preservation of form, then no doubt the former wins. But if our concern is with the continuity of process – that is with the *perdurance* or life expectancy of a thing, or with how long it can keep on going – then the *Infestation Piece* is easily the victor, since it gained a new lease of life from its sojourn underwater, whereas the *Warrior*'s life was already over by the time the sculpture was completed. So, too, did Twomey's pots come alive, if only for a brief while, when water was poured into them.[5]

Joshua Pollard (2004: 51–53) describes how contemporary environmental artists have challenged our assumptions about the durability of things by producing works that are transitory and ephemeral. When Andy Goldsworthy, for example, throws a handful of sticks into the air, the resulting work lasts no longer than the gesture that animates it, and can be fixed only as a photographic record. Yet as a gathering of materials in motion, of sticks and air, it is undoubtedly a thing (Figure 7.9). For Goldsworthy, the strength of a work lies precisely in the 'energies' emanating from materials in their movement, growth and decay, and in the fleeting moments when they come together as one (quoted in Friedman 1996: 10). Here it is the materials that perdure, not the more or less transitory forms into which they are cast. Throwing, as Goldsworthy shows us, and as our experiments in kite-flying proved, is not so much the outward effect of an embodied agency as the propulsion of animate being as it spills out into the world. Such, indeed, is the propulsion of life itself.

FIGURE 7.9 A bundle of sticks thrown in the air, on the shore of Lake Pielinen in eastern Finland. (Courtesy of Susanna Ingold.)

Interaction and correspondence

In the days before the keyboard severed all traces of writing from the hand, and before email lifted them from the page, people used to send handwritten letters to one another. In them, they would tell of their affairs, of how they were doing, at the same time answering to recollections and sentiments expressed in letters most recently received. For such a drawn-out exchange of letters, it was customary to use the word *correspondence*. This is a word to which I have also had recourse at a number of points in my argument, and I would like to conclude this chapter by explaining more fully what I mean by it. The case of letter writing highlights two aspects that I take to be central to correspondence: first, that it is a movement in real time; and second, that this movement is sentient. On the first point: writing letters takes time, as does waiting for them and reading them when they arrive. A correspondence is rather like a relay, in which each participant takes it in turns to pick up the baton and carry it forward, while others remain temporarily quiescent, awaiting their turn. They may of course wait forever, and gradually give up hope, yet there is no knowing whether, or when, a lapsed correspondence may be rekindled. Thus while letters may go back and forth, the correspondence has no starting point or end point. It simply carries on. On the second point: the lines of correspondence are lines of feeling, of sentience, evinced not – or not only – in the choice of words but in the manual gestures of the writing and their traces on the page. To read a letter is not just to read *about* one's respondent, but to read *with* him or her. It is as though the writer was speaking from the page, and you – the reader – were there, listening.

Long ago, Alfred Schutz, phenomenologist of the social world, hit on much the same idea in his characterisation of social life as a process of 'growing older together'. Sharing a community of time, Schutz maintained, every consociate participates in the on-rolling life of every other (Schutz 1962: 16–17). In a celebrated paper, he compared this participation to making music. The players in a string quartet, for example, are not exchanging musical ideas – they are not *inter*acting, in that sense – but are rather moving along together, listening as they play, and playing as they listen, at every moment sharing in each other's 'vivid present' (Schutz 1951). In our studies of everyday walking, my colleague Jo Vergunst and I came to a very similar conclusion (Lee and Ingold 2006). We found that walking abreast was generally experienced as a particularly companionable form of activity. Even while conversing, as they often did, companions would rarely make immediate eye-to-eye contact, at most inclining their heads slightly towards one another, while co-ordinating their gait and pace by means of peripheral vision, which is especially sensitive to movement. Direct face-to-face interaction, by contrast, was found to be far less sociable. A key difference is that in walking along together, companions share virtually the same visual field, whereas in face-to-face interaction, each can see what is behind the other's back, opening up possibilities for deceit and subterfuge. As they turn to face one another, stopped in their tracks, each blocking the other's path, they appear to be locked in a contest in which views are no longer shared but batted back and forth.

Now in a classic essay on 'visual interaction', dating from 1921, the sociologist Georg Simmel argued that eye-to-eye contact 'represents the most perfect reciprocity in the entire field of human relationships', inducing a kind of union between the persons involved. This union, he surmised 'can only be maintained by the shortest and straightest line between the eyes' (Simmel 1969: 146). Do lovers, then, look straight at one another? Not according to John Donne who, in his poem *Exstasie*, penned three centuries earlier, described their vision thus:

> Our hands were firmely cimented
> With a fast balme, which thence did spring,
> Our eye-beames twisted, and did thred
> Our eyes, upon one double string;

> (in Grierson 1947: 16)

Donne's poem begins with the two lovers joined by the hands and yet entirely separate, over and against one another, lying immobile – 'like sepulchrall statues'. The conjunction of their bodies was not enough to make them one. To achieve the union they crave, their souls must rise up from their bodily moorings and stream out through the eyes, whence they twist around one another in a space between, 'hung 'twixt her, and mee', as between two opposed armies. Negotiating there, on their double eye-beams, while the bodies they have exited remain stationary, they eventually achieve a blend wherein each soul speaks with the other's voice. Only when they have thus come into unison can the two souls descend back into the bodies from whence they came, bringing about the desired unity of body and soul in the consummation of love and its ensuing bounty.

We do not have to subscribe to Donne's complex and somewhat esoteric metaphysics to appreciate the force of the distinction he draws between the 'overagainstness' (the

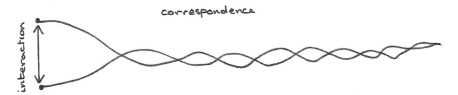

FIGURE 7.10 Interaction and correspondence.

word Donne used was *entergraft*) of embalmed, cemented bodies and the entwinement of evanescent, light-borne souls. In our terms, this is the distinction between interaction and correspondence – that is, between the dance of agency and the dance of animacy (Figure 7.10). A straight line drawn between two points, as Simmel describes eye-to-eye contact, leaves each point motionless and unfeeling. Such contact may be rational, but it cannot be sentient. Like walkers who have turned in discord to square up to one another, or passengers in that kind of carriage known as the *vis-à-vis*, or indeed like Donne's lovers as they hold hands, or even Moore's *Warrior*, there is no way forward. The implication of the prefix *inter-*, in 'interaction', is that the interacting parties are closed to one another, as if they could only be connected through some kind of bridging operation. Any such operation is inherently detemporalising, cutting across the paths of movement and becoming rather than joining along with them. In correspondence, by contrast, points are set in motion to describe lines that wrap around one another like melodies in counterpoint. Think, for example, of the entwined melodic lines of the string quartet. The players may be seated opposite one another, and their bodies fixed in place. But their movements and the ensuing sounds correspond, seeking a blend not unlike that of Donne's souls in ecstasy, neither here nor there but in-between.

The notion of correspondence, admittedly, comes with a certain amount of theological baggage. It was central, for example, to the thought of the eighteenth century mystic Emanuel Swedenborg, for whom it described the relations of mutuality and harmony between all things natural and spiritual, earthly and celestial. From there it found its way into the writings of Charles Baudelaire, whose celebrated poem *Correspondences* has man making his way in the natural world, surrounded by a polyphony of voices and a forest of eyes, in which 'perfumes, sounds and colours correspond' (in Aggeler 1954). Perhaps it was at the back of Johann Wolfgang von Goethe's mind when he wrote of the relation between sunlight and vision that 'were the eye not sun-like, it could not see the sun' (Luke 1964: 282). By this he did not mean that the eye resembles the sun, but that it is so formed as to be able to respond to its light. In his *Bedeutungslehre* ('Theory of Meaning') of 1940, the Estonian-born biologist Jakob von Uexküll turned this around to argue that 'were the sun not eye-like, it could not shine in any sky'. His point was that the sky, and the sun as a celestial light that illuminates the sky, could exist only in the phenomenal world – what he called the *Umwelt* – of creatures with eyes. In just the same way, the bee corresponds with the pollen-bearing flower, and the spider with the fly. The lives of creatures, von Uexküll suggests, proceed contrapuntally, each taking into itself something of the characteristics of the other so as to be able to respond to it (von Uexküll 2010: 190).

In a recent meditation on the same theme, Lars Spuybroek imagines that as he walks through a field, he comes across a little group of stones with a seedling growing between them, and he likes what he sees:

> Clearly the stones are lying there in a certain correspondence, if not accordance, because the wind and water have moved them, rolled them over the ground and made them find an impression, create a little group, a little nest where a plant could start growing and be protected – but where does my liking fit in? Is it merely in me, subjectively enjoying the sight, or is it an ... extended correspondence? I am with the stones and plant immediately, fitting in with them ... What ... flows in and out, like the enjoyment of the stones? Feeling does. All relations are *felt* relations.
>
> (Spuybroek 2011: 152)

My argument in this chapter has been that in the same way, too, the potter's feeling flows in and out in a correspondence with the clay, the herdsman's in correspondence with the airborne rope, the flyer's running with the wind, and the cellist's bowing with musical sound.[6] Even the *Musselled Moore* develops a feeling for the waters of Lake Ontario. To correspond with the world, in short, is not to describe it, or to represent it, but to *answer to it*. Thanks to the mediating work of transduction, it is to mix the movements of one's own sentient awareness with the flows and currents of animate life. Such mixture, where sentience and materials twine around one another on their double thread until – like lovers' eye-beams – they become indistinguishable, is of the essence of making.

8

TELLING BY HAND

Personal knowledge

It is a fact, declared Michael Polanyi, introducing a series of lectures on *The Tacit Dimension*, 'that *we can know more than we can tell*' (Polanyi 1966: 4). Polanyi was referring to those ways of knowing and doing that grow through the experience and practice of a craft, but which adhere so closely to the person of the practitioner as to remain out of reach of explication or analysis. His argument was that knowledge of the sort that can be rendered formally and self-consciously explicit is but the tip of an iceberg compared with the immense reservoir of know-how that lies beneath the surface and without which nothing could be practically accomplished. Whereas Polanyi, however, was primarily interested in what it means to *know*, my concern just now is with what it means to *tell*. In his reflections on the nature of personal knowledge, Polanyi seems to have assumed that telling is tantamount to putting what one knows into words, in speech or writing, and that this entails two things: *specification* and *articulation*. Thus he regards as the unspecifiable part of knowledge 'the residue left unsaid by defective articulation' (Polanyi 1958: 88). In this chapter I want to argue, to the contrary, that we *can* tell of what we know through practice and experience, precisely because telling is itself a modality of performance that *abhors* articulation and specification. It follows that personal knowledge is not quite as tacit as Polanyi thought. Part of the problem is that the term 'tacit' has many shades of meaning, ranging from the silent through the unspoken to the implicit. What remains unspoken need not be left unvoiced; nor need what remains unwritten be left without any inscriptive trace. Moreover, what is not explicated may still find expression in spoken or written words. As anthropologists who have worked with skilled practitioners are all too aware, their mentors are often inclined to expound upon their crafts vociferously, demonstrably and at very great length. The figure of the silent craftsman who is struck dumb when asked to tell of what he does, or how he does it, is largely a fiction sustained by those who have a vested interest in securing an academic monopoly over the spoken and written word.

The verb 'to tell' has two related senses. On the one hand, a person who can tell is able to recount the stories of the world. On the other hand, to tell is to be able to recognise subtle cues in one's environment and to respond to them with judgement and precision. Hunters, for example, are compulsive storytellers, but they can also tell the whereabouts and recent movements of animals from their tracks. Archaeologists tell of the inhabitants of past settlements, but they can also tell where the wooden posts of buildings once stood from subtle discolorations in the earth. Letter writers tell of their affairs, but they can also tell from the inflections of the handwritten line how a correspondent who has written to them is feeling. And so on. These two senses of telling are closely related. They are related because for those who listen, watch or read – including of course the anthropologist engaged in participant observation (see Chapter 1, p. 2) – the telling of stories is an education of attention. Through it, things are pointed out to novices, so that they can discover for themselves what meanings the stories might hold in the situations of their current practice. Making their ways in the company of those more knowledgeable than themselves, and hearing their stories, novices grow into the knowledge of their predecessors through a process that could best be described as one of 'guided rediscovery', rather than receiving it ready-made through some mechanism of replication and transmission (Ingold 2011a: 162). To tell, in short, is not to explicate the world, to provide the information that would amount to a complete specification, obviating the need for would-be practitioners to inquire for themselves. It is rather to trace a path that others can follow. Thus the hunter, educated in stories of the chase, can follow a trail; the trained archaeologist can follow the cut; the competent reader can follow the line of writing.

The key thing about stories is that they provide practitioners with the means to tell of what they know *without* specifying it. They do not so much carry encrypted information as offer pointers of where to go and what to look out for.[1] This is why they are so efficacious as media of education. A complete specification would offer no guidance: indeed it would leave the novice as perplexed as to how to proceed as do the technical specifications that often accompany mechanical or electronic instruments, which are incomprehensible to anyone not already thoroughly familiar with their operation. *In place of specification without guidance, the story offers guidance without specification.* The distinction exactly parallels the one we introduced earlier, in Chapter 5 (p. 69), between predictive and anticipatory foresight. The former might yield a plan, but it is the latter that allows the practitioner to carry on, or as Polanyi put it (1958: 62), to 'feel our way forward' in the accomplishment of a task. Specifications provide information *about* the specified, about the materials to be used, about parts and their dimensions, about movements to be made. They define a project. But stories issue *from* moving bodies and vital materials, in the telling. They lay down an itinerary. It is precisely because both their knowledge and their practice have the same itinerant character that, in storytelling, practitioners can bring them into correspondence with one another. In the case of making a handaxe, we saw in Chapter 3 how the process of flaking is a carrying on, a procession along a path, rather than a building up of parts into a predetermined whole. And in Chapter 4, we saw how the medieval cathedral better resembles a patchwork quilt than a completed jigsaw puzzle. No more does the form of the axe result from the concatenation of discrete operations than does the structure of the cathedral from the assembly of pre-cut pieces. Neither axe nor cathedral is, in this sense, 'joined up'.

This is where the issue of articulation comes in. For the assembly or concatenation of rigid elements, bolted at the joints, into a larger totality is exactly what articulation *means*. What linguists call 'articulate speech', for example, is supposed to be assembled in the mind of the speaker, prior to its vocal expression, by joining phonemes to form morphemes, morphemes to form words, words to form phrases and phrases to form whole sentences or syntactic chains. But if all speaking were like that, we would have no stories, no myth, no poetry, indeed no verbal arts of any kind. If all making were like that, we would have no axes and no cathedrals. And if all thinking were like that, we would have no sympathy. Articulation – or what nowadays goes under the name of 'joined up thinking' – may be the friend of reason, but it is the enemy of sentience. It arrests feeling. Thus what Polanyi correctly identified as the mismatch between articulate and personal knowledge is, more fundamentally, between the lateral integration of interconnected propositions and the longitudinal correspondence of entwined movements. Whereas articulate knowledge takes the form of statements *about* the known, personal knowledge both grows *from* and unfolds *in* the field of sentience comprised by the correspondence of practitioners' awareness and the materials with which they work. Relative to articulate knowledge, then, personal knowledge is not buried deep down in the psyche rather than raised up at the forefront of consciousness. Indeed it is not submerged at all, as the iceberg analogy suggests, but rather swirls *around and between* the islands that articulate knowledge joins up. The skilful practitioner knows how to negotiate the passages. It is the gravest of errors to regard such know-how as subconscious, as though practitioners could 'do it without thinking', when in fact their work involves the most intense concentration. Recall the watchmaker whom we encountered in Chapter 5, in amongst his cogs and springs! He is thinking with his eyes and with his fingers. Like every other craftsman, he is a go-between.

I have no quarrel, therefore, with Polanyi's distinction between personal and articulate knowledge. My only objections are to his identification of articulation with telling, and to the inference he draws, namely that what is not articulated remains untold and therefore tacit. In truth, telling is just the opposite of articulation. For in both of its senses – both in the verbal relating of stories and in the coupling of sensory awareness with material variations – telling is a practice of correspondence. At the personal level, knowing and telling are one and the same. This is the level of knowing from the inside that, as we saw in Chapter 1, unites the four As of anthropology, archaeology, art and architecture. And my contention, which motivates my entire endeavour in bringing these disciplines together, is that they can be taught, learned and studied precisely because ways of knowing that grow from the inside of being do *not* commit their practitioners to silence. Like makers generally, scholars of the four As *can* tell of what they know. They can tell *all* of it. The one thing they cannot do, however – or not without great difficulty and potential loss of meaning – is articulate it.

The humanity of the hand

We have eyes to watch and look, ears to listen and noses to sniff the air. Each of these organs of perception is located in the head. They enable us to tell in one of its senses, of the way things are going. But they are of not much help when it comes to telling in the other. Noses and ears cannot tell stories, and nor can eyes, unless with Jacques Derrida (1993: 126–128), we hold that the proper function of the eyes is not to see but to weep. Behind the veil of tears that blurs the vision of the sighted, says Derrida, the eyes can tell of grief, loss and suffering, but also of love, joy and elation. Even the blind can weep. Let us admit, then, that eyes can sometimes tell more in the latter sense than the former: they might not see so well, but look into them, and there's a story. Portrait painters have always known this. But to find the most consummate organ of storytelling we have to go lower down, from head to larynx. In humans, the vocal cords function only marginally, and very much in the background, as organs of perception. Working in conjunction with the ear, they comprise a system of echolocation that enables us to tell, for example in pitch darkness, whether we are in an open or enclosed space. But it is the voice that enables us to speak and sing. In earlier times, it would also have enabled us to read. Medieval readers did not see the words ready-formed on paper, as we moderns do. They had rather to perform from the inscriptions on the page, rather as a musician performs from a score, allowing the words to emerge or 'fall out' from the very process of their vocal utterance so that they could then be identified by ear (Saenger 1982: 384). It was not the voice of the reader that created these inscriptions, however. It was the hand of the scribe.

Compared with eyes, ears and nose on the one hand, and the voice box on the other, the hand is unique in so far as it combines telling in both of its aspects.[2] The more eloquent the eyes, the less they see; the more they see, the less they give away. But with the hand there is no such trade-off. Not only is it supreme among the organs of touch, the hand can also tell the stories of the world in its gestures and in the written or drawn traces they yield, or in the manipulation of threads as in weaving, lacemaking and embroidery. Indeed, the more gesturally animate the hand, the more it feels. Regarded anatomically, the hand is a marvellously intricate arrangement of skin, bone, muscle tissue and nerves, fed with blood that pulses through the arteries of the wrist. But we should not make too much of the contrast between hand and head. Hands are not instruments operated remotely from a command and control centre located in the cerebrum. As the anatomist Frank Wilson explains, 'the brain does not live inside the head, even though it is its formal habitat. It reaches out to the body, and with the body it reaches out to the world' (Wilson 1998: 307). Thus right down to the fingertips, and indeed beyond, the hand is an extension of the brain, not a separate device that is controlled by it. But if, as Wilson goes on to declare, 'brain is hand and hand is brain', then the question that has so exercised philosophers and psychologists, of whether mind and brain are the same or different, and if different, how the one exceeds the other, must be addressed to the hand as well. Adapting Wilson's declaration, could we say that 'mind is hand and hand is mind'? The *hand of the human* may be an extension of the brain, but is not the *humanity of the hand* a phenomenon of mind?

The story has often been told of how the human hand has evolved, in tandem with bipedal locomotion, the increasing use of tools and, ultimately, the expansion of the cerebral cortex, and I shall not repeat it here (Napier 1993). There can be no doubt that compared with the hands of other primates, not to mention the paws, claws, talons and equivalent prostheses of other animal orders, the hands of human beings are truly without parallel, and for three reasons in particular. First, they have flexible fingers that can be moved independently; second they have nails instead of claws, allowing greater play to sensitive pads at the fingertips; and thirdly and most importantly, every hand has a thumb that can turn, thanks to a saddle joint at the base, so as perfectly to oppose the tip of the bent index finger, which is of the right relative length to receive it. This latter property allows for the precision grip of which human hands are uniquely capable, and that is involved in nearly every instance of skilled making (Tallis 2003: 267). In the words of Sir Charles Bell, professor of surgery at the University of Edinburgh, from his Bridgewater Treatise of 1833,

> in the human hand ... we have the consummation of all perfection as an instrument. This, we perceive, consists in its power, which is a combination of strength with variety and extent of motion; we see it in the forms, relations and sensibility of the fingers and thumb; in the provisions for holding, pulling, spinning, weaving and constructing; properties which are found in other animals, but which are combined to form this more perfect instrument.
>
> (Bell 1833: 209)

Yet for all that, Bell remained convinced that the essence of humanity lay not in the hand but in the mind, in the service of which the hand is but an instrument, obedient to its every wish and command.

However, in a meditation on the hand in the course of his lectures on *Parmenides*, delivered at the University of Freiburg in 1942–1943, Martin Heidegger (1992) turned this view on its head. The hand, for Heidegger, is no mere instrument; rather its role is to establish the very possibility of instrumentality, such that things can be 'at hand'. The hand of the human may be distinguished by the precision grip; however, the humanity of the hand, Heidegger argued, lies in its possession by the word. 'Man does not "have" hands, but the hand holds the essence of man, because the word as the essential realm of the hand is the ground of the essence of man' (Heidegger 1992: 80). Thus language holds the hand, and the hand holds man. Thanks to language, and by way of the hand, the world opens up to the human being in a way that it does not and cannot to the animal. It was in an earlier course of lectures on *The Fundamental Concepts of Metaphysics*, delivered at Freiburg in 1929–1930 but unpublished until 1983, that Heidegger set out his unequivocal stance on the question of human uniqueness. Animals, he said, are *poor in world*, whereas only humans are *world-forming* (Heidegger 1995: 177). Caught up or 'captivated' (ibid.: 239) in a world of which it knows nothing, the animal can only behave according to its bent. It is slave to its own instinctive drives, and the world exists for it only as an environment of 'disinhibitors' (ibid.: 255) that trigger their release. The human, by contrast, is emancipated from the bonds that hold the animal captive, but by the same token is cast into a world that is not simply given but must be revealed or disclosed for what it is. It is the hand that betokens this opening, that conducts what Heidegger (ibid.: 237) called a *comportment* towards the world, as distinct from a behaviour within it. Thanks to the hand's humanity, to its possession by the word, humans alone can be 'handy', they can be world-forming, or in short, they can *tell*, in the sense of disclosure or revelation. But more than that, they can tell in the other sense, of recollection. In a word, they can *write*. It follows, for Heidegger, that writing tells only when it is written by the hand. To our eyes, writing that tells appears in the manifest form of script; hence 'the word as script is handwriting' (Heidegger 1992: 80). This is a crucial point, and I shall come back to it towards the end of this chapter. At this juncture, however, I want to turn to another thinker who has dwelled at length on the humanity of the hand, namely, the prehistorian André Leroi-Gourhan.

The intelligence of gestures

We have already encountered Leroi-Gourhan in Chapter 3 (pp. 36–37), tying himself in knots over the question of whether his 'Archanthropian' handaxe makers were capable of intelligent design or whether their technical activity merely oozed from their bodies, only to excuse his failure to resolve the issue by admitting to the limitations of his *Homo sapiens* brain. These limitations, we concluded, in fact have more to do with the framing of the question within the classical antinomies of nature/culture, body/soul, and matter/form. This frame encloses the world of nature within a frontier that it appears to have been humanity's singular privilege (or misfortune) to have crossed. On one side of the frontier, technicity is taken to be subject to the genetic imperatives of the species; on the other side it is subject to the traditional imperatives of the social group. Ostensibly, Leroi-Gourhan's *Gesture and Speech* (1993)[3] is an account of how an ascendant humanity broke through the bounds of purely zoological existence, of its expansion into the domains of social life and symbolic culture, and of the consequent reconfiguration of the relations between hands and face, liberating the former for technical operations and the latter for language and speech. 'The emergence of tools as a species characteristic', Leroi-Gourhan writes (1993: 90), 'marks the frontier between animal and human, initiating a long transitional period during which sociology slowly took over from zoology.' How, then, are we to understand the technicity of those creatures, ancestral to ourselves, whose lives were caught up in the transition? Inevitably from this perspective, the denizens of this period figure as anomalous zoo-sociological hybrids, as neither one thing nor the other but a bundle of contradictions. They are intelligent, yet their technicity seems to be devoid of creative thought; the forms of their tools are tied to the body plan and yet are represented as images in their minds.

These contradictions can be multiplied indefinitely, and they leave us with one fundamental question unanswered. Can we, even in principle let alone empirically, recognise what Leroi-Gourhan calls 'a radical turning point in our biological evolution as a zoological species' (1993: 137), whence the history of technology literally took off from its foundations in innate capacities? Leroi-Gourhan thinks we can, and repeatedly identifies it with an event in the evolution of the cranium, namely, the enlargement of the cortex and, with it, the disappearance of the 'prefrontal bar', the bony ridge above the eye sockets that in pre-human hominins divides the convexity of the skull from the facial bloc. Indeed the prefrontal bar takes on a quite extraordinary – and in hindsight, preposterous – significance in Leroi-Gourhan's account. More than a mere bump on the skull, it figures as a barrier whose removal opened the floodgates of symbolic imagination, and launched humankind upon the tide of fully social life. This, the 'prefrontal event', was the final liberation. However, Leroi-Gourhan is nothing if not contradictory, for no sooner has he pronounced upon 'the essential fact that we belong to two worlds, the zoological and the sociological', than he sets off down what he calls a 'third track', along which we would perceive that the lives of both humans and non-human animals are 'maintained within a body of "traditions" whose basis is neither instinctive nor intellectual but, to varying degrees, zoological and sociological at one and the same time'. Only then, he suggests, will we be truly able to progress beyond the preoccupation with 'the search for the dividing line between the natural and the cultural' that has dominated the last two centuries of scientific thought, to break down the disciplinary barrier between animal psychology and ethnology, and to really understand 'what is animal and what is human' (1993: 220).

The second part of *Gesture and Speech* is entitled 'Memory and Rhythms', and it is above all in Leroi-Gourhan's attention to the rhythmicity and mnemonic character of technical activity, rather than to its foundation in either genetic programming or intelligent design, that this third-track argument appears. A great many operations, he observes, entail the regular repetition of certain manual gestures: these include hammering, sawing and scraping. And whether or not the artisan has an idea in mind of the final form of the artefact he is making, the actual form emerges from the pattern of rhythmic movement, not from the idea. This view had, in fact, already been adumbrated by the ethnologist Franz Boas in his classic work of 1927 on *Primitive Art*. Boas was concerned to show how the perfectly controlled rhythmic movement of the accomplished craftsman guarantees a certain constancy of form. 'In flaking, adzing, hammering, in the regular turning and pressing required in the making of coiled pottery, in weaving, regularity of form and rhythmic repetition of the same movement are necessarily connected' (Boas 1955: 40). Leroi-Gourhan seems to have alighted on much the same conclusion in his assertion, to which I have already alluded (Chapter 3, p. 45), that 'rhythms are ... the creators of forms' (1993: 309).[4] The rhythmic repetitions of gesture entailed in handling tools and materials are not, however, of a mechanical kind, like the oscillations of the pendulum or metronome. For they are set up through the continual sensory attunement of the practitioner's movements to the inherent rhythmicity of those components of the environment with which he or she is engaged. As Leroi-Gourhan himself remarks, in the course of a discussion of the relation between function and style in the aesthetic evaluation of artefacts, 'the making of anything is a dialogue between the maker and the material employed' (1993: 306). This dialogue is like a question and answer session in which every gesture aims to elicit a response from the material that will help lead the craftsman towards his goal. It is, in short, a correspondence. The final form, far from having been known to him all along and forced upon the material, is only fully revealed once the work is finished.

It follows that technical intelligence is to be found neither in the brain nor in the hand, nor even in the tool it holds. An object that might be used as a tool is, in and of itself, no more than an inert lump of stone, wood or metal of a certain shape. Likewise anatomically speaking, as we have already observed, the hand is merely an arrangement of skin, bone and muscle tissue and the brain an immense tangle of neurons. Intelligence belongs to none of these things, taken singly. It rather inheres in the technical act, the gesture, in which they are brought together. 'The human hand is human', Leroi-Gourhan declares (1993: 240), 'because of what it makes, not of what it is.' In other words, whilst the *hand of the human* may be an anatomical organ, the *humanity of the hand* is a compendium of capacities, each particular to one of the many tasks in which it is brought into use and to the gestures it entails. Concentrated in skilled hands are capacities of movement and feeling that have been developed through life histories of past practice. Herein lies the mnemonic aspect of technicity. Put a saw in my hand and the hand knows how to saw (Ingold 2011a: 58), put a knife and fork into my hands and they know how to cut and pick up food, put a pen in my hand and it knows how to write – how to shape the letters and allow them to run into one another. In the intelligent gesture, at once technically effective and perceptually attentive, hand and tool are not so much used as *brought into use*, through their incorporation into a regular pattern of rhythmic, dextrous movement. And the intelligence of this use is not placed in advance of the technical act as a capacity of the individual mind in isolation, but arises as an emergent property of the entire 'form-creating system' (Leroi-Gourhan 1993: 310) comprising the gestural synergy of human being, tool and material. Hands, in a word, can *tell*, both in their attentiveness to the conditions of a task as it unfolds, and in their gestural movements and the inscriptions they yield. Leroi-Gourhan brings such inscriptions – the relatively durable traces of dextrous manual movement in a solid medium – under the general rubric of *graphism*. It is an idea to which we shall return in the next chapter (p. 129).

Grip and touch

So what can hands do? The answer, I suppose, is 'almost anything'. The hand, as philosopher–physician Raymond Tallis (2003: 267) says, 'is totipotential and so can develop in whatever direction will be of benefit'. Scholars have, from time to time, tried to come up with lists of things that hands can do – of its various grips, grasps and grabs – but every list is different. Leroi-Gourhan (1993: 328), for example, lists wounding with the fingernails, grasping with the fingers and palm, and gripping between the fingers. To these he adds the leverage that can be exerted by hand and forearm working together, as in throwing a spear. One cannot help but notice a certain gender bias in this list: with all its scratching, seizing, wounding and piercing, it seems to embody an ideal of masculinity that could have come straight out of classical Greece! Where, I wonder, is the squeezing employed in everything from milking cows to wringing out laundry, the pounding used for kneading dough or clay, or the digging used in grubbing up root vegetables, which in so many societies are things that women do? More recently, in his exploration of craftsmanship, Richard Sennett (2008: 151) has focused on grip and touch as the key capacities that make hands human. Referring to the work of physical anthropologist Mary Marzke (1997), he notes that there are three basic ways to grip things: pinching between the tip of the thumb and the side of the index finger (this is the precision grip involved, for example, in threading a needle); cradling an object in the palm and moving it around with pushing and massaging actions between thumb and fingers; and holding the object in a rounded hand, with the thumb and index finger placed on opposite sides of the object (the cupping grip).

However this classification, too, is hardly exhaustive. For example, not one of the three grips listed suffices to describe the way to hold a pen. This is how it is done. First rest the lower shaft in the notch between the tips of the third and fourth fingers, and the upper shaft in the saddle between the base of the thumb and index finger; then bring the tips of both thumb and index finger together into the precision position, not to grip the pen between them but to bear down upon the shaft from above. Of course, though these directions work on a general level, they are no more than that – *directions* – indicating a way to go rather than prescribing a fixed and final destination. In its actual performance, every kind of manual gesture admits infinite variation. Thus in the practice of drawing or handwriting each of us finds our own way to hold a pen, and every way is a little bit different. That is why it is possible to identify a person from their script. Likewise, everyone is identifiable from their voice. Phoneticians and speech therapists may direct us in the gestures and positions of the tongue and lips required to produce particular vowels or consonants, but in performance, every speaker has their own voice, as recognisable and distinctive as their face, their demeanour, and especially their handwriting.

Turning from grip to touch, and from what hands do to how they feel, it would seem at first glance that since they generally proceed fingers-first into their engagements with things, making initial contact at the extremities, the hands' tactility lies first and foremost at the fingertips. As a cellist like myself, Sennett has much to say about what he calls the 'truthfulness' of touch at the fingertips (Sennett 2008: 157). On this he makes one observation that seems counter-intuitive but which certainly resonates with my own experience. Practitioners often develop calluses of thickened skin at places on the fingers or palms that constantly rub against tools or materials. Likewise, people who go barefoot develop calluses on those parts, primarily the balls of the big toes and the heels, which are most in contact with the ground. You would think that calluses would deaden touch, or at least reduce its sensitivity: thus for those accustomed to walk barefoot, they would act rather like the soles of shoes for the rest of us. But in fact, Sennett suggests (2008: 153), it is just the other way around. Calluses allow greater sensitivity since they make the act of probing or treading less hesitant. The cellist can bring his fingers down on the fingerboard with assurance, and really commit to the strings, because his fingers are not deterred by the anticipation of soreness. Not only that; he can also lift his fingers with the same poise, thus ensuring a note that is pure and not rough around the edges (ibid.: 151). Likewise the callus-footed walker can tread without hesitation where his normally shod counterpart, having removed his shoes, would step only gingerly, and is able thereby to establish a full-bodied rapport with the ground. So too the rower, whose initial blisters at the base of the fingers – where they wrap around the oars – have given way to hard patches, can propel his craft with confidence through the water.

As in rowing, however, and in countless other tasks from milking and doing the laundry to carpentry and stonemasonry, the hands' tactility is by no means confined to the fingertips but extends over their entire surfaces, front and back. Gnarled and weathered by the exactions of their respective tasks as are the limbs of a tree by the elements, the hands of skilled practitioners bear witness to years of repetitive effort. Not only, then, in touch and gesture, can hands tell. In their bumps and creases they can also be told, both as histories of past practice and, in the telling of fortunes, as prophecies for the future. Hands open to reveal, in their creases, the fold lines of their closing positions. With penetrating vision, the clairvoyant can enter these lines and follow them, as though they were the threads of a labyrinth, and can tell both where the hand owner has been and where he or she might be going (Hallam 2002).

Making string

We decided – the students taking the 4 As course and I – to find out more about the hand's capacities by learning to make string. Of all the proceeds of human artifice, string is perhaps the most widespread and least appreciated. No one knows when our ancestors began making it, since the organic fibres from which it is made do not lend themselves to preservation. But there is no reason why creatures capable of fashioning handaxes should not also have been able to wind string. Like the great apes of today, our very earliest ancestors were likely to have been fibre users before they were tool users. Nor should it have been beyond them to tie string into knots, since this same facility is found in the apes, albeit only among those living in close proximity with humans (Herzfeld and Lestel 2005). In her ethno-archaeological study of traditional basketry in Egypt, involving techniques little changed since pharaonic times, Willeke Wendrich (1999: 298–300) describes in detail how the maker of coiled baskets winds the string he uses to sew together adjacent turns of the coil. The string, made from veins stripped from leaves of the date palm and prepared by soaking in water, is a simple but immensely strong two-ply, each strand comprising a bundle of fibres twisted in the direction opposite to that in which they twist around one another. The counter-valence of these twists holds the string together and prevents it from unravelling: the strands could only unravel by further tightening the string; the string could only unravel by further tightening the strands. Each – string and strands – wants to unwind, and in so doing winds up the other.

I took the leaves of a palm – yes, palm trees grow even in cold and windswept Aberdeen, and we had one in our garden until two hard winters in a row, 2009–2010 and 2010–2011, finished it off – and holding a leaf between the thumb and forefinger of the left hand, I pinched the edge between the thumbnail and the pad of the third finger of my right. Using the nail to slice the edge of the leaf, I then pulled it away in a millimetre-thin but leaf-long strip. Having in this way made a sufficient quantity of strips I left them to soak overnight in a bucket of water and brought them along to my 4 As class the next day. We had been reading Wendrich's description of Egyptian string-winding and had also watched the accompanying video of the basket maker at work. With these as guides, we set to work with our palm-leaf fibres. The technique is to lay the two bundles of fibres comprising each strand across the outstretched palm of the left hand, and then to bring up the flattened palm of the right so that it slides over the left from base to tip. As it does so, it rolls and twists the two strands. But as the right hand nears the end of its slide, its thumb and forefinger pick up the distal strand and pull it over to the basal position, nearest the wrist, allowing the originally basal strand to slide up to the distal. The effect is to half-twist the two strands in the reverse direction (Figure 8.1). This elementary double movement – slide-roll and pickup-pullover – is then repeated over and over again, while continually introducing additional fibres into the strand-bundles as necessary. Needless to say, our efforts were laboured and clumsy, and we could only look on in envy at the way in which the string of the basket maker in the video seemed to spool out effortlessly from his hands as they rolled and pulled, rolled and pulled, in a steady, almost hypnotic rhythm. Nevertheless, string was made (Figure 8.2), and we were astonished by its strength and pliability.

What did we learn? Four things, really: about how the hands get to know materials, or acquire a 'feel' for them; about how they impart a rhythm to these materials in the iteration of their own movements, and how the materials, in turn, carry a memory of their manipulation; about how the forces and energies bound into the materials through these gestural movements hold them together – that is, how the friction of opposed torsions makes things stick; and about the correspondence of materials in making. I will conclude this section with a few words on each of these four lessons.

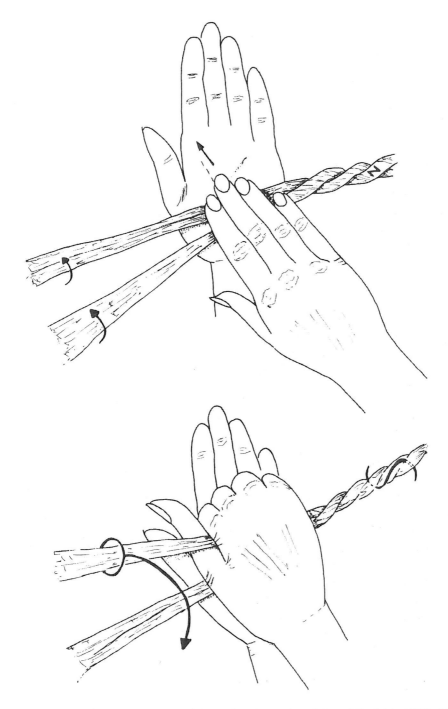

FIGURE 8.1 Hand movements in making string. Reproduced from Wendrich (1999: 299), courtesy of the author.

FIGURE 8.2 A length of string wound from palm-leaf fibres. (Courtesy of Susanna Ingold.)

First, our experiment offered an experience of tactility quite different from that of the blindfold inspection of objects or artefacts, where the task of exploring fingertips is to extract the form of the object and to cast it as an image in the mind. Here, the whole hand was in play (and not just one hand but both), including the palms, and the impressions were of texture rather than form, in an entwinement of bodily sensing and material flexion that could carry on indefinitely. We had already touched upon this difference in our experiments with objects and materials described in Chapter 2 (p. 18), and our exercise of making string seemed only to lend further weight to it. One of the reasons, we discovered, why we found the task so difficult was that our soft scholars' hands, unused to the abrasions of agrarian toil, were so smooth that they tended to slip over the bundles of fibres in our palms rather than rolling them. Friction, then, is essential to technically effective tactility (Wendrich 1999: 300). The experience, secondly, offered vivid confirmation of the conclusion to which both Boas and Leroi-Gourhan had independently arrived, of the relation between rhythmic movement and emergent form. There is, as Sennett observes (2008: 176), a 'rhythm involved in concentration', which is far from the dull routine of rote habituation. As long as concentration is sustained and the rhythm remains unbroken, then the string will be even. But when it lapses, causing the rhythm to falter, jar or miss a beat, then the string will kink and bend. Thus, in its inclinations and dispositions, its regularities and imperfections, the string retains a complete and unflinching record of the gestures that went into its formation. Nothing escapes it. As the 'cord' in re-*cord* reminds us, and as we already saw in Chapter 6 (pp. 81–82), there is memory in a length of string (Figure 8.2), and to remember is to rewind it.

Third, as in our experiments in basketry (see Chapter 2, pp. 22–23), the twist of the string was generated in a kind of force field that included both the forces imparted by our manual movements and those intrinsic to the material itself. The fibres have no inherent inclination to twist. The string coheres not because of the inertia of materials but because of the contrary forces of torque and friction imparted to them by the hands. Making string is rather like winding two spirals at once, which are parts of a larger spiral that is simultaneously wound in the opposite direction. As a result of this contrariness, a dynamic equilibrium is sustained. Bodies are wound and held together in much the same way. They are a tissue of twisted fibres at every level of resolution from the DNA of the chromosomes to the coils of the guts, and to the vocal cords and heartstrings. There is an ancient etymological connection between the Latin words for the heart, *cor*, and for cord or string, *chorda*, and both – in 'learning by heart' as in rewinding – are involved in the production of memory (Carruthers 1990: 172). Topologically, the heart is a tube twisted into a knot. But as source of feeling it also puts us in mind of the twisted eye-beams of Donne's lovers, with whom we brought the last chapter to a close. And this was our fourth lesson. For the eye-beams show that a perception that inheres in the entwinement of materials and awareness rather than in the projection of objects as images – that is, in this sense, haptic rather than optical – is by no means confined to the modality of the tactile. As Gilles Deleuze and Félix Guattari remind us (2004: 543–544), 'the eye itself may fulfill this nonoptical function'. Conversely of course, as in the blindfold inspection of objects, the hands can fulfil an optical one. Projection is optical, but telling is haptic – whether by hand or by eye. It is feeling-full. The strands of our string, as they twisted around one another, had a feel for each other in their correspondence no less than that of eye-beams or heartstrings. They are but species of the same phenomenon. The language of feeling is as appropriate, and as literal, for the twisted eye-beams of lovers as it is for the entwined strands of string.

The regression of the hand

Nowadays, most of us buy our string ready-made, and it will have been spun by machine, not by hand, very probably from synthetic materials. Moreover, string itself has fewer uses, as other things also come ready-made, in parts pre-designed to slot together. String is for things that are not already parts of a whole but have to be made to cohere by tying them up. It is for bringing things together in a world of non-parts: for correspondence. But in a world where everything is already joined up, in principle if not in practice, balls of string seem an anachronism. You find them hidden away in household drawers. The string that the mason or the carpenter once used for plotting foundations, for his plumb line, or for the alignment of walls or timbers (see Chapter 4, pp. 54–55), has long since been superseded by mechanical instruments of projection. We are not even allowed to use string, these days, for tying parcels, since it could snag the machines that the post office uses for sorting! Not having to wind our own string – not even needing it – certainly saves us time, which can be used for other tasks. But have we also lost something? Once, to have said that an article is 'made by hand' would have been a statement of the obvious. How else would you have made it? By foot? In today's world, however, 'handmade' is a mark of distinction. It connotes a kind of authenticity and devotion that people, increasingly cast as passive consumers rather than active citizens, feel is otherwise missing from their lives. With citizenship comes moral responsibility, yet how can we be responsible for a world that comes to us ready-made? At the very same moment when the whole world is at our fingertips, it also seems completely out of our hands.

This is the point at which we can return to Heidegger's credo that the hand is the cradle of our humanity. It holds our humanity, he thought, as it holds a pen. When the pen writes, it tells. It discloses a way of sentient being. Yet 'modern man', observes Heidegger (1992: 80) with scarcely disguised revulsion, 'writes "with" the typewriter'. He puts the 'with' in inverted commas to indicate that typing is not really a writing *with* at all. It is merely the mechanical transcription of words to paper. What is lost, in this transcription, is the *ductus* of the hand itself. The very movement by which the hand tells, when it holds a pen, is annihilated when it strikes the keyboard, for it leaves no trace upon the page. The correspondence of gesture and inscription, of hand and line, is broken. The words of the typescript may of course tell you how to move, and even how to feel. They may instruct, like a diagram. However, as assemblies of letters, the shapes of which bear no relation to the percussive or impressive gestures entailed in their transfer to the page, they are static and immobile. The typescript is inhuman because the words spelled out upon the page are devoid of manual movement and feeling. Or as Heidegger puts it, 'the typewriter tears writing from the essential realm of the hand' (ibid.: 81). Anyone who thinks that there is no difference between a typed word and a handwritten one, Heidegger implies, has failed to understand the essence of the word. This is to let us *be* in the world and, in being, to *feel*, and in feeling, to *tell*. Rather than carrying the current of human being-feeling-telling, which the pen picks up and converts into the inflexions of the handwritten line, words are reduced in the operation of the typewriter to mere 'means of communication' whose function is to transmit encoded information.

Heidegger was of course an incorrigible pessimist who missed no opportunity to moan about how technology was eating away at the very foundations of our humanity. Leroi-Gourhan, by contrast, was a technological optimist who revelled in the thought of what humans could become once they had cast aside the sluggishly evolving, physiological bodies that had held them captive for so long, and had managed to 'exteriorise' their being into the mechanical and computational prostheses of their own creation. They might by then have come to the end of the line as a zoological species, but with the centre of gravity of human being shifted from the body to the extra-somatic apparatus, imagine what else they could do! Nevertheless Leroi-Gourhan shared with Heidegger a profound respect for human craftsmanship – a respect that owed much to his observations of the work of sword makers and potters in the course of his early ethnological research in Japan. It was this that led him to question the assumed superiority of head over hands that had underpinned mainstream accounts of the rise of human civilisation, and eventually to adopt his 'third-track' approach that attributed the origination of artefactual forms not to the priority of intellectual conception over mechanical execution but to the generative potential of rhythmic manual activity. Whilst Heidegger's humans wrapped themselves up in the homely embrace of the word, Leroi-Gourhan's were always up to something, whether using tools, talking, gesticulating, writing, or just walking around. But it was above all in the handiwork of artisans, he thought, that the essence of their humanity was to be found.

What is found, however, can also be lost. Having spelled out the technological progression leading from manipulation with bare hands, through the hand's directly (as with a handheld instrument) or indirectly (by way of a pulley or crank) working a tool, to its initiating a motor process (driven by water, wind or animal power) and eventually to its merely pushing a button to set off a preprogrammed process (as in the automatic machine), Leroi-Gourhan concludes that by the end of it, something is indeed lost as well as gained. Imagine a machine for producing standard pieces of parquet flooring. You could feed wood into it without having to pay any attention to the grain or knots, and out would come perfectly shaped blocks. The machine, says Leroi-Gourhan, 'undoubtedly represents a very important social advance' (1993: 254). And yet, he goes on, it leaves us with no other option than 'that of ceasing to be *sapiens* and becoming something else, something that may perhaps be better but will certainly be different'. Post-human, perhaps? Indeed there is a sense, Leroi-Gourhan concludes, in which 'not having to "think with one's fingers" is equivalent to lacking a part of one's normally, phylogenetically human mind'. In short, the button-pushing finger that operates the automatic machine is part of a hand that, although still anatomically human, has lost something of its humanity. Herein lies the *problem of regression of the hand*. Technicity has become 'demanualized' (ibid.: 255).

Comparing hand writers to typists, or the makers of prehistoric handaxes to the push-button operators of the parquet flooring machine, we might suppose that the overall trend of technological progress has been from hands to fingertips. 'The hand holds', wrote Heidegger in his essay of 1951, *What Calls for Thinking*. 'The hand carries' (Heidegger 1993: 381). With our hands, we can keep things fast and take them along with us. Above all, we can hold the hands of others, and in this way both guide and be guided in the conduct of life: this is what medieval rhetoric knew as *manuduction* (Candler 2006: 5). The hand that holds and carries is a retentive and caring hand. Fingertips, by contrast, while they can touch, are unable either to hold or to carry – not, at least, without calling the thumb to their aid. This contrast, however, is not sufficiently precise. The key question is whether the hands, or the fingertips, can *feel*. We cannot deny feeling to the cellist as he stops the strings with his fingertips or to the pianist as she presses or strokes the keys with hers. There is, here, an uninterrupted continuity from the technically effective gesture to the ensuing sound.[5] But does the driver of a forklift truck feel the weight of the load he is lifting? Does the parquet-machine operator feel the bite of the saw as it slices the wood? Does the typist feel the different shapes of the letters she is typing? If the answer, in each case, is 'no', then the touch of the finger, however sensitive and precise, is without feeling. The fingertip interacts with the machine, through the 'interface' of button or key, but its gestures do not correspond with the material movements or traces that ensue. The finger is but a 'prod' and its contact with the interface a 'hit'. As in eye-to-eye contact, the hit establishes a relation that is optical rather than haptic, rational rather than sentient.

The drift of technological enhancement has been to substitute touch sensitivity at the fingertips for the sentient correspondence of telling by hand. In this substitution, handling, reach and grasp become metaphors of understanding, modelled on bodily experience, rather than animate movements in their own right (Johnson 2007: 166; Brinkmann and Tanggaard 2010: 249). We say we 'reach' a certain level of knowledge by 'handling' ideas and 'grasping' concepts, not however by doing anything constructive with our hands. Likewise, while we academics are fond of convening so-called 'workshops' to discuss our ideas, you can be sure that apart from much earnest tapping on keyboards and optical data projection, no handwork ever gets done in them. In an act of sheer, short-sighted vandalism, university managements have even commanded the removal of blackboards and chalk from classrooms, to make way for sleek white screens, so that even that final possibility of telling by hand is removed. We are not allowed to get our hands dirty by mixing them with materials, even if we wanted to! Sensitivity and sentience – touch and feeling – need not, however, be in inverse ratio. We could, for example, hand write with a sensitive pen, rather than abandoning the pen for a touch-sensitive keyboard, and get the best of both worlds. A technologically enhanced sensitivity, brought into the service of hands-on engagement with materials in making, could genuinely enlarge the scope of humanity, rather than further eroding it.

9

DRAWING THE LINE

Draw and tell

We have seen that a hand that tells is also one that feels and draws. Is all drawing, then, a way of telling by hand? Yes and no, depending on what you mean by drawing. And that depends, in turn, on what you want to compare drawing with – that is, on what you want to say it is *not*. If, for example, you want to compare drawing with writing, you might be interested in the limits of language or syntax, or in whether any hard and fast distinctions can be made between verbal and non-verbal inscriptions. If you were comparing it with sculpture, you might be interested in the difference between working with line and working with surface or volume, or between scribing and carving. Comparison with painting might lead to reflections on the difference between marking a surface and covering it or between line and colour; whereas comparison with photography would undoubtedly lead one to think about what it takes to make an image, and about the temporality of drawing as against the relative instantaneity of the photograph. Comparison with music would lead to a focus on the expressive gesture and its duration, but would also bring up the question of what difference it makes when the gesture leaves no enduring trace at all. Each comparison would prompt a somewhat different characterisation of drawing. They may share a family resemblance, but it would be unrealistic to expect them to converge upon a single, essential definition that holds once and for all.

I am interested in drawing as a way of telling. But that means excluding, from the outset, a whole class of drawings that do not and are not intended to tell, but rather to specify and articulate. Such are the technical drawings of architects and engineers (Henderson 1999), which convey precise details of what is to be made or built, with measurements and angles. When Leon Battista Alberti introduced the idea of the architectural drawing as an assembly of 'lineaments', comprising a complete specification of the form and appearance of the building as conceived by the mind in advance of the labour of construction, it was to this kind of drawing that he referred, and it also underlay the sense of drawing as *disegno* in the writings of such Renaissance authors as Giorgio Vasari (see Chapter 4, p. 51). The importance of this kind of drawing cannot be overestimated. Without it, as Patrick Maynard observes, 'it is hard to see how there could *be* a modern world' – a world, that is, in which anything that gets made, every manufactured item, must first be drawn (Maynard 2005: 7). Maynard goes on to define drawing as what happens when 'an object such as fingertip, piece of chalk, pencil, needle, pen, brush ... having something like a tip, which we therefore refer to as a "point", is intentionally moved (drawn) over a fairly continuous track on a surface. This action leaves, as the trace of its path, a mark of some kind, and is done for that purpose' (Maynard 2005: 62).

Every hand-drawn line, then, is the trace of a gesture, even if it is done with the aid of a ruler and compass, or a stencil that acts as a jig by steering the path of the point. Yet not every line has as its purpose to express that gesture. In a study of her own drawing practice through attempts to copy the work of others, artist Patricia Cain found that she needed to distinguish between what she called 'gestural' and 'non-gestural' lines. This was a distinction not so much of practice as of intent. Gestural lines were meant to express the movements that generated them, whereas with non-gestural lines any such expression was merely a side effect, incidental to their primary purpose of specification (Cain 2010: 126). Drawings comprised of non-gestural lines are, in effect, propositions: they make statements *about* what is to be, or what has been, made. Drawings comprised of gestural lines are, by the same token, non-propositional. They issue *from* things (including bodies) rather than making statements *about* them. Commonly known as sketches, they are *drawings that tell*, in both senses. They call for close and attuned observation, and trace paths that others can follow. Sketching, as Juhani Pallasmaa points out, is a haptic exercise: 'As I sketch a contour of an object, human figure or landscape', he writes (2009: 89), 'I actually touch and feel the surface.'

Architects and engineers typically sketch, often collaboratively, in the process of working out an idea. For them it is a vital part of the design process (Henderson 2007: 8). We could say that sketches are *on their way* towards proposition. But at the point where the sketch gives way to the technical drawing, all movement is stilled. The lines of the technical drawing may encode instructions on how to move, but convey no movement in themselves. And for the same reason, such drawings are devoid of feeling. They establish a relation with the world that is optical rather than haptic. What happens when the two kinds of drawing are confused – that is, when sketches are taken for specifications – is vividly illustrated by a complaint from the architect Adolf Loos. Architecture, he laments, has become so much a graphic art that 'bricklayers and masons have to scratch out and retouch the graphic nonsense with their own painstaking efforts' (Loos 1985: 105–106). He means that architects, on the one hand, have become so obsessed with their drawings that they have become ends in themselves, while on the other hand builders, taking the architect's sketches for specifications, find themselves having to render, in the material, every nuance of the architect's line – from the hardness or softness of the pencil used to textures of shading and cross-hatching – with ludicrous consequences.

The drawing is not an image

In an interview with Patricia Cain, sculptor and draughtsman Richard Talbot commented: 'I don't think I think with images. But the drawings ... when I'm setting out to do the drawing, I don't have a pre-conceived image ... I might have just a hunch' (in Cain 2010: 89). Elsewhere, Talbot likens his approach to making a drawing to medieval cathedral building, noting – as we have done (Chapter 4, p. 57) – how the form of the building, once laid out on the ground, 'developed organically, ... the result of varying amounts of intention, pragmatism, accident and ambition'. It is the same, says Talbot, with his drawing. 'The drawing's meaning, if such a thing exists, is not in my control' (Talbot 2008: 56). This observation, which tallies with what many graphic artists have to say about their work, flies in the face of the common belief among non-practitioners, not least historians and anthropologists of art, that the essence of drawing lies in the projection onto the page of interior mental pictures. They would have us suppose that in drawing an object, the draughtsman would first obtain an image in his mind, by way of the intromission of light through the eye, fix it in visual memory, and then, in a reverse movement of extromission, would shine the image onto the page, going on to draw around its outline. Philip Rawson, for example, is convinced that when children draw, 'they always project, out onto the surface, images from inside themselves, made up from memories' (Rawson 1979: 7). Nor is it any different in principle, he thinks, for grown-up artists: the difference is only of degree, in the density of the image. The drawings of major artists exhibit many layers of meaning, whereas children's drawings are 'only one concept thick' (ibid.: 8). Thus unlike the child whose expression is accomplished, as it were, in a single act, the artist has to build up an image from its constituent marks, so as to create an assembly in which every mark has meaning in relation to the whole. Ultimately, says Rawson, it is the 'overall image' that is important, for it is this that the artist 'wishes to plant in the viewer's mind' (ibid: 22, 29).

He could not be more wrong! For one thing, as art historian Norman Bryson has stressed, drawing does not seek overall coverage: it is not subject – as painting is – to the 'law of the all-over' (Bryson 2003: 151), nor do its marks take on meaning only in relation to a completed totality. On the contrary, it is inherently anti-totalising, committed to carrying on. In drawing, completion is an asymptote that is never finally reached. 'We can only use the word "finished"', says artist Yves Berger, in a dialogue with his father John, 'to say that we have arrived as close as possible to the drawing's own identity' (in Berger 2005: 130).[1] And for another thing, it is doubtful whether the intention of the artist is to plant anything in the viewer's mind, save perhaps the seed from which the work grew, so that viewers can follow it through for themselves, looking *with* it rather than *at* it, all the while recognising that at any moment in the process of growth, it could have taken a path other than the one actually followed (Rosenberg 2008: 123). It is not as though the hand, in drawing, gradually empties out what first fills the head, such that the entire composition slides like a transfer from mind to paper; rather both hand and head are together complicit throughout in the work's unceasing generation (Roque 1994: 46; Badmington 2007). Rawson himself admits as much when he points out that drawing's very uniqueness among the visual arts lies in its expression of time and movement. 'If we do not follow through in time the traces left by the artist's moving hand we are bound to miss the point' (Rawson 1979: 24). In this regard, despite its conventional classification among the visual arts, drawing is closer to music and dance than it is to, say, painting or photography. The photograph arrests time, says writer and critic John Berger; the drawing flows with it.

'Could we not think of drawings', he suggests (2005: 124), 'as eddies on the surface of the stream of time?' The drawing that tells is not an image, nor is it the expression of an image; it is the trace of a gesture.

If drawing that tells is like music, then it follows that the pencil – or whatever other mark-making implement is used – is analogous to a musical instrument. The great pioneer of modern abstract art, Wassily Kandinsky, drew the parallel explicitly in his essay on *Point and Line to Plane* (Kandinsky 1982: 612). Just as in playing a stringed instrument such as my cello the movement of the bowing arm issues, by way of the bow hairs' contact with the strings, into the stream of melodic sound, so in the flow of the pencil line, the *ductus* of the hand finds its way onto the page. And likewise, as the pressure on the bow is mirrored in the amplitude of sound, so the pressure of the draughtsman's pencil is reflected in the thickness of his lines (Ingold 2011a: 188). Thus the pencil serves in the draughtsman's hands precisely as the cello in mine, as a *transducer*.[2] To recall our definition from Chapter 7 (p. 102), the transducer converts the kinetic quality of the gesture – its *ductus* – from the register of bodily movement and awareness to that of material flux. The one thing the pencil is *not*, then, is a vector of projection, or what Pallasmaa (2009: 17) claims it to be for the architect: 'a bridge between the imagining mind and the image that appears on paper'.[3] The exact same argument could be made for the archaeologist's trowel, which in skilled hands does not simply translate from mind to site or vice versa but *follows the cut*. Just like the draughtsman's line (ibid.: 111), the cut moves in directions that are sometimes foreseen but 'at other times wildly at variance with expectations' (Edgeworth 2012: 78). And the same, too, goes for building. Taking Simon Unwin's (2007: 108) point that 'all buildings are drawings; not the built realization of drawing but drawings in and of themselves' – their walls and pathways drawn out in the very process of building and moving – then in the hands of the builder, the trowel serves as a transducer just as it does for the archaeologist. Only in the eyes of the architect is the trowel a bridge between the initial design and the final construction. For the builder it allows him to navigate the treacherous waters that flow beneath.

From here it is but a short step to the conclusion that drawing that tells is a correspondence, of kinaesthetic awareness and the line of flight. In this correspondence, as Bryson says (2003: 154), 'the mark on paper leads as much as it is led', alternately sewing the line into the mind and the mind into the line in a suturing action that grows ever tighter as the drawing proceeds. Thus the drawing is not the visible shadow of a mental event; *it is a process of thinking, not the projection of a thought*.[4] Whereas the project implies a *throwing forward*, a cast into the future, drawing is a *gathering*, pulling closer (Phipps 2006: 4). 'Instead of dictating a thought', writes Pallasmaa (2009: 111), 'the thinking process turns into an act of waiting, listening, collaboration and dialogue [in which] one gradually learns the skill of co-operating with one's own work.' *Co-operating with one's work* – now there's a good definition of correspondence! This thinking, this imagining, goes on as much in the hands and fingers as in the head. It is strung out in the lines of practice. 'The creator', according to Serge Tisseron (1994: 37), 'is the one who agrees to venture forth with no certainty and follow this thread unwinding ahead of him like Ariadne's thread, and falling behind him like a spider's web.' Are not thoughts veritable spiders' webs? Are they not, as John Berger puts it (2005: 133), 'like strings all tangled together?' Not only that, says Berger, but in this drawing-thinking you become what you draw: not in shape but in affect (ibid.: 126). You know it from the inside, and in your gesture you relive its movement. Drawing is transformative (Cain 2010: 76).

Let me return for a moment, with this thought uppermost in mind, to the distinction I introduced right at the start of this book, between anthropology and ethnography (Chapter 1, pp. 3–4). The objective of ethnography, I argued, is description; that of anthropology, transformation. Now drawing that tells describes a line – it is a graphic act – but that line is descriptive of nothing but itself. It is, however, transformative. It transforms the draughtsman, in making the work, and it transforms those who follow, in looking with it. To correspond with the world through drawing, therefore, is to practise not ethnography but graphic anthropology or, to coin a term, *anthropography*.

Drawing and handwriting

In the last chapter (p. 116) I remarked on how André Leroi-Gourhan had selected the word *graphism* to refer to the durable traces of manual gestures of all kinds. He chose wisely. Long before any of his contemporaries, Leroi-Gourhan recognised the fallacy of positing, at the origins of graphic inscription, a distinction between drawing and writing that emerged only at a late stage of its development – in the phonetisation of the word and the alphabetisation of its representations – and which depends for its modern meaning on the technology of print. This is a complex story that is tangential to our current concerns, and I shall not repeat it here.[5] However, I do want to return to an issue raised at the outset of Chapter 8, concerning the meaning of the tacit. I observed there that what is unspoken may still be voiced, and, correspondingly, that what is unwritten can still be drawn. Just as singing and speaking are ways of telling with the voice, so both drawing and writing are ways of telling by hand. We can imagine a time in deep prehistory when speech had yet to crystallise from the inflections of the voice and writing from the inflections of the line. In those days, there were just vocalisation and graphism, issuing from gestures respectively oral and manual, each commenting upon or amplifying the other. But that time is no more, and now we have writing and drawing, as we have speech and song. How, then, are they distinguished? How do writing and drawing differ as varieties of graphism?

There can be no picture, it could be argued, that cannot also be read, and no written text that cannot be looked at. But it is difficult, if not impossible, to do both at once. This argument has been proposed, on the side of text, by the literary scholar Jean-Gérard Lapacherie. 'It is impossible to read a text in a sustained fashion', Lapacherie writes (1994: 65), 'and at the same time look at the printed characters.' These characters can be regarded, on the one hand, as signs representing units of language (phonemes) and, on the other, as graphs – that is, as characters that have their own proper and autonomous meaning. But if you stop to focus attention on the typography of the characters – on their expressive shape or calligraphic form – your reading will be interrupted and you will lose the track. If, conversely, you concentrate on reading, then it is the typography that will evade your attention. On the side of pictures, James Elkins (1999: 91) has proposed something rather similar. Just as there can be no 'pure writing', uncontaminated by non-verbal meaning, so – Elkins argues – the 'purely visual picture' is also a fantasy. Pictures are always comprised of signs that can be read. These signs may be disordered, or even layered over one another so as to make them virtually indistinguishable. But they are necessarily *there*, else the image would make no sense. Similarly and with specific reference to drawing, Rawson insists that like language, the art of drawing has its grammar and syntax, with a knowledge of which it is possible for the informed viewer to read off the many different messages it concurrently conveys (Rawson 1979: 11). Every inscription we might come across, then, is a mixture of the pictorial and the textual, in proportions that vary along a continuum between the practically unrealisable poles of pure picture and pure text. 'Any sufficiently close look at a visual artefact', Elkins concludes (1999: 84), 'discloses *mixtures* of reading and seeing.'

On this continuum, however, seeing means looking *at*, while reading means the disaggregation of the whole into its parts and arranging them in their proper syntactic sequence. These operations are the precise reverse, respectively, of *projection* and *articulation*. The former retrojects, from world to mind, what has been projected from mind to world; the latter disarticulates and reconnects what has first been articulated. Both projection and articulation, as I argued in the last chapter, are inimical to telling. So let us ask: what would happen to the continuum if we were to substitute, for seeing, the looking *with* (or watching) of telling, and for reading, a sensibility that would follow the line of writing rather than breaking it down into segments and reassembling the pieces? For a clue to the answer, we could turn to the parallel case of speech and song. When you listen to a song – even a song with words – it is the song you hear, not two parallel lines of words and melody (although this is how it is notated according to modern western conventions). It is not as though to hear the words you cannot help but lose track of the melody, or vice versa. Why should this be so? Why should the problem that seems to afflict us when we read disappear when we listen? The answer, of course, is that to listen is to harness your awareness to the current of sound. It is the aural analogue of looking *with*, of watching, not of looking *at*. And the words of the song are gestures of the voice launched on this current. To hear the song is to hear the words because the words *are* sound, in specific modulations and inflections. Likewise, the words of handwriting or calligraphy *are* specific modulations and inflections of the letter-line, as it is traced by the dextrous hand of the writer. To read is to retrace the line, once again to 'go over' the movements of its formation.[6] But the line, and the letters and words into which it twists and loops, are brought forth in drawing, just as much as the words of the song are brought forth in singing. Drawing that tells, therefore, slides easily into handwriting and just as easily out of it. There is no great barrier to be overcome (Tisseron 1994). Nor does it present itself as a mix that requires us to do two things simultaneously – look and read – which cannot practicably be combined. We need do only one thing – follow the hand-drawn line – and if that line is a letter-line of writing, then the words will 'fall out' from it.

Many analysts, however, have a curious blind spot when it comes to vision: they seem to assume that there can be only one kind of looking, namely looking *at*. The assumption is that vision can only be optical, never haptic; that there is no vision other than the spectacular. This is what leads Martine Reid, introducing a collection of papers on the theme of writing and drawing, to insist that there is a conflict between legibility and visibility, as though writing that 'drifts off course' (Reid 1994: 7) and reverts to drawing – as in doodling, scribbling, marginal sketching or the excessive embellishment of letters – at once breaks out into the realm of visibility, only to sink back into invisibility at the moment when the writing becomes legible again. If even ordinary writing is invisible when we read it, then how invisible, I wonder, is writing in invisible ink? As noted above, the same assumption leads Lapacherie (1994: 65), in a contribution to Reid's collection, to claim that one cannot simultaneously see and read, as though reading did not involve the exercise of eyesight. But if you have to stop reading in order to see words on paper, then what are we to make of the sign language of the deaf? You cannot stop a sign to look at it. Are signs, then, invisible? If so, by what mysterious sense do deaf people communicate? For Elkins (1999: 81), built into every image is a vacillation between showing and saying – that is, between 'pure visuality' and 'legible systems of signs' – which pull in opposite directions. It is as though the eyes found employment only in the fixating of images, and not in the reading of signs. Indeed Elkins (1996: 222) is convinced that we are all blind to a degree, in so far as much of what we see passes in our wake and is not fixed in memory in the form of what he calls a 'final image'. In rather similar vein, Jacques Derrida (1993: 3) claims that not just the eye of the reader but the hand of the writer, too, is blind: 'it feels its way, it gropes, it caresses as much as it inscribes ... as if a lidless eye had opened at the tip of the fingers ... right next to the nail' (ibid.). Even drawing, at that moment when the hand with its inscribing point ventures forth upon the surface of the page, must necessarily proceed in the night. On the threshold of emergence – in its inaugural or path-breaking aspect – drawing, Derrida tells us, 'escapes the field of vision'. Our eyes are opened, it seems, only when we can turn and look *back* on lines already drawn, or on what remains of them. For only then do they enter the realm of what he calls 'spectacular objectivity' (ibid.: 45).

How come, then, that the slide in the work of the drawing hand both in and out of writing has been transmuted into a continuum from picture to text, where every gradation figures as an incongruous hybrid – part picture, part text, in varying proportions – the comprehension of which depends upon twin operations, of seeing and reading, or showing and saying, which are fundamentally incompatible? The answer, I believe, lies in our modern tendency to assimilate the picture to the photograph and the text to the typewritten or printed word. Hand and eye have been replaced by keyboard and camera. In drawing, as we have already seen, the pencil serves as a transducer, converting the kinaesthetic awareness of the draughtsman into the flow and inflection of the line. I referred above, in the words of John Berger, to the difference between the drawing and the photograph: to repeat, the still camera arrests a moment in both the consciousness of the photographer and the things that hold his attention, and effects an instantaneous capture, of the latter by the former. And as we saw from Heidegger's diatribe against the typewriter, reviewed in Chapter 8 (p. 122), this machine does something similar, breaking up the flow of manual gesture and the corresponding letter-line into discrete and momentary 'hits'. As the poet Billy Collins explains (cited in Pallasmaa 2009: 111), 'the keyboard, to me, makes everything kind of look done ...writing on a page gives me a feeling of fluidity'. That is why he always writes with pen or pencil. For my part, I asked the students taking the 4 As course to experiment with using handwriting to record their observations, and to compare their experience with using a keyboard. They reported, with a degree of unanimity that was remarkable, that writing by hand brought them closer to and into greater sympathy with the observed. My own experience is much the same (Ingold n.d.).

In short, if anything has torn writing from the *ductus* of the hand, and reassembled it as an articulation of jointed segments, it is the typewriter. And if anything has torn drawing from the *ductus* of the hand and re-established it as a projected image, it is the camera. A return to drawing, then, would also be a return to handwriting, replacing the antinomies of projection and articulation, image and text, with a continuum of inscriptive practices, or processes of line-making, ranging from handwriting through calligraphy to drawing and sketching, with no clear points of demarcation between them (Ingold 2011a: 225). Our next task is to focus on the nature and quality of the lines themselves.

The meshwork

In the mornings, on the flagstones outside our house, and especially after rain, I often find an intricate tracery of interlaced trails, as though someone had scribbled all over them with a slime pen (Figure 9.1). They are actually made by slugs, which come out at night to make their forays into the vegetation, only to vanish again at dawn into the mysterious depths from whence they came. The tracery of slime trails on the flagstones comprises a *meshwork*. By this I mean an entanglement of lines (Ingold 2011a: 63–65). These lines may loop or twist around one another, or weave in and out. Crucially, however, they do not connect. This is what distinguishes the meshwork from the network. The lines of the network are connectors: each is given as the relation between points, independently and in advance of any movement from one towards the other. Such lines therefore lack duration: the network is a purely spatial construct. The lines of the meshwork, by contrast, are of movement or growth. They are temporal 'lines of becoming' (Deleuze and Guattari 2004: 224–225). Every animate being, as it threads its way through and among the ways of every other, must perforce improvise a passage, and in so doing it lays another line. We can do the same. From a distance, the meshwork might look like a matted surface. Up close, however, with our eyes next to our fingernails (to recall Derrida's allegory of 'blind' drawing), we find ourselves entangled in a 'system of sympathies and longings, with no dots whatever, just lines, all curving, shooting in and out of knot stations consisting of all kinds of textile art: braids, knots of every type, loops, crossings and interlaces' (Spuybroek 2011: 321).

Where the network has nodes, the meshwork – as Lars Spuybroek intimates here – has knots. Knots are places where many lines of becoming are drawn tightly together. Yet every line overtakes the knot in which it is tied. Its end is always loose, somewhere beyond the knot, where it is groping towards an entanglement with other lines, in other knots. What is life, indeed, if not a proliferation of loose ends! It can only be carried on in a world that is not fully joined up, not fully articulated. Thus the very continuity of life – its sustainability, in current jargon – depends on the fact that nothing ever quite fits. As we saw in Chapter 4 in the specific case of medieval cathedral building, the world is not assembled like a jigsaw puzzle in which every 'building block' slots perfectly into place within an already pre-ordained totality. To be sure, we are always being told these days that the world we inhabit is built from blocks: thus biologists speak of the building blocks of cellular organisms, psychologists

FIGURE 9.1   Slug trails, photographed in the early morning on an Aberdeen pavement.

of the building blocks of thought, physicists of the building blocks of the universe itself.[7] But a world built from perfectly fitting blocks could harbour no life at all. The reality, again as in the case of the cathedral, is more akin to a quilt in which ill-fitting elements are sewn together along irregular edges to form a covering that is always provisional, as elements can at any time be added or taken away.

Gilles Deleuze and Félix Guattari (2004: 526) take up the history of the quilt in developing their idea of a topology that is smooth rather than striated, showing how early embroidered fabrics gave way to a patchwork technique where scraps of leftover material or fragments salvaged from worn-out garments were sewn together. With its regular and rectilinear intersections of woof and weft, fabric – for Deleuze and Guattari – is the epitome of the striated. But in the patchwork, 'an amorphous collection of juxtaposed pieces that can be joined together in an infinite number of ways', the principle of striation is subordinated to that of the smooth. No material better exemplifies the principle of the smooth, however, than felt. Comprised of a mélange of entangled woollen fibres, with no consistent orientation and extending without limit and in all directions, felt – say Deleuze and Guattari – is everything that fabric is not. It is an anti-fabric (ibid.: 525). Could the same, then, not be said of the meshwork? Are the wayward trails left by slugs in their nocturnal meanderings not comparable to the fibres of felt, which in turn seem reminiscent of the tracks worn in the ground, in their pastoral wanderings, by the very sheep upon whose backs the wool was grown? This is indeed what Deleuze and Guattari would have us believe. Yet the constitutive lines of the smooth, they say, are *abstract*, as distinct from lines that are either *geometric* or *organic*. In order to appreciate what they are getting at, we need to examine these three kinds of line a little more closely.

The abstract line

We begin with the line of geometry – the Euclidean line – that inhabits a mathematical space defined by the regular intersection of dimensional co-ordinates. Like both Alberti's lineament and its contemporary counterpart, the computer-generated line (Pallasmaa 2009: 100), it is defined as the connection between two points. As its name implies, the geometric line has its origin in the practices by which the surveyors of ancient Egypt measured the earth after every annual flood of the Nile. They would stretch a cord between stakes hammered in the ground (Ingold 2007: 159). From this, too, as philosopher Michel Serres (1995: 59) reminds us, comes the legal notion of *contract*: a 'cord that draws or tracts us together'. The stretched cord, string or thread, however, retains a certain tactility: you can *feel* the tension; pluck it, and it vibrates. As textile artist Victoria Mitchell has put it, taut thread is a kind of 'hinge' between feeling and form, between bodily kinesis and speculative reason (Mitchell 2006: 345). But as geometry was drawn into the art and science of optics, and as the earth-measurer's cord was joined by the optical instruments of the seafarer, the once tangible, taut thread morphed into its intangible and insensible spectre, the ray of light. For long, both thread and ray, the material line and its spectral double, appeared together, like a thing and its shadow. Even Alberti thought of lines of sight as threads, like those of a veil stretched between the eye and the thing seen, yet so fine that they could not be split (Alberti 1972: 38). But as a vector of projection, the geometric line was eventually divested of all remnants of tactility. We can recognise it today in Georg Simmel's (1969: 146) definition of eye-to-eye contact: 'the shortest and straightest line between the eyes' (see Chapter 7, p. 106).

In making connections and setting limits, the geometric line lies at the root of law, reason and analytic thought. It is laconic and always to the point. Organic lines, by contrast, trace the envelopes or contours of things as though they were contained within them: they are outlines. They are also separators, dividing the surfaces on which they are drawn between what is on one side of the line and what is on the other: in this sense they are analogous to cuts (Rawson 1979: 34; Maynard 2005: 63–64). Such lines, however, have no presence on or in things themselves. I might draw an egg in outline as an oval, the trunk of a tree as two parallel lines or the sky as an arc, but would look in vain to find their counterparts on egg or trunk, or in the heavens. Or I might want to draw an apple or the border between a meadow and a ploughed field, yet as Maurice Merleau-Ponty observes in his essay 'Eye and mind' (1964: 182), I would be deluded to think that the outer contour of the apple or the field boundary is actually present, 'such that, guided by points taken from the real world, the pencil or brush would only have to pass over them'. For if we look, there are no lines to be seen. '*Lines?* I see no lines', the great artist Francisco Goya – himself a consummate draughtsman – is reputed to have declared (cited in Laning 1971: 32). This and similar observations have led numerous authorities (reviewed in Maynard 2005: 99) to conclude that *line does not exist in nature*, and therefore that the lines of drawing have only a symbolic connection to their referents, based on artifice or convention rather than phenomenal experience. 'Line itself', asserts artist and curator Deanna Petherbridge in her magisterial survey of histories and theories of drawing practice, 'does *not* exist in the observable world. Line is a representational convention...' (Petherbridge 2010: 90).

In short, if the geometric line is the mark of reason, then the outline looks more like a cultural construct: the visible expression of a process by which the mind, according to a well-worn anthropological paradigm (Leach 1964), more or less arbitrarily divides the continuum of nature into discrete objects that can be identified and named. The lines of those familiar 'join-the-dot' puzzles, designed for children, manage to be both geometric and organic simultaneously, at once connecting points and outlining objects. Rather as children join the dots, surveyors make maps, outlining such features as riverbanks and coasts (Ingold 2007: 86). But the lines of the meshwork – such as the slime trails of slugs (Figure 9.1) – are not outlines, nor are they point-to-point connectors. To my eyes, however, they seem entirely real and indeed natural. Surely, there *are* lines in the observable world, for they are unmistakably *there*. In what conceivable sense, then, can they be said to be abstract?

For an answer we can return to Kandinsky. In his essay 'On the spiritual in art', Kandinsky insists that abstraction does not mean draining a work of content so as to leave only an empty outline or a pure geometrical form. On the contrary, it means removing all those figurative elements that refer only to the externalities of things, that is to their outward appearances, in order to reveal what he called their 'inner necessity' (Kandinsky 1982: 160). By this he meant the life force that animates them and that, since it animates us too, allows us to join with them and experience their affects and pulsations from within. In a charming sketch penned in 1935, Kandinsky (ibid.: 774–775) asks us to consider the similarities and differences between a line and a fish. They do have certain things in common: both are animated by forces internal to them that find expression in the linear quality of movement. A fish streaking through the water could be a line. Yet the fish remains a creature of the external world – a world of organisms and their environments – and depends on this world to exist. The line, by contrast, does not. The line is no more, and no less, than life itself. That, says Kandinsky, is why he prefers the line to the fish, at least in his painting (Ingold 2011a: 208). And this, too, is why Deleuze and Guattari, following Kandinsky, can say of '*a line that delimits nothing, that describes no contour*, that no longer goes from point to point but passes between points, … that is without outside or inside, form or background, beginning or end and that is alive as a continuous variation', that it is *abstract* (Deleuze and Guattari 2004: 549, 550–551 fn. 38). Such is the line of the river current, or of the ebb and flow of the tide, as distinct from the riverbank or coastline plotted on the cartographer's chart.

In words attributed to Leonardo da Vinci, Merleau-Ponty writes that the secret of drawing any thing is to discover 'the particular way in which a certain flexuous line, which is, so to speak, its generating axis, is directed through its whole extent'.[8] Such a line, he continues, is neither here nor there, neither in this place nor that, but 'always between or behind whatever we fix our eyes upon' (Merleau-Ponty 1964: 183). One could almost treat line as a verb, and say that in the thing's growing – in its issuing forth, in its making itself visible, as Paul Klee (1961: 76) would say – *it lines*. That would certainly accord with the view of the nineteenth century draughtsman-critic John Ruskin. In his massive three-volume compendium *The Stones of Venice* (1851–1853), Ruskin assembled a collection of what he called 'abstract lines' into a single figure, combining his observations of things great and small, from a glacier and a mountain ridge, through a spruce bough, to a willow leaf and a nautilus shell (Figure 9.2). In every case, he contended, the line is 'expressive of action or *force* of some kind' (Ruskin 1903: 268). These lines of action and force, as he would go on to explain in his treatise of 1857 on *The Elements of Drawing*, are to be discerned in 'the animal in its motion, the tree in

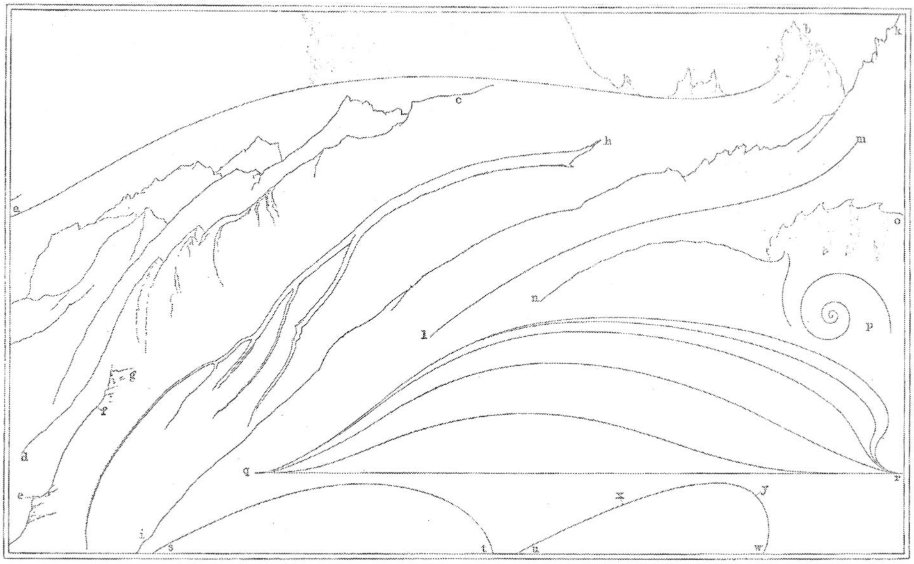

FIGURE 9.2 Abstract lines. Reproduced from Ruskin (1903), Plate VII, facing page 268.

its growth, the cloud in its course, the mountain in its wearing away'. Thus he went on to advise the novice: 'try always, whenever you look at a form, to see the lines in it which have had power over its past fate and will have power over its futurity. Those are its *awful* lines; see that you seize on those, whatever else you miss' (Ruskin 1904: 91). Wisdom, for Ruskin, lay in grasping not just the way things are but *the way they are going* – that is, in anticipation – and this meant concentrating not on the outlines of shape but on the centrelines of force. These are the awful lines. If they abstract from the real, as Spuybroek points out (2011: 115), it is not by reduction but by the precise registration of its variation. The awesome power of such lines lies precisely in their capacity to break the bounds that otherwise hold things captive within their envelopes, thus releasing them into the fullness of their being.

Such are the lines that comprise the meshwork and that, for Deleuze and Guattari, constitute the topology of the smooth. It is a topology, they argue, that is haptic rather than optical, that relies not on points that might be connected geometrically, nor on objects that might be outlined organically, but on the tactile and sonorous qualities of a world of wind and weather, where there is no horizon separating earth and sky, no intermediate distance, no perspective or contour (Deleuze and Guattari 2004: 421). We have already encountered this world in Chapter 6: it is what we called the *earth-sky*, in contradistinction to the *landscape*. In the landscape, the geometric line defines the disposition of elements and the organic line delimits their projected forms. The abstract line, however, anticipates the becoming of things in the earth-sky world. In such a world, lines are not imposed by representational convention, nor are they plotted between points. They are rather laid down in growth and movement. Look *at* nature, as landscape, and there are, as Goya said, no lines to be seen. They exist only in its graphic representations. Look *with* it, however, as a manifold of earth and sky, join in the movements of its formation, and lines are everywhere. For they are the very lines along which we and other creatures live.

Lines and beasts

In what must be one of the founding statements of architectural modernism, Le Corbusier headed his manifesto for urban planning, *The City of Tomorrow*, with the following declaration: 'Man walks in a straight line because he has a goal and knows where he is going; he has made up his mind to reach some particular place and he goes straight to it' (Le Corbusier 1947: 11). And a man who does not? His way, says Le Corbusier, is that of the pack donkey, who has no thought in its scatter-brained head save to follow the line of least resistance, wherever it goes. The pack donkey's way is always winding, never straight, governed, Le Corbusier contends, by feeling, not by reason. When we look at the layout of almost every continental city, we find in its meandering streets that the donkey has been there first, lumbering along in its aimless and distracted way, and creating tracks in the process along which people then settled. But in a modern city, fit for the age of the automobile, there can be no place for these wriggling, zigzag lines. They are difficult and dangerous, and induce paralysis. A modern city, Le Corbusier insisted, can only live by the straight line (ibid.: 16).

I will return to Le Corbusier in a moment. But first let me introduce a contemporary compatriot whose influence was equally far-reaching, extending far beyond his discipline of anthropology as did Le Corbusier's beyond his of architecture. I refer of course to Claude Lévi-Strauss. In his memoir, *Tristes Tropiques*, Lévi-Strauss recounts the stories of his travels among the Nambikwara, an indigenous people of Brazilian Amazonia. One chapter, entitled 'A writing lesson' (Lévi-Strauss 1955: 294–300), folds together two concurrent stories, both of which are about lines. The first is about inscriptions on paper; the second about the paths of animals. I shall summarise each very briefly.

Story 1: Lévi-Strauss has persuaded the chief of the group he is with to take him to their village, where he can meet with other groups to whom they are related by kinship and marriage. With four oxen laden with gifts intended for distribution to the relatives, the party sets off across the plateau, along a straight route specially devised for the occasion, since the vegetation along the usual winding tracks following the valley bottoms would be too dense to allow the animals through. Despite the Indians' losing their way en route, they eventually make it to the appointed meeting place, and the chief – urged along by the anthropologist – commences with the distribution of gifts. Taking from a basket a piece of paper completely covered with wavy lines, the chief proceeds to 'read out', as if from a checklist, each gift, for whom it is intended, and for what received in exchange. This 'farce' – as Lévi-Strauss does not hesitate to call it – goes on for two hours.

Story 2: Recall that on the way out, the natives had managed to get lost. On the return journey, however, it is Lévi-Strauss himself who goes astray. His mule, irritated by mouth ulcers, is ill-behaved: one moment it comes to an abrupt halt; the next it rushes ahead. Before knowing it, Lévi-Strauss is alone in the bush with no idea of his whereabouts. He fires a shot to attract attention, but this only frightens the mule, which trots off. He runs to catch it, but every time he is about to seize the reins, the mule flees. Eventually, after grabbing the animal by the tail, he is able to remount, but neither he nor the mule has a notion of the direction in which to go in order to rejoin the party. The two of them, alternately leading and led, end up going around in circles until – just as the sun is about to set – a couple of Lévi-Strauss's Nambikwara companions who, with no difficulty at all, have been following his and the mule's tracks since midday, catch up and lead both him and the mule back to safety.

That night, Lévi-Strauss recalls, restless and unable to sleep, the events of the previous day – and especially the episode involving the exchange of gifts – were preying on his mind. He remembered how, on an earlier occasion, he had handed out pencils and sheets of paper to the Nambikwara, who had proceeded to cover them with horizontal, wavy lines. Of course, having no understanding of writing or its purpose, they were only using their pencils as they had seen Lévi-Strauss use his. The chief, however, had cottoned on to the fact that these lines, though meaningless in themselves, conferred some kind of authority on his subsequent words. He had therefore requested a writing pad, and would always scribble a few lines first before proffering information in response to the anthropologist's questions. It is no wonder, then, that he read from his sheet while conducting the formalities of gift exchange. But what if the chief, while uncomprehending of words and their meanings, had nevertheless chanced upon the true purpose of writing – the purpose for which, somewhere between the fourth and third millennia BC, it had originally been invented?

We might be tempted to suppose that writing, in so far as it allows people to store up memories and to place their achievements on record, would make it possible for literate civilisations, as it were, to set their history straight, and to advance with increasing rapidity towards the goals they have set for themselves. Without writing, would people not be condemned – as Lévi-Strauss (1955: 296) puts it – 'to remain imprisoned in a fluctuating history which will always lack both a beginning and any lasting awareness of an aim'? On reflection, he concludes that there would be nothing to justify such a conclusion, for not only have some of the greatest achievements of human history – in the fields of production, arts and crafts, and even building – been won in periods when writing was still unknown, but for the majority of people in the literate world, history has also continued to fluctuate much as it always did, with no consistent sense of direction. So what is the purpose of writing? What great innovation was it linked to? The answer, Lévi-Strauss conjectures, lies in architecture. If we want to find the link between the origins of writing and the birth of architecture, it is to be found in the possibility that writing confers to organise large numbers of people, and to exploit their labour, in the construction of monuments. Thus, Lévi-Strauss concludes, 'the primary function of written communication is to facilitate slavery' (ibid.: 299). It is a means of exploitation, not of enlightenment, and any possible intellectual benefits that writing conferred were but a spin-off, a secondary consequence.

Reading Lévi-Strauss today, his account of Nambikwara writing strikes one as both patronising and ethnocentric. In a critical commentary on Lévi-Strauss's text, Derrida (1974: 118–126) points out that the very idea of 'people without writing' is founded on a split between writing and drawing that, as we have already seen, only emerged in consequence of the phonetisation and alphabetisation of the word. Indeed in his doctoral thesis, Lévi-Strauss had admitted that the term the Nambikwara used for the act of writing translates literally as 'drawing lines' (cited in Derrida 1974: 123).

If we were to trace the etymology of the words for writing in the western tradition, we would find much the same: both the Old English *writan* and the Greek *graphein* carried connotations of scratching, engraving or incising a surface with a sharp point (Howe 1992: 61; Elkins 1999: 83). Should we suppose that people lacked writing because their word for 'to write' was literally 'to scratch' or 'to scribble'? That, as Derrida (1974: 123) caustically remarks, would be like saying that people cannot speak because the verb they use for speaking translates as 'to sing'! Rather than invoking the idea of a great leap into history, separating people with writing from those without, it would surely make more sense to follow the precedent of Leroi-Gourhan, and to speak of a transition, *within graphism*, that involves crossing no frontier. For as we have seen, so long as it is done by hand, all writing is drawing. And if that is so, would not the same apply to architecture? Recall Unwin (2007: 108): 'all buildings are drawings'.

Let us now return to Le Corbusier. Juxtaposing the great architect's vision for the city of the future with the great anthropologist's lesson in writing, what might we learn about the relation between writing and architecture? The architectural theorist Catherine Ingraham (1992) finds that Le Corbusier and Lévi-Strauss, in their respective accounts, have two things in common: an obsession with linearity and curious encounters with beasts of burden. And for both, these beasts – the donkey and the mule – 'come to bear the burden of the line' (ibid: 143): a line that, far from connecting points, arises in the midst of things and simply carries on from there. For Le Corbusier, such a line is inimical to the orthogonality proper to architecture and urbanity. He has no time for the errant donkey, or for the uncouth folk who once followed its ways. Lévi-Strauss, too, is a man of the straight line, unlike both his mule and the Nambikwara. They get lost following the straight route on the outward journey, whereas Lévi-Strauss gets lost following his mule on the return. They find the lost anthropologist with ease by tracking the mule; he writes straight while they can only draw wavy lines. But Lévi-Strauss is much less sanguine about the benefits the straight line has brought to humanity. He laments the loss of the native line; Le Corbusier is happy to see it wiped out. For all his disdain for the 'farcical' machinations of the Nambikwara and their chief, and for their wavy lines and fluctuating, directionless history, Lévi-Strauss is all too aware of the havoc and destruction wrought upon indigenous populations by people with a clear-cut civilising mission, who have a goal and aim directly for it. For the problem with the straight line is simply this: once it has reached its end, what then?

From A to B, and beyond

During a conference held in June 2009 at the University of Aberdeen (Ingold 2011b), Maxine Sheets-Johnstone ran a workshop in which, among other things, participants were asked to dance their names. We had to move across the floor, flexing this way and that, in such a way that we would speak our names with our entire bodies, and not just our voice. Mine was simple enough, with one emphatic sweep for the 'Tim', followed by a brief hesitation, a short hop for the 'In-', and a more drawn-out, upward-rising flourish for the '-gold'. What took me quite by surprise, however, was the discovery that when I sign my name, holding a pen in my hand, the rhythm and shape of the gesture is exactly the same. I realised that my written name does not simply stand for the spoken one, but rather that in both speaking and writing it, I enact a sense of self –

an identity, if you will – that is primarily kinaesthetic. The difference between speaking and writing, of course, is that the latter leaves a lasting trace. Yet as we have already seen, the quality of movement when we write by hand, or for that matter when we draw, extends into the lines that appear on the paper. The duration, the rhythm, the varying tempo, the pauses and attenuations, the pitch and amplitude are all there. These lines are both inspired by, and carry forth, our affective lives. And most importantly, what they describe is ongoing movement rather than a connection between one point and another, between an origin and a destination, or between A and B.

It is for precisely this reason that our most fundamental knowledge of movement cannot be grasped in terms of what linguist George Lakoff and philosopher Mark Johnson call the 'source-path-goal' schema (Lakoff and Johnson 1999: 33–34). In this schema the body is understood not as movement in itself, or as a constellation of movements, but rather as an object – self-contained and externally bounded – that moves. They call it a 'trajector'. And this trajector, located at any particular moment in a certain position, is on its way from one point (the source) to another (the goal). In life, however, there are no start points and end points. There are only horizons that vanish as you approach them, while further horizons loom ahead. As infants we come into the world moving, and continue on our way, now in pursuit, now in retreat, carried along and in turn carrying, approaching and leaving, or just going around, continually overtaking any destinations to which we might be drawn in the very course of reaching them. The trouble with the source-path-goal schema, as Sheets-Johnstone (2011: 121–123) explains, is that it leaves no place for the kinetic quality of lifelines that continually issue forth in the midst of things but which *do not connect*. How can our knowledge of movement possibly be grounded in a schema that eliminates the very qualitative dynamics that constitute the experience of kinaesthesia?

By way of contrast, our own experience in dancing our names revealed in stark outline the values of a digitally enhanced society that ranks objects over things, mobility over movement, and the printed word over handwriting and drawing. In such a society, the network reigns supreme, and all lines connect: objects into assemblies, destinations into road maps, letters into words or acronyms. As Le Corbusier foretold, the inhabitants of tomorrow's city would all be straight-line people, launched from A to B, single-minded in purpose and oblivious to what goes on from side to side. Yet had he practised what he preached, I wonder, would we have his architecture? And what of those who stray, who do not go straight to the point but choose to meander, who behave – as Le Corbusier insinuated – like pack donkeys? Such people wander through fields instead of sticking to the road, their eyes and noses are distracted by the colours and scents of flowers, and their ears by the song of birds; they periodically pause to rest, to talk to people, and to look around. They wave their hands about, embracing the air, rather than keeping them well to their sides. They fall in love and have children. Suppose we set them side by side: straight-line people and pack-donkey people. Which of them are stupid, and which wise?

Straight-line people are addicted to innovation and change – to what the poet T. S. Eliot, in *Choruses from the Rock*, called 'the endless cycle of idea and action; endless invention, endless experiment'. Were it not for novelty, they'd be stuck. Restlessly, like molecules in motion, they race from point to point, or instantly communicate. They are all connected, these avatars, in a networked world. Their motto's 'joined up thinking'. They have the information, mistaking it for knowledge. What need have they to ask the world, when they already know? Blinded by information and dazzled by images, they fail to see what's happening before their very eyes. 'Where is the wisdom we have lost in knowledge', continued Eliot, 'where is the knowledge we have lost in information?'[9] Truly, never in the history of the world has so much information been married to so little wisdom. To me, wisdom runs not in straight lines but along the ways of the donkey. This humble beast, slow but nimble, cross-eyed but big-eared, capable of traversing the most rugged ground without mishap, without need of road or rail, or fossil fuel, has served mankind for many thousand years. Whereas the automobile, once it has reached the end of the road, can go no further, the donkey just keeps on going. Non-human it may be, but should we not pay heed to what it has to tell us? All true scholars are donkeys: obdurate, capricious, dogged, curious, petulant, at once captivated and astonished by the world in which they find themselves. They will not be hurried but go at their own pace. They live in hope, not under the illusion of certainty. Their paths may go this way or that, unpredictably. They find the grain of things and follow it, and in so doing find themselves. All learning, as I hope that you have found by now, is self-discovery. Where next? *Know for yourself!*

NOTES

1 Knowing from the inside

1 Emphasis in the original. In all further direct quotations throughout this book, emphases are in the original unless otherwise stated.

2 Of the participants in the seminar, I would like to mention three in particular: Stephanie Bunn, Wendy Gunn and Amanda Ravetz. All three, since completing their doctorates, have gone on to make important professional contributions in their own right, and I am indebted to them for their continued stimulus and support.

3 We are very grateful for generous funding from the Arts and Humanities Research Board (grant reference B/RG/AN8436/APN14425). I would also like personally to acknowledge the support of Murdo Macdonald, Professor of the History of Scottish Art at the University of Dundee, who was the principal applicant for the project and played a major role throughout.

4 See for example Blier (1987), Wilson (1988), Oliver (1990), Coote and Sheldon (1992), Carsten and Hugh-Jones (1995), Waterson (1997). Two recent studies by Trevor Marchand are notable exceptions, in that they focus on the actual building process, along with the organisation of labour and the acquisition and deployment of the skills of masons (Marchand 2001, 2009).

5 See, for example, Hallowell (1955: 178–181) on dreaming among Ojibwa people of north-central Canada.

6 The reason for calling the focus of the project a 'thing', and not – for example – an 'object', will become clearer later (Chapter 6, p. 85).

7 In my teaching I have referred to the work of scholars such as Jerome Bruner (1986), Barbara Rogoff (1990, 2003), Jean Lave and Etienne Wenger (1991), and Gisli Palsson (1994), as well as my own (Ingold 2001, 2008b).

2 The materials of life

1 In English: *Individuation in the light of notions of form and information*. The first part of the thesis was published in 1964, but the second not until 1989; only in 2005 was the work published in its entirety (Simondon 1964, 1989, 2005). With a long-promised English translation still awaited, it remains little known and is barely cited in Anglophone anthropological literature. Yet Simondon's work has the potential to revolutionise the field (Knappett 2005: 167).

2 The concept of *chaîne opératoire* was introduced into anthropology and archaeology by André Leroi-Gourhan, and has remained central to the comparative study of techniques, especially among Francophone scholars (Naji and Douny 2009).

3 'Substance', according to literary scholar Daniel Tiffany (2001: 75), 'is the solution to the conundrum posed by things that speak in riddles'. As Tiffany points out (ibid.: 78), the word 'riddle' is etymologically linked to the verb 'to read', both derived from the Old English *raedan*, meaning to attend and to take counsel.

3   On making a handaxe

1 The literature on chimpanzee nut cracking is very extensive. Some key sources include Sugiyama and Koman (1979), Boesch and Boesch (1990), McGrew (1992) and Joulian (1996). For a description of split-breaking to obtain blanks among contemporary stone adze makers, see Stout (2002: 697).

2 In recent years the inclusive term *hominins* has been introduced in place of the more traditional *hominids*, to denote both human beings and closely related but now extinct ancestral species that shared such human-like characteristics as bipedalism. This is a consequence of the recognition that the genealogical connections between humans and the great apes (orang-utans, gorillas and chimpanzees) are closer than previously thought, leading to calls to expand the range of the *Hominidae* to include the latter. A new term had then to be introduced to refer to the narrower group, previously known as the hominids. These are the hominins.

3 Published in English as *Gesture and Speech* in 1993, in a superb translation by Anna Bostock Berger.

4 As Aristotle explains, at the very start of Book 2 of *De Anima* ('On the Soul'): 'Now there is one class of things which we call substance, including under the term, firstly, matter, which in itself is not this or that; secondly shape or form, in virtue of which the term this or that is at once applied; thirdly the whole made up of matter and form. Matter is identical with potentiality, form with actuality' (Hicks 1907: 49).

5 This is not to say that the hypothesis has been finally disproved. A spirited defence has been mounted by Tony Baker (2006). His argument is that *Homo erectus* would have lacked the manual dexterity to hold a core steady with one hand while striking with the other. The axe maker had therefore to rely on the inertia of the mass of the core to resist each strike, which had in turn to be directed towards the centre of the mass rather than tangentially – else the core would simply have been displaced by the force of the blow. Such a technique favoured larger cores with greater mass rather than smaller ones which – for contemporary knappers – are easier to hold. And the removal of flakes from these large cores would have yielded serviceable tools.

6 Dietrich Stout and his colleagues have recently argued, along the same lines, that Acheulean toolmaking 'requires the intentional shaping of the core to achieve a predetermined form' and that this calls for 'elaborate planning including the subordination of immediate goals to long-term objectives'. In their view, elementary acts of percussion are governed by subordinate goals of bifacial edging, which nest within intermediate goals of thinning, themselves encompassed by the overarching goal of shaping (Stout, Toth, Schick and Chaminade 2008).

7 This is also true of the brick maker's moulds, discussed in the last chapter (pp. 24–25).

8 The metaphor of the 'string of beads', to describe an operational sequence, was first proposed by John Gatewood, in a study of the acquisition of technical skills on board a commercial salmon trawler (Gatewood 1985: 206). It has been further elaborated by Wynn (1993: 392–396).

4   On building a house

1 Ironically, although *tekton* referred generically to the maker, it also referred more specifically to carpentry, *tekton* having been derived from the Sanskrit *taksan*, meaning 'carpenter'. So perhaps the first 'architects' were carpenters, after all! For a more extended discussion of the etymology of *tekton*, and of the evolution of its meaning from carpentry in particular to making in general, leading eventually to the emergence of the notion of master builder or *arkhitekton*, see Frampton (1995: 3–4).

2 When the humanists Poggio Bracciolini and Cencio Rustici found a manuscript of Vitruvius's *Ten Books* at the monastery of St Gall in 1416, they thought they had rediscovered a long lost

classical work, which Alberti then did much to promulgate as part of the contemporary revival of interest in Roman art and architecture. We now know, however, that copies of Vitruvius were in wide circulation throughout the Middle Ages (Harvey 1972: 20–21).

3   This is not to deny that the medieval architect as master mason was already distinguished from his underlings in so far as he would direct the work without dirtying his own hands, while being more handsomely recompensed. In a sermon dating from 1261, the Dominican friar Nicolas de Biard even saw fit to complain about it (cited in Erlande-Brandenburg 1995: 61)!

4   The top two rows appear not to have been drawn by Villard himself but were added perhaps fifty years later, by an unknown hand, having first scraped away the original drawings. The written inscriptions are also later additions. Villard himself may well have been illiterate, in which case he would have had to have dictated to a scribe (Barnes 2009: 11, 24).

5   Medieval sources refer exclusively to 'moulds', from which is derived the word 'moulding' for shaped stone. It appears that the word 'template' or 'templet' was introduced more recently, as a synonym for 'mould' (Pacey 2007: 219).

6   Lambros Malafouris makes precisely the same point with reference to the Cyclopean wall that surrounds the ancient citadel of Mycenae, in the Peloponnese. 'In building a Cyclopean wall, the choice of the appropriate block of stone was determined by the gap left by the previous one in the sequence of action rather than, or at least as much as by, any preconceived mental plan to which these choices are but subsequent behavioural executions' (Malafouris 2004: 60).

7   The analogy between architectural drawing and musical notation, though a powerful and productive one, could actually backfire on Harvey's argument. This is because in medieval times, musical notation did not so much specify a composition as provide a series of mnemonic cues to assist the musicians in the performance of a work (Parrish 1957: 21; see Ingold 2007: 21–23). It is likely that drawings, such as there were, assisted the builders of the period in much the same way.

8   In a more recent study of medieval cathedral building, architectural historian Nigel Hiscock makes the same assumption, namely 'that such building will have needed to be thought out and possibly drawn out in advance for it to have been set out on site' (Hiscock 2000: 172). That so few of the inferred plans have survived is attributed to the fact that they would have been drawn on expensive parchment, which would have been repeatedly reused. In this, the initial plan would have been the first drawing to be erased, to make way for its successors (ibid.: 174).

5   The sighted watchmaker

1   Turnbull (1993: 319) is thus mistaken in thinking that in disproving the creative agency of God as an intelligent designer, evolutionary theory has disproved the argument from design. It has not. On the contrary, the theory – at least in its current neo-Darwinian incarnation – depends on it.

6   Round mound and earth sky

1   Even if we were in possession of a time machine, we would not immediately have all the answers. As Gavin Lucas notes, it would merely substitute one set of problems for another (Lucas 2005: 118–119).

2   In an ode, *Exegi monumentum aere perennius*, the Roman poet Quintus Horatius Flaccus describes the perfect monument: it 'cannot be destroyed by gnawing rain nor by the wild north wind, nor by the unnumbered procession of the years and flight of time. I shall not wholly die' (West 2002: 259).

7   Bodies on the run

1   I am grateful to Janice Tsui for drawing my attention to this work.

2   Paul Connerton, for example, argues that in the formation of what he calls 'habit-memory', postures and gestures 'become sedimented in bodily conformation' (Connerton 1989: 94).

3 This is by no means my first attempt to understand what happens when you fly a kite (see, for example, Ingold 2011a: 214–215). I have long been puzzled by it. This attempt, however, supersedes my previous efforts, and should be read in that light.

4 The concept of transduction has recently been introduced into anthropology through the work of Stefan Helmreich, who borrowed it, in turn, from the field of acoustics, 'where it refers to the conversion of sound signals from one medium to another' (Helmreich 2009: 214). The concept also plays a central role in the philosophy of Gilbert Simondon, for whom it denotes 'a process – be it physical, biological, mental or social – in which an activity sets itself in motion, propagating within a given area, through a structuration of the different zones of the area over which it operates' (Simondon 1992: 313). An example would be the growth of a crystal as it extends in all directions in a solution. Simondon's usage is idiosyncratic, to say the least, and I do not follow it here.

5 The same could be said of Laura Vinci's *Máquina do Mundo*, discussed in the last chapter (pp. 75–76). The machine can, at least in principle, keep on going forever, although the heaps of ground marble it creates undergo ceaseless transformation. A statue carved from solid marble, on the other hand, while it may retain its form in perpetuity, is rendered effectively lifeless.

6 César Giraldo Herrera (personal communication) reminds me that the word *cogito*, in Latin, is a compound of *co-* (implying togetherness and mutuality) and *-agito* (to stir up, guide, lead or care about). Thus *cogito* would literally mean to co-agitate, to lead and be led, stir up and be stirred, care and be cared for; and the phrase *cogito ergo sum*, which is much older than Descartes, could well be translated as 'I correspond, therefore I am'.

8 Telling by hand

1 Not infrequently, stories are couched in the deliberately tantalising form of riddles, which can only be resolved – as we have already seen in the case of materials (see Chapter 2, p. 31) – by close observation of what is there. See also Ingold (2011a: 172–174).

2 I have, perhaps unfairly, omitted the tongue, which is both an organ of taste and intimately involved in the production of speech. It deserves more credit than it has generally received.

3 For a detailed review of this work, see Ingold (1999).

4 Whether Leroi-Gourhan reached this conclusion independently of Boas is hard to say. Though none of the latter's writings is listed in the bibliography appended to *Gesture and Speech*, Leroi-Gourhan was certainly familiar with Boas's research on the native art and design of the American Northwest Coast, to which he referred in his doctoral thesis on the archaeology of the northern Pacific.

5 The technique of *vibrato*, which most string players use most of the time, allows movement at the fingertip to carry on beyond the point at which the string is stopped, so as to yield a sound that registers with the listener as full of feeling. To play without *vibrato*, by contrast, is to produce a sound that is eerily insentient, as though one had entered a world of dead souls in which no correspondence is possible.

9 Drawing the line

1 The illustrator John Vernon Lord reports a rather similar experience. Wondering how he knows when a drawing is finished, he answers that it is the drawing itself that tells him when to stop, often when least expected. By that stage, he reports, 'I am too close to the drawing to see it any more ... When I look at it now it is not so much as what I had in mind but more to do with what the drawing itself tells me about its own mind' (Lord 2005: 36).

2 In addition, of course, the pencil incorporates a reservoir of material, in its graphite centre or 'lead'. In a detailed account of the history and engineering of the pencil, Henry Petroski (1989: 6) comments on the peculiar suitability of graphite for drawing, as compared with ink. Solid rather than liquid, but soft enough to leave a mark, it neither runs nor leaves an indelible stain. It is therefore admirable for work in progress, which can be inked in when finished. 'Ink', Petroski writes, 'is the cosmetic that ideas will wear when they go out in public. Graphite is their dirty truth.' See also Faure Walker (2008).

3 In fairness to Pallasmaa, this passing remark should not be taken out of context, for the whole tenor of his argument points in the opposite direction. Indeed in the very same paragraph he moves to qualify what he has just said, suggesting that it is perhaps the hand, holding the pencil, which really imagines. Later on, Pallasmaa attributes the idea that the drawing is the projection of a mental image to the arrogance of youth: 'When one is young and narrow-minded, one wants the text and the drawing to concretise a preconceived idea, to give the idea an instant and precise shape' (2009: 111). Now he is old and wise enough to know better!

4 This contrast invites some reflection on the relation between line and colour. Art historian Georges Roque (1994) has documented a tendency among western writers on art to regard colour as mere embellishment or 'make-up', with the power to seduce or charm but not, like drawing or writing, to convey the processes of thought. It seems to me, however, that there is more to it than that. Colour, I suggest, saturates consciousness; line leads it. Thus if the line traces a process of thought, then colour is its temperament. Both line and colour are modalities of feeling, but where line is *haptic*, colour is *atmospheric*. Further development of this suggestion, however, will have to be the subject of another work.

5 For a detailed discussion, see Ingold (2004).

6 Research in neuropsychology supports this contention. Testing experimental subjects with an imaginary alphabet of 'pseudoletters', never before encountered, showed that experience with forming letters by hand contributed significantly to letter recognition. Subjects with such experience performed better in recognition tasks that those whose experience was limited to typing the equivalent letters on a keyboard. Had the visual apprehension of letters been unconnected to the movements of their formation, then hand writers and typists should have performed equally well (Longcamp, Zerbato-Poudou and Velay 2005; James and Atwood 2009).

7 So pervasive has this metaphor become that we are inclined to forget how recent it is. According to architectural historian Witold Rybczynski (1989: 29–36), it did not come into common use until the middle of the nineteenth century, when a domestic architecture of prosperous homes equipped with dedicated nurseries made it possible for building with blocks to become child's play. Before that time, most play was out of doors, and even when it took place indoors, floors were too uneven, busy and cluttered for any construction to stand up. From the 1850s onwards, however, the architectural profession actively promoted the development and marketing of sets of building blocks for children. Inculcated from our earliest years, the assumption that the world is built from blocks has since become part of the stock in trade of modern thought.

8 These words come, in fact, from M. L. Andison's translation of Henri Bergson's *The Creative Mind* (Bergson 1946: 229). Bergson, in turn, was referring to the work of the nineteenth century philosopher-archaeologist Félix Ravaisson. Whether the quoted words are actually da Vinci's, or Ravaisson's, or even Bergson's, is moot.

9 In T. S. Eliot, *The Waste Land and Other Poems* (1940: 72).

REFERENCES

Adamson, G. 2007. *Thinking Through Craft*. Oxford: Berg.

Aggeler, W. 1954. *The Flowers of Evil*. Freno, CA: Academy Library Guild.

Alberti, B. 2007. Destabilising meaning in anthropomorphic forms from northwest Argentina. In *Overcoming the Modern Invention of Material Culture*, eds. V. O. Jorge and J. Thomas (special issue of *Journal of Iberian Archaeology* 9/10). Porto: ADECAP, pp. 209–223.

Alberti, B. and Y. Marshall 2009. Animating archaeology: local theories and conceptually open-ended methodologies. *Cambridge Archaeological Journal* 19(3): 345–357.

Alberti, L. B. 1972. *On Painting*, trans. C. Grayson, ed. M. Kemp. Harmondsworth: Penguin.

Alberti, L. B. 1988. *On the Art of Building in Ten Books*, trans. J. Rykwert, N. Leach and R. Tavernor. Cambridge, MA: MIT Press.

Anderson, B. and J. Wylie 2009. On geography and materiality. *Environment and Planning A* 41: 318–335.

Andrews, F. B. 1974. *The Mediaeval Builder and his Methods*. Totowa, NJ: Rowman and Littlefield.

Badmington, N. 2007. Declaration of ink dependence. *Writing Technologies* 1(1), http://www.ntu.ac.uk/writing_technologies/back_issues/Vol.%201.1/Badmington/51321p.html

Bailey, G. 2007. Time perspectives, palimpsests and the archaeology of time. *Journal of Anthropological Archaeology* 26: 198–223.

Baker, T. 2006. The Acheulean handaxe. http://www.ele.net/acheulean/handaxe.htm

Barad, K. 2003. Posthumanist performativity: toward an understanding of how matter comes to matter. *Signs: Journal of Women in Culture and Society* 28: 801–831.

Barad, K. 2007. *Meeting the Universe Halfway*. Durham, NC: Duke University Press.

Barnes, C. F. Jr. 2009. *The Portfolio of Villard de Honnecourt: A New Critical Edition and Color Facsimile*. Farnham: Ashgate.

Bateson, G. 1973. *Steps to an Ecology of Mind*. London: Fontana.

Baudelaire, C. 1986. *The Painter of Modern Life and Other Essays*, trans. and ed. J. Mayne. New York: Da Capo.

Bell, C. 1833. *The Hand: Its Mechanism and Vital Endowments as Evincing Design* (2nd edition). London: William Pickering.

Bennett, J. 2010. *Vibrant Matter: A Political Ecology of Things*. Durham, NC: Duke University Press.

Berger, J. 2005. *Berger on Drawing*, ed. J. Savage. Cork: Occasional Press.

Bergson, H. 1946. *The Creative Mind*, trans. M. L. Andison. New York: Philosophical Library.

Billeter, J. F. 1990. *The Chinese Art of Writing*, trans. J.-M. Clarke and M. Taylor. New York: Rizzoli International.

Blier, S. P. 1987. *The Anatomy of Architecture*. Cambridge, UK: Cambridge University Press.

Boas, F. 1955. *Primitive Art*. New York: Dover Publications (original 1927).

Boesch, C. and H. Boesch 1990. Tool use and tool-making in wild chimpanzees. *Folia Primatologica* 54: 86–99.

Boivin, N. 2008. *Material Cultures, Material Minds: The Impact of Things on Human Thought, Society and Evolution*. Cambridge, UK: Cambridge University Press.

Bourdieu, P. 1977. *Outline of a Theory of Practice*, trans. R. Nice. Cambridge, UK: Cambridge University Press.

Brand, S. 1994. *How Buildings Learn: What Happens to Them after They're Built*. New York: Penguin.

Brinkmann, S. and L. Tanggaard 2010. Toward an epistemology of the hand. *Studies in the Philosophy of Education* 29: 243–257.

Bruner, J. 1986. *Actual Minds, Possible Worlds*. Cambridge, MA: Harvard University Press.

Bryson, N. 2003. A walk for walk's sake. In *The Stage of Drawing: Gesture and Act*, ed. C. de Zegher. London: Tate Publishing; New York: The Drawing Center, pp.149–158.

Bucher, F. 1979. *Architector: The Lodge Books and Sketchbooks of Medieval Architects*, Volume 1. New York: Abaris Books.

Bunn, S. 2010. From enskillment to houses of learning. *Anthropology in Action* 17(2/3): 44–59.

Cain, P. 2010. *Drawing: The Enactive Evolution of the Practitioner*. Bristol: Intellect.

Calvin, W. 1993. The unitary hypothesis: a common neural circuitry for novel manipulation, language, plan-ahead and throwing. In *Tools, Language and Cognition in Human Evolution*, eds. K. R. Gibson and T. Ingold. Cambridge, UK: Cambridge University Press, pp. 230–250.

Candler, P. M. Jr. 2006. *Theology, Rhetoric, Manuduction, or Reading Scripture Together on the Path to God*. Grand Rapids, MI: William B. Eerdmans.

Carruthers, M. 1990. *The Book of Memory: A Study of Memory in Medieval Culture*. Cambridge, UK: Cambridge University Press.

Carruthers, M. 1998. *The Craft of Thought: Meditation, Rhetoric and the Making of Images, 400-1200*. Cambridge, UK: Cambridge University Press.

Carsten, J. and S. Hugh-Jones eds. 1995. *About the House: Lévi-Strauss and Beyond*. Cambridge, UK: Cambridge University Press.

Clark, A. 1997. *Being There: Putting Brain, Body and World Together Again*. Cambridge, MA: MIT Press.

Clark, A. 1998. Where brain, body and world collide. *Daedalus: Journal of the American Academy of Arts and Sciences* 127: 257–280.

Clark, A. 2001. *Mindware: An Introduction to the Philosophy of Cognitive Science*. Oxford: Oxford University Press.

Clark, A. and D. Chalmers 1998. The extended mind. *Analysis* 58: 7–19.

Conneller, C. 2011. *An Archaeology of Materials: Substantial Transformations in Early Prehistoric Europe*. London: Routledge.

Connerton, P. 1989. *How Societies Remember*. Cambridge, UK: Cambridge University Press.

Coote, J. and A. Sheldon eds. 1992. *Anthropology, Art and Aesthetics*. Oxford: Clarendon.

Crapanzano, V. 2004. *Imaginative Horizons: An Essay in Literary-Philosophical Anthropology*. Chicago, IL: University of Chicago Press.

Darwin, C. 2008. *The Autobiography of Charles Darwin: From the Life and Letters of Charles Darwin*. Teddington, Middlesex: The Echo Library.

Davidson, I. and W. Noble 1993. Tools and language in human evolution. In *Tools, Language and Cognition in Human Evolution*, eds. K. R. Gibson and T. Ingold. Cambridge, UK: Cambridge University Press, pp. 363–388.

Dawkins, R. 1986. *The Blind Watchmaker*. Harlow, Essex: Longman Scientific & Technical.

Deleuze, G. and F. Guattari 2004. *A Thousand Plateaus: Capitalism and Schizophrenia*, trans. B. Massumi. London: Continuum.

Derrida, J. 1974. *Of Grammatology*, trans. G. C. Spivak. Baltimore, MD: Johns Hopkins University Press.

Derrida, J. 1993. *Memoirs of the Blind: The Self-Portrait and Other Ruins*, trans. P.-A. Brault and M. Nass. Chicago, IL: University of Chicago Press.

Dibble, H. 1987a. Reduction sequences in the manufacture of Mousterian implements of France. In *The Pleistocene Old World: Regional Perspectives*, ed. O. Soffer. New York: Plenum Press, pp. 33–44.

Dibble, H. 1987b. The interpretation of Middle Palaeolithic scraper morphology. *American Antiquity* 52(1): 109–117.

Dormer, P. 1994. *The Art of the Maker: Skill and its Meaning in Art, Craft and Design*. London: Thames & Hudson.

Douglas, M. 1966. *Purity and Danger: An Analysis of Concepts of Pollution and Taboo*. London: Routledge & Kegan Paul.

Edgeworth, M. 2012. Follow the cut, follow the rhythm, follow the material. *Norwegian Archaeological Review* 45(1): 76–92.

Eisenberg, L. 1972. The *human* nature of human nature. *Science* 176: 123–128.

Eliot, T. S. 1940. *The Waste Land and Other Poems*. London: Faber & Faber.

Elkins, J. 1996. *The Object Stares Back: On the Nature of Seeing*. New York: Simon & Schuster.

Elkins, J. 1999. *The Domain of Images*. Ithaca, NY: Cornell University Press.

Elkins, J. 2000. *What Painting Is: How to Think About Painting, Using the Language of Alchemy*. London: Routledge.

Erlande-Brandenburg, A. 1995. *The Cathedral Builders of the Middle Ages*, trans. R. Stonehewer. London: Thames & Hudson.

Fagan, B. 1989. *People of the Earth: An Introduction to World Prehistory* (6th edition). Glenview, IL: Scott, Foresman.

Farnell, B. 2000. Getting out of the *habitus*: an alternative model of dynamically embodied social action. *Journal of the Royal Anthropological Institute* (N.S.) 6: 397–418.

Faure Walker, J. 2008. Pride, prejudice and the pencil. In *Writing on Drawing: Essays on Drawing Practice and Research*, ed. S. Garner. Bristol: Intellect, pp. 71–92.

Flusser, V. 1995. On the word design: an etymological essay (trans. J. Cullars). *Design Issues* 11(3): 50–53.

Flusser, V. 1999. *The Shape of Things: A Philosophy of Design*. London: Reaktion.

Frampton, K. 1995. *Studies in Tectonic Culture: The Poetics of Construction in Nineteenth and Twentieth Century Architecture*. Cambridge, MA: MIT Press.

Frascari, M. 1991. *Monsters of Architecture: Anthropomorphism in Architectural Theory*. Savage, MD: Rowman and Littlefield.

Friedman, T. 1996. Stonewood. In *Wood*, by A. Goldsworthy. London: Viking, pp. 6–12.

Gatewood, J. 1985. Actions speak louder than words. In *Directions in Cognitive Anthropology*, ed. J. Dougherty. Urbana, IL: University of Illinois Press, pp. 199–220.

Gell, A. 1998. *Art and Agency: An Anthropological Theory*. Oxford: Clarendon.

Gibson, J. J. 1979. *The Ecological Approach to Visual Perception*. Boston, MA: Houghton Mifflin.

Gosden, C. 2010. The death of the mind. In *The Cognitive Life of Things: Recasting the Boundaries of the Mind*, eds. L. Malafouris and C. Renfrew. Cambridge: McDonald Institute for Archaeological Research, pp. 39–46.

Gowlett, J. 1984. Mental abilities of early man: a look at some hard evidence. In *Hominid Evolution and Community Ecology*, ed. R. Foley. London: Academic Press, pp. 167–192.

Graves-Brown, P. 2000. Introduction. In *Matter, Materiality and Modern Culture*, ed. P. M. Graves-Brown. London: Routledge, pp. 1–9.

Grierson, H. J. C. 1947. *Metaphysical Lyrics and Poems of the Seventeenth Century: Donne to Butler*. Oxford: Clarendon Press.

Gunn, W. 2007. Learning within the workplaces of artists, anthropologists and architects: making stories for drawings and writings. In *Skilled Visions: Between Apprenticeship and Standards*, ed. C. Grasseni. Oxford: Berghahn, pp. 106–124.

Hägerstrand, T. 1976. Geography and the study of the interaction between nature and society. *Geoforum* 7: 329–334.

Hallam, E. 2002. The eye and the hand: memory, identity and clairvoyants' narratives in England. In *Temporalities, Autobiography and Everyday Life*, eds J. Campbell and J. Harbord. Manchester: Manchester University Press, pp. 169–192.

Hallowell, A. I. 1955. *Culture and Experience*. Philadelphia, PA: University of Pennsylvania Press.

Harman, G. 2005. Heidegger on objects and things. In *Making Things Public: Atmospheres of Democracy*, eds. B. Latour and P. Weibel. Cambridge, MA: MIT Press, pp. 268–271.

Harvey, J. 1972. *The Mediaeval Architect*. London: Wayland.

Harvey, J. 1974. *Cathedrals of England and Wales*. London: B. T. Batsford.

Heidegger, M. 1971. *Poetry, Language, Thought*, trans. A. Hofstadter. New York: Harper and Row.

Heidegger, M. 1992. *Parmenides*, trans. A. Schuwer and R. Rojcewicz. Bloomington, IN: Indiana University Press.

Heidegger, M. 1993. *Basic Writings*, ed. D. F. Krell. London: Routledge.

Heidegger, M. 1995. *The Fundamental Concepts of Metaphysics: World, Finitude, Solitude*, trans. W. McNeil and N. Walker. Bloomington, IN: Indiana University Press.

Helmreich, S. 2009. *Alien Ocean: Anthropological Voyages in Microbial Seas*. Berkeley, CA: University of California Press.

Henderson, K. 1999. *On Line and on Paper: Visual Representations, Visual Culture, and Computer Graphics in Design Engineering*. Cambridge, UK: Cambridge University Press.

Henderson, K. 2007. Achieving legitimacy: visual discourses in engineering design and green building code development. *Building Research and Information* 35(1): 6–17.

Herzfeld, C. and D. Lestel 2005. Knot tying in great apes: etho-ethnology of an unusual tool behaviour. *Social Science Information* 44(4): 621–653.

Hicks, R. D. 1907. *Aristotle, De Anima*, trans. R. D. Hicks. Cambridge, UK: Cambridge University Press.

Hiscock, N. 2000. *The Wise Master Builder: Platonic Geometry in Plans of Medieval Abbeys and Cathedrals*. Aldershot: Ashgate.

Hockey, J. and M. Forsey 2012. Ethnography is not participant observation: reflections on the interview as participatory qualitative research. In *The Interview: An Ethnographic Approach*, ed. J. Skinner. New York: Berg, pp. 69-87.

Holloway, R. 1969. Culture, a *human* domain. *Current Anthropology* 10(4): 395–412.

Holtorf, C. 2002. Notes on the life history of a pot sherd. *Journal of Material Culture* 7: 49–71.

Holtorf, C. 2009. On the possibility of time travel. *Lund Archaeological Review* 15: 31–41.

Howe, N. 1992. The cultural construction of reading in Anglo-Saxon England. In *The Ethnography of Reading*, ed. J. Boyarin. Berkeley, CA: University of California Press, pp. 58–79.

Hugh of St Victor 1961. *The Didascalicon of Hugh of St. Victor: A Medieval Guide to the Arts*, trans. J. Taylor. New York: Columbia University Press.

Ingold, T. 1990. Editorial. *Man* (N.S.) 26: 1–2.

Ingold, T. 1993. The reindeerman's lasso. In *Technological Choices: Transformation in Material Cultures Since the Neolithic*, ed. P. Lemmonier. London: Routledge, pp. 108–125.

Ingold, T. 1999. 'Tools for the hand, language for the face': an appreciation of Leroi-Gourhan's *Gesture and Speech*. *Studies in the History and Philosophy of Biological and Biomedical Science* 30(4): 411–453.

Ingold, T. 2000. *The Perception of the Environment: Essays on Livelihood, Dwelling and Skill*. London: Routledge.

Ingold, T. 2001. From the transmission of representations to the education of attention. In *The Debated Mind: Evolutionary Psychology Versus Ethnography*, ed. H. Whitehouse. Oxford: Berg, pp. 113–153.

Ingold, T. 2004. André Leroi-Gourhan and the evolution of writing. In *Autour de l'homme: contexte et actualité d'André Leroi-Gourhan*, eds. F. Audouze and N. Schlanger. Antibes: APDCA, pp. 109–123.

Ingold, T. 2007. *Lines: A Brief History*. London: Routledge.

Ingold, T. 2008a. Earth, sky, wind and weather. In *Wind, Life and Health: Anthropological and Historical Perspectives*, eds. E. Hsu and C. Low. Oxford: Blackwell, pp. 17–35.

Ingold, T. 2008b. The social child. In *Human Development in the Twenty-First Century: Visionary Ideas from Systems Scientists*, eds. A. Fogel, B. J. King and S. G. Shanker. Cambridge, UK: Cambridge University Press, pp. 112–118.

Ingold, T. 2010. The man in the machine and the self-builder. *Interdisciplinary Science Reviews* 35(3/4): 353–364.

Ingold, T. 2011a. *Being Alive: Essays on Movement, Knowledge and Description*. London: Routledge.

Ingold, T. ed. 2011b. *Redrawing Anthropology: Materials, Movements, Lines*. Farnham: Ashgate.

Ingold, T. n.d. In defence of handwriting. In *Writing Across Boundaries*, eds. R. Simpson and R. Humphrey, Department of Anthropology, University of Durham, http://www.dur.ac.uk/writingacrossboundaries/writingonwriting/timingold/

Ingraham, C. 1992. The burdens of linearity. In *Strategies of Architectural Thinking*, eds. J. Whiteman, J. Kipnis and R. Burdett. Cambridge, MA: MIT Press, pp. 130–147.

Irigaray, L. 1999. *The Forgetting of Air in Martin Heidegger*, trans. M. B. Mader. London: Athlone.

James, J. 1985. *Chartres: The Masons Who Built a Legend*. London: Routledge & Kegan Paul.

James, K. H. and T. P. Atwood 2009. The role of sensorimotor learning in the perception of letter-like forms: tracking the causes of neural specialization for letters. *Cognitive Neuropsychology* 26(1): 91–110.

James, P. ed. 1966. *Henry Moore on Sculpture: A Collection of the Sculptor's Writings and Spoken Words*. London: Macdonald.

Johannsen, N. 2012. Archaeology and the inanimate agency proposition: a critique and a suggestion. In *Excavating the Mind: Cross-sections Through Culture, Cognition and Materiality*, eds. N. Johannssen, M. D. Jessen and H. J. Jensen. Aarhus: Aarhus University Press, pp. 305–347.

Johnson, M. 2007. *The Meaning of the Body: Aesthetics of Human Understanding*. Chicago, IL: University of Chicago Press.

Jones, A. M. 2004. Archaeometry and materiality: materials-based analysis in theory and practice. *Archaeometry* 46: 327–338.

Jones, A. M. 2007. *Memory and Material Culture*. Cambridge, UK: Cambridge University Press.

Jones, A. M. and N. Boivin 2010. The malice of inanimate objects: material agency. In *The Oxford Handbook of Material Culture Studies*, eds. D. Hicks and M. C. Beaudry. Oxford: Oxford University Press, pp. 333–351.

Joulian, F. 1996. Comparing chimpanzee and early hominid techniques: some contributions to cultural and cognitive questions. In *Modelling the Early Human Mind*, eds. P. A. Mellars and K. R. Gibson. Cambridge: McDonald Institute for Archaeological Research, pp. 173–189.

Kandinsky, W. 1982. *Kandinsky: Complete Writings on Art, Vols. 1 (1901-1921) and 2 (1922-1943)*, eds. K. C. Lindsay and P. Vergo. London: Faber & Faber.

Klee, P. 1961. *Notebooks, Volume 1: The Thinking Eye*, ed. J. Spiller, trans. R. Manheim. London: Lund Humphries.

Knappett, C. 2005. *Thinking Through Material Culture: An Interdisciplinary Perspective*. Philadelphia, PA: University of Pennsylvania Press.

Knappett, C. and L. Malafouris eds. 2008. *Material Agency: Towards a Non-Anthropocentric Approach*. New York: Springer.

Lakoff, G. and M. Johnson 1999. *Philosophy in the Flesh: The Embodied Mind and its Challenge to Western Thought*. New York: Basic Books.

Laning, E. 1971. *The Act of Drawing*. New York: McGraw Hill.

Lapacherie, J.-G. 1994. Typographic characters: tension between text and drawing, trans. A. Lehmann. *Yale French Studies* 84: 63–77.

Latour, B. 1999. *Pandora's Hope: Essays on the Reality of Science Studies*. Cambridge, MA: Harvard University Press.

Latour, B. and A. Yaneva 2008. 'Give me a gun and I will make buildings move': an ANT's view of architecture. In *Explorations in Architecture: Teaching, Design, Research*, ed. R. Geiser. Basel: Birkhäuser, pp. 80–89.

Lave, J. 1990. The culture of acquisition and the practice of understanding. In *Cultural Psychology: Essays on Comparative Human Development*, eds. J. W. Stigler, R. A. Shweder and G. Herdt. Cambridge, UK: Cambridge University Press, pp. 309–327.

Lave, J. and E. Wenger 1991. *Situated Learning: Legitimate Peripheral Participation*. Cambridge, UK: Cambridge University Press.

Le Corbusier 1947. *The City of Tomorrow and its Planning*, trans. F. Etchells. London: Architectural Press.

Leach, E. R. 1964. Anthropological aspects of language: animal categories and verbal abuse. In *New Directions in the Study of Language*, ed. E. H. Lennenberg. Cambridge, MA: MIT Press, pp. 23–63.

Leary, J., T. Darvill and D. Field eds. 2010. *Round Mounds and Monumentality in the British Neolithic and Beyond*. Oxford: Oxbow Books.

Lee, J. and T. Ingold 2006. Fieldwork on foot: perceiving, routing, socialising. In *Locating the Field: Space, Place and Context in Anthropology*, eds. S. Coleman and P. Collins. Oxford: Berg, pp. 67–85.

Lefebvre, H. 2004. *Rhythmanalysis: Space, Time and Everyday Life*. London: Continuum.

Leroi-Gourhan, A. 1993. *Gesture and Speech*, trans. A. Bostock Berger, ed. R. White. Cambridge, MA: MIT Press.

Lévi-Strauss, C. 1955. *Tristes Tropiques*, trans J. and D. Weightman. London: Jonathan Cape.

Longcamp, M., M. Zerbato-Poudou and J. L. Velay 2005. The influence of writing practice on letter recognition in preschool children: a comparison between handwriting and typing. *Acta Psychologica* 119: 67–79.

Loos, A. 1985. *The Architecture of Adolf Loos*. London: Precision Press.

Lord, J. V. 2005. A journey of drawing: an illustration of a fable. In *Drawing: The Process*, eds. J. Davies and L. Duff. Bristol: Intellect, pp. 29–37.

Lucas, G. 2005. *The Archaeology of Time*. London: Routledge.

Luke, D. 1964. *Goethe*, ed., trans. and intr. D. Luke. London: Penguin.

Malafouris, L. 2004. The cognitive basis of material engagement: where brain, body and culture conflate. In *Rethinking Materiality: The Engagement of Mind with the Material World*, eds. E. DeMarrais, C. Gosden and C. Renfrew. Cambridge: McDonald Institute for Archaeological Research, pp. 53–62.

Malafouris, L. 2008. At the potter's wheel: an argument for material agency. In *Material Agency: Towards a Non-Anthropocentric Approach*, eds. C. Knappett and L. Malafouris. New York: Springer, pp. 19–36.

Malafouris, L. and C. Renfrew eds. 2010. *The Cognitive Life of Things: Recasting the Boundaries of the Mind*. Cambridge: McDonald Institute for Archaeological Research.

Marchand, T. H. J. 2001. *Minaret Building and Apprenticeship in Yemen*. London: Curzon.

Marchand, T. H. J. 2009. *The Masons of Djenné*. Bloomington, IN: Indiana University Press.

Marzke, M. W. 1997. Precision grips, hand morphology and tools. *American Journal of Physical Anthropology* 102(1): 91–110.

Massumi, B. 2009. 'Technical mentality' revisited: Brian Massumi on Gilbert Simondon (with A. de Boever, A. Murray, J. Roffe). *Parrhesia* 7: 36–45.

Maynard, P. 2005. *Drawing Distinctions: The Varieties of Graphic Expression*. Ithaca, NY: Cornell University Press.

McGrew, W. C. 1992. *Chimpanzee Material Culture: Implications for Human Evolution*. Cambridge, UK: Cambridge University Press.

Merleau-Ponty, M. 1964. Eye and mind, trans. C. Dallery. In *The Primacy of Perception, and Other Essays on Phenomenological Psychology, the Philosophy of Art, History and Politics*, ed. J. M. Edie. Evanston, IL: Northwestern University Press, pp.159–190.

Merleau-Ponty, M. 1968. *The Visible and the Invisible*, ed. C. Lefort, trans. A. Lingis. Evanston, IL: Northwestern University Press.

Mills, C. W. 1959. *The Sociological Imagination*. New York: Oxford University Press.

Mitchell, V. 2006. Drawing threads from sight to site. *Textile* 4(3): 340–361.

Miyazaki, H. 2004. *The Method of Hope: Anthropology, Philosophy and Fijian Knowledge*. Stanford, CA: Stanford University Press.

Naji, M. and L. Douny 2009. Editorial. *Journal of Material Culture* 14: 411–432.

Napier, J. 1993. *Hands*, revised edition, ed. R. H. Tuttle. Princeton, NJ: Princeton University Press.

Nonaka, T., B. Bril and R. Rein 2010. How do stone knappers predict and control the outcome of flaking? Implications for understanding early stone tool technology. *Journal of Human Evolution* 59: 155–167.

Norman, D. A. 1988. *The Design of Everyday Things*. New York: Basic Books.

Oliver, P. 1990. *Dwellings: The House Across the World*. Austin, TX: University of Texas Press.

Olsen, B. 2003. Material culture after text: re-membering things. *Norwegian Archaeological Review* 36: 87–104.

Olsen, B. 2010. *In Defense of Things*. Plymouth, UK: Altamira Press.

Olwig, K. 2008. The Jutland cipher: unlocking the meaning and power of a contested landscape. In *Nordic Landscapes: Region and Belonging on the Northern Edge of Europe*, eds. M. Jones and K. R. Olwig. Minneapolis, MN: University of Minnesota Press, pp. 12–49.

Pacey, A. 2007. *Medieval Architectural Drawing: English Craftsmen's Methods and their Later Persistence (c.1200-1700)*. Stroud: Tempus.

Paley, W. 2006. *Natural Theology; or, Evidences of the Existence and Attributes of the Deity, Collected from the Appearances of Nature*. Oxford: Oxford University Press.

Pallasmaa, J. 1996. *The Eyes of the Skin: Architecture and the Senses*. London: Academy Editions.

Pallasmaa, J. 2009. *The Thinking Hand: Existential and Embodied Wisdom in Architecture*. Chichester: Wiley.

Palsson, G. 1994. Enskilment at sea. *Man* (N.S.) 29: 901–927.

Panofsky, E. 1968. *Idea: A Concept in Art Theory*, trans. J. J. S. Peake. Columbia, SC: University of South Carolina Press.

Parrish, C. 1957. *The Notation of Medieval Music*. New York: W. W. Norton.

Pelegrin, J. 1993. A framework for analysing prehistoric stone tool manufacture and a tentative application to some early stone industries. In *The Use of Tools by Human and Non-Human Primates*, eds. A. Berthelet and J. Chavaillon. Oxford: Clarendon Press, pp. 302–314.

Pelegrin, J. 2005. Remarks about archaeological techniques and methods of knapping: elements of a cognitive approach to stone knapping. In *Stone Knapping: The Necessary Conditions for a Uniquely Hominin Behaviour*, eds. V. Roux and B. Bril. Cambridge: McDonald Institute for Archaeological Research, pp. 23–33.

Petherbridge, D. 2010. *The Primacy of Drawing: Histories and Theories of Practice*. New Haven, CT: Yale University Press.

Petroski, H. 1989. *The Pencil: A History of Design and Circumstance*. London: Faber & Faber.

Pevsner, N. 1942. The term 'architect' in the Middle Ages. *Speculum* 17(4): 549–562.

Phipps, B. 2006. *Lines of Enquiry: Thinking Through Drawing*. Cambridge: Kettle's Yard.

Pickering, A. 1995. *The Mangle of Practice: Time, Agency and Science*. Chicago. IL: University of Chicago Press.

Pickering, A. 2010. Material culture and the dance of agency. In *The Oxford Handbook of Material Culture Studies*, eds. D. Hicks and M. C. Beaudry. Oxford: Oxford University Press, pp. 191–208.

Polanyi, M. 1958. *Personal Knowledge: Towards a Post-critical Philosophy*. London: Routledge & Kegan Paul.

Polanyi, M. 1966. *The Tacit Dimension*. London: Routledge & Kegan Paul.

Pollard, J. 2004. The art of decay and the transformation of substance. In *Substance, Memory, Display*, eds. C. Renfrew, C. Gosden and E. DeMarrais. Cambridge: McDonald Institute for Archaeological Research, pp. 47–62.

Pye, D. 1968. *The Nature and Art of Workmanship*. Cambridge, UK: Cambridge University Press.

Pye, D. 1978. *The Nature and Aesthetics of Design*. London: Herbert Press.

Rawson, P. 1979. *Seeing Through Drawing*. London: British Broadcasting Corporation.

Reid, M. 1994. Legible/visible (trans. N. P. Turner). *Yale French Studies* 84: 1–12.

Roche, H. 2005. From simple flaking to shaping: stone-knapping evolution among early hominins. In *Stone Knapping: The Necessary Conditions for a Uniquely Hominin Behaviour*, eds. V. Roux and B. Bril. Cambridge: McDonald Institute for Archaeological Research, pp. 35–48.

Rogoff, B. 1990. *Apprenticeship in Thinking: Cognitive Development in Social Context*. New York: Oxford University Press.

Rogoff, B. 2003. *The Cultural Nature of Human Development*. Oxford: Oxford University Press.

Roque, G. 1994. Writing/drawing/color (trans. C. Weber). *Yale French Studies* 84: 43–62.

Rosenberg, T. 2008. New beginnings and monstrous births: notes towards an appreciation of ideational drawing. In *Writing on Drawing: Essays on Drawing Practice and Research*, ed. S. Garner. Bristol: Intellect, pp. 109–124.

Ruskin, J. 1903. *The Stones of Venice, Volume 1, The Foundations* (Volume 9 of *The Works of John Ruskin*, eds. E. T. Cook and A. Wedderburn). London: George Allen.

Ruskin, J. 1904. *The Elements of Drawing* (Volume 15 of *The Works of John Ruskin*, eds. E. T. Cook and A. Wedderburn). London: George Allen.

Rybczynski, W. 1989. *The Most Beautiful House in the World*. New York: Penguin.

Saenger, P. 1982. Silent reading: its impact on late medieval script and society. *Viator* 13: 367–414.

Sanabria, S. L. 1989. From Gothic to Renaissance stereotomy: the design methods of Philibert de l'Orme and Alonso de Vandelvira. *Technology and Culture* 30(2): 266–299.

Schama, S. 1995. *Landscape and Memory*. London: HarperCollins.

Schick, K. and N. Toth 1993. *Making Silent Stones Speak: Human Evolution and the Dawn of Technology*. New York: Simon & Schuster.

Schneider, A. and C. Wright eds. 2006. *Contemporary Art and Anthropology*. Oxford: Berg.

Schneider, A. and C. Wright eds. 2010. *Between Art and Anthropology: Contemporary Ethnographic Practice*. Oxford: Berg.

Schutz, A. 1951. Making music together: a study in social relationship. *Social Research* 18: 76–97.

Schutz, A. 1962. *The Problem of Social Reality*, collected papers volume I, ed. M. Nathanson. The Hague: Nijhoff.

Sennett, R. 2008. *The Craftsman*. London: Penguin (Allen Lane).

Serres, M. 1995. *The Natural Contract*, trans. E. MacArthur and W. Paulson. Ann Arbor, MI: University of Michigan Press.

Sheets-Johnstone, M. 1998. *The Primacy of Movement*. Amsterdam: John Benjamins.

Sheets-Johnstone, M. 2011. The imaginative consciousness of movement: linear quality, kinaesthesia, language and life. In *Redrawing Anthropology: Materials, Movements, Lines*, ed. T. Ingold. Farnham: Ashgate, pp. 115–128.

Shelby, L. R. 1970. The education of medieval English master masons. *Mediaeval Studies* 32: 1–26.

Shelby, L. R. 1971. Mediaeval masons' templates. *Journal of the Society of Architectural Historians* 30(2): 140–154.

Shelby, L. R. 1972. The geometrical knowledge of mediaeval master masons. *Speculum* 47(3): 395–421.

Simmel, G. 1969. Sociology of the senses: visual interaction. In *Introduction to the Science of Sociology* (3rd edition), eds. E. W. Burgess and R. E. Park. Chicago, IL: University of Chicago Press, pp. 146–150.

Simondon, G. 1964. *L'individu et sa génèse physico-biologique*. Paris : Presses Universitaires de France.

Simondon, G. 1989. *L'individuation psychique et collective*. Paris: Aubier.

Simondon, G. 1992. The genesis of the individual (trans. M. Cohen and S. Kwinter). In *Incorporations*, eds. J. Crary and S. Kwinter. New York: Zone, pp. 297–319.

Simondon, G. 2005. *L'individuation à la lumière des notions de Forme et d'Information*. Grenoble: Editions Jérôme Millon.

Siza, A. 1997. *Alvaro Siza: Writings on Architecture*. Milan: Skira Editore.

Sperber, D. 1985. *On Anthropological Knowledge: Three Essays*. Cambridge, UK: Cambridge University Press; Paris: Maison des Sciences de l'Homme.

Spuybroek, L. 2011. *The Sympathy of Things: Ruskin and the Ecology of Design*. Rotterdam: V2_ Publishing.

Steadman, P. 1979. *The Evolution of Designs: Biological Analogy in Architecture and the Applied Arts*. Cambridge, UK: Cambridge University Press.

Stewart, K. 1983. *Katie Stewart's Cookbook*. London: Victor Gollancz.

Stout, D. 2002. Skill and cognition in stone tool production. *Current Anthropology* 43: 693–722.

Stout, D., N. Toth, K. Schick and T. Chaminade 2008. Neural correlates of early Stone Age toolmaking: technology, language and cognition in human evolution. *Philosophical Transactions of the Royal Society B* 363: 1939–1949.

Suchman, L. 1987. *Plans and Situated Actions*. Cambridge, UK: Cambridge University Press.

Sugiyama, Y. and J. Koman 1979. Tool-using and -making behaviour in wild chimpanzees at Boussou, Guinea. *Primates* 20: 513–524.

Summers, D. 2003. *Real Spaces: World Art History and the Rise of Western Modernism*. London: Phaidon.

Talbot, R. 2008. Drawing connections. In *Writing on Drawing: Essays on Drawing Practice and Research*, ed. S. Garner. Bristol: Intellect, pp. 43–57.

Tallis, R. 2003. *The Hand: A Philosophical Inquiry into Human Being*. Edinburgh: Edinburgh University Press.

Thomas, J. 2007. The trouble with material culture. In *Overcoming the Modern Invention of Material Culture*, eds. V. O. Jorge and J. Thomas (special issue of *Journal of Iberian Archaeology* 9/10). Porto: ADECAP, pp. 11–23.

Tiffany, D. 2001. Lyric substance: on riddles, materialism, and poetic obscurity. *Critical Inquiry* 28(1): 72–98.

Tilley, C. 2004. *The Materiality of Stone: Explorations in Landscape Archaeology*. Oxford: Berg.

Tilley, C. 2007. Materiality in materials. *Archaeological Dialogues* 14: 16–20.

Tilley, C., S. Hamilton and B. Bender 2000. Art and the re-presentation of the past. *Journal of the Royal Anthropological Institute* (N.S.) 6: 35–62.

Tisseron, S. 1994. All writing is drawing: the spatial development of the manuscript. *Yale French Studies* 84: 29–42.

Turnbull, D. 1993. The ad hoc collective work of building Gothic cathedrals with templates, string, and geometry. *Science, Technology and Human Values* 18(3): 315–340.

Turnbull, D. 2000. *Masons, Tricksters and Cartographers*. Amsterdam: Harwood Academic.

Turnbull, D. 2002. Performance and narrative, bodies and movement in the construction of places and objects, spaces and knowledges: the case of Maltese megaliths. *Theory, Culture and Society* 19(5/6): 125–143.

Uexküll, J. von 2010. *A Foray into the Worlds of Animals and Humans (with 'A Theory of Meaning')*, trans. J. D. O'Neil. Minneapolis, MN: University of Minnesota Press.

Unwin, S. 2007. Analysing architecture through drawing. *Building Research and Information* 35(1): 101–110.

Vergunst, J. 2012. Seeing ruins: imagined and visible landscapes in north-east Scotland. In *Imagining Landscapes: Past, Present and Future*, eds. M. Janowski and T. Ingold. Farnham: Ashgate, pp. 19–37.

Vitruvius 1914. *The Ten Books on Architecture*, trans. M. H. Morgan. Cambridge, MA: Harvard University Press.

Waterson, R. 1997. *The Living House: An Anthropology of Architecture in South-East Asia*. New York: Watson-Guptill.

Webmoor, T. and C. L. Witmore 2008. Things are us! A commentary on human/things relations under the banner of a 'social' archaeology. *Norwegian Archaeological Review* 41(1): 53–70.

Wendrich, W. 1999. *The World According to Basketry: An Ethno-Archaeological Interpretation of Basketry Production in Egypt*. University of Leiden: CNWS.

West, D. A. 2002. *Horace Odes III. Dulce Periculum*. Oxford: Oxford University Press.

Whitehead, A. N. 1938. *Science and the Modern World*. Harmondsworth: Penguin.

Willerslev, R. 2006. 'To have the world at a distance': reconsidering the significance of vision for social anthropology. In *Skilled Visions: Between Apprenticeship and Standards*, ed. C. Grassemi. Oxford: Berghahn, pp. 23–46.

Wilson, F. R. 1998. *The Hand: How Its Use Shapes the Brain, Language and Human Culture*. New York: Pantheon.

Wilson, P. J. 1988. *The Domestication of the Human Species*. New Haven, CT: Yale University Press.

Wynn, T. 1993. Layers of thinking in tool behavior. In *Tools, Language and Cognition in Human Evolution*, eds. K. R. Gibson and T. Ingold. Cambridge, UK: Cambridge University Press, pp. 389–406.

Wynn, T. 1995. Handaxe enigmas. *World Archaeology* 27(1): 10–24.

Zumthor, P. 2006. *Atmospheres: Architectural Environments: Surrounding Objects*. Basel, Boston, Berlin: Birkhäuser.

INDEX